ORDINARY WOMEN

Ordinary Women

AN ARCTIC ADVENTURE

Sue Carter

Michigan State University Press • *East Lansing*

⊛ The paper used in this publication meets the minimum requirements of
ANSI/NISO z39.48-1992 (R 1997) (Permanence of Paper).

  Michigan State University Press
East Lansing, Michigan 48823-5245

Printed and bound in the United States of America.

11 10 09 08 07 06 05   1 2 3 4 5 6 7 8 9 10

LIBRARY OF CONGRESS CATALOGING-IN-PUBLICATION DATA
Carter, Sue, 1950–
Ordinary women : an arctic adventure / Sue Carter.
p. cm.
Includes bibliographical references and index.
ISBN 0-87013-748-4 (cloth : alk. paper)
1. Polar Trek (2001) 2. Carter, Sue, 1950– —Travel—Arctic regions. 3. Women
adventurers—Travel—Arctic regions. 4. Arctic regions—Description and travel.
5. North Pole—Description and travel. I. Title.
G627.C27 2005
910'.92—dc22
2004025621

Cover design by Erin Kirk New
Book design by Sharp Des!gns, Lansing, Michigan

**g green
press** INITIATIVE Michigan State University Press is a member of the Green Press
Initiative and is committed to developing and encouraging eco-
logically responsible publishing practices. For more information about the
Green Press Initiative and the use of recycled paper in book publishing, please
visit *www.greenprressinitiative.com*.

Visit Michigan State University Press on the World Wide Web at *www.msu-
press.msu.edu*

ORDINARY WOMEN

To my mother, Jane, on whose
shoulders I stood
So that my daughter, Amanda,
can see into the future.
And, to Linda.

CHAPTER ONE

Day One: April 16, 2001

Those who have gone before tell us that the hardest moment will be when the huge Russian Mi-8 helicopter takes off, leaving us on the ice. We will be alone on the frozen Arctic Ocean. Our band of women, trying to ski the last distance to the North Pole from the Russian side of the planet, will be on its own. As I sit in the jump seat in the helicopter's cockpit, between the pilot and the copilot, I know that the warning was wrong. The timing was off.

The absolute hardest moment comes just after the helicopter lifts off from the frozen pad at Ice Station Borneo. At that moment, there is really no possibility of making a round trip. Like a chair on a ski lift, there is no downloading. "This is it, baby," my stomach tells me. "We're on the way now." It might as well be a journey to Mars, for all the loneliness that wells up. The moment that I and the rest of the Polar Trek 2001 team have dreamed about and worked hard for is suddenly here. The hollow pit inside me says so.

For nearly eight years, the vision of skiing to the North Pole with only women has danced in front of me—a tantalizing, terrifying prospect. An all-women team would make a statement and show everyone who ever doubted whether "girls" could do it. It could be just the challenge I need to confront my discomfort about turning fifty. And it would be a gift to the next generation of women.

The whir of the helicopter blades brushes all that aside. I am scared.

Despite my inner desire to glue the helicopter to the ice, it takes off from Ice Station Borneo shortly after noon. The orange and blue Aeroflot chopper looks a bit like a New York subway car with a rotor strapped to the top. The interior is devoid of seats, but jammed with nineteen skiers, most of them as nervous as I am. The chatter and camaraderie of our past two weeks together has diminished into silence; now all we can hear is the noise of the machine. Packed in cheek by jowl, we have to sit on our skis, sleds, and backpacks. But we are all determined to reach the North Pole. Our WomenQuest group is flying with the Weber-Malakhov Expedition to our respective drop-off points. Everything we will need for our expedition to the North Pole is crammed in along with us. It seems improbable that we can lift off with such a load.

My momentary flash of I-want-to-be-anywhere-else-but-here eases a bit as we fly, and I feel some confidence returning. After all, wasn't I the organizer of this expedition? Hadn't Misha Malakhov, Hero of Russia, called me "Sue Carter, Arctic Explorer"? It is up to me to be brave and assertive. Still, I feel more like a drugstore cowgirl.

The thunderous roar of the two rotors drives us deeper into silence. Occasionally, a nervous smile or a camera's flash breaks our meditation, but mostly we quietly crane to look out the portholes of the helicopter. The light that blazes through is a brilliant contrast to the dark interior. Back and forth, inside and out we look, wondering how much farther until we land. The first drop-off will be for the Weber-Malakhov group.

Focusing on the flying instead of the trek ahead calms me and puts me back in charge of my feelings. Flying has always been exciting to me, ever since I was a child. My father worked for the Air Force, and much of my childhood was spent around airplanes and people who flew them. I had longed for their thrills and yearned to be among the boys who could get close to them. Now, after years of spectating, my desire to fly has been fulfilled at last: my private pilot's license is less than four months old. And even though I am not in the pilot's seat on this aircraft, I feel as though I have entered the inner circle.

Of the members of the two teams on board the helicopter, Ray and I are the only pilots, though we couldn't be further apart in experience. Ray, a Brit, has flown Boeing 747s for a living for Cathay Pacific Airways and was a helicopter pilot in the RAF. The Russians are intrigued by our status, particularly by mine as a woman aviator, and they invite us into the cockpit to sit between the pilots. Because Ray will be leaving with the Weber-Malakhov team, he takes the jump seat first. I am close enough to the front of the craft that I can see him grin as he absorbs the immense icescape less than a thousand feet below.

Twenty minutes, a half hour, and then the helicopter starts to descend. Vladimir, the pilot, cocks his head and talks with Konstantin, the copilot, through the headsets. Ray is tensing with excitement, a signal that we are going to land. For the first time.

Slowly, slowly, the craft eases its way down. Vladimir sets the three wheels deftly on the ice pack. A crewmember leaps out the door before the helicopter settles, and with a thin rod he probes the surface around each wheel to make sure that the chopper is putting down on *glacies firma* and not on thin ice—or worse yet, an open lead, a break in the ice where the water is exposed.

A check all around, and the crewman gives the sign to the cockpit that the surface is firm. It is time for the Weber-Malakhov team to leave the mother ship. It isn't WomenQuest's time yet, but the knot forming inside me says the next landing will be ours.

With the helicopter on thick, frozen ice and the ladder in place, both teams shift in order to pile out. A few trekkers remain inside and form a human chain. Skis, sleds, and backpacks are passed out, fire-brigade style. All the while, the whomp-whomp of the rotating blades scatters snow and leaves everyone ducking slightly, as the Weber-Malakhov gear is massed into a pile on the left side of the craft.

There are hugs between groups, words of encouragement—"See you at the Pole!"—and a kiss between Arctic veteran Richard Weber and his wife, Josée Auclair. He will be co-leading another expedition, and she is the woman I have chosen to guide my group. A native of Quebec, Josée is a Canadian ski champion with several Artic expeditions under her belt, and I am trusting her experience and stamina to get us through.

The members of WomenQuest's Polar Trek 2001 then clamber back aboard the helicopter for one last flight to our drop-off point. We are only a liftoff and a landing from beginning our own trek. Suddenly, it starts to be exciting.

Konstantin motions me to come up to the front, to the seat between his and Vladimir's. Konstantin is a Dolgan, a member of one of the groups native to the region. We have been told that he was the first of his people to become a pilot. He speaks some English and likely understands much more. In earlier social gatherings between the Russian helicopter crews and our team on Ice Station Borneo, Konstantin has been very circumspect and polite with our women. He may have done this as much to spare himself the scrutiny of his Russian crewmates as out of concern for us. More likely, though, Konstantin is a gentleman.

Vladimir, a fine pilot and a bit of a roué, is in the left seat. Vladimir misbehaved earlier in the week, to the point where Josée told him during one of our training breaks that if he couldn't behave around the team, we would not come back to visit his crew in their tent. We would spend our available social time with the crew of the other Russian helicopter based at Ice Station Borneo. The loss of my team's favors was clearly too great a risk to take. On a subsequent visit, Vladimir declined even a *chut-chut*—the smallest taste of vodka.

Thoughts of socializing, though, are far distant at the moment. Beyond the windscreen of the cockpit lies an enormous desert of white. Above it is a sharp blue sky with only traces of clouds. But the ice itself is staggeringly vast.

Having spent nearly a week training around Ice Station Borneo, I know what the features are like at ground level. From the air, it is possible to get a rich sense of the wide sweep of the Arctic Ocean, frozen in grandeur. The pressure ridges—little uplifts of ice rubble that come from the melting and reforming of ice pans—are decisively clear from this altitude. They snake along the surface like hedgerows dividing fields in Normandy. A huge sense of challenge washes over me.

Some of the pressure ridges can reach thirty feet high and are devilish to cross. The leads, and there are several of them, also stand out. Leads present real difficulties because they are open water in an otherwise frozen territory. Some expeditioners on Ice Station Borneo, and in Khatanga, our Siberian training ground, have blamed global warming in the polar region for the increase in leads. Global warming or not, there is open water down there.

I shift my gaze back inside the cockpit, away from the ice that might jolt me again into terror if I look too long. The instruments in the cockpit are labeled in Russian, but some of them are still recognizable. There is an altimeter, an air-speed indicator, and a tachometer, as well as a compass. The heading hovers around 330 degrees, a bearing of north. We are moving along the ground swiftly now toward our drop-off point. We have settled on N89.10 and E118.00 as a point of departure. Konstantin is checking the charts for the location on the surface. Though hardly featureless, the Arctic Ocean has neither great variety nor many distinguishing aspects. After a while, the pressure ridges tend to look alike. Working with his charts and talking with Vladimir through headsets, Konstantin is homing in on our drop-off point. It has been less than a half hour since we deposited the other team on the ice. Their plan is to ski from N89.00, a slightly longer distance.

With a gesture from Konstantin and a nod from Vladimir, the craft swings down, circles around to the left, and settles. Again, a crewmember with his measuring stick hops out before the helicopter lands firmly on the ice. Thumbs up from the outside, and with a furiously beating downdraft, the craft rests and the ladder is put into place.

There is no one else left to deposit on the ice. This stop is meant for us. My butterflies return. I don't want to be an Arctic Explorer. I want to be back home, back in my classroom; but it is too late. It is time to perform.

With a high energy fueled by anxiety and anticipation, we again link ourselves in a human chain and quickly pass skis, backpacks, and sleds from the rear of the helicopter and onto the frozen ocean surface. It is eerie to think of this spot as waves frozen into place, rather than as an ice pack. But it is the top of the ocean, and it will be our environment and our home from now until we reach the Pole.

As the rotors whir above our heads, we amass our gear a safe distance from the body of the helicopter. Vladimir and Konstantin look out from the warm cockpit and watch as my team steps away from the craft. Ladder up, door closed, and the huge ship gingerly lifts off the surface, far lighter than when we left Ice Station Borneo less than two hours ago. As the helicopter ascends, the twelve of us turn our backs and brace against the powerful downdraft that threatens to push us over. My fear of the void is dissipating. This is the beginning of the last stage of a long journey. Josée's eyes mist over as the helicopter waggles good-bye, then wheels away for Borneo. From now on, it's one ski in front of the other until it is time to stop. Long after the helicopter escapes from sight, the beat of its rotor hangs in the air.

CHAPTER TWO

1993

One year and counting until NATAS-Michigan member Frida Waara of Marquette plans to lead the first all-female expedition to the North Pole.

Not without me, she wasn't.

I tore the notice out of the Detroit National Academy of Television Arts and Sciences bulletin and got directory assistance on the line.

"Do you have a listing for Frida Waara in Marquette?"

"Please hold for the number."

I wrote it on the paper, remembering to include the area code, and dialed.

"Hi, is Frida there?"

"This is Frida."

Lord, what do I say now? In the excitement of getting a number, I hadn't thought about what to say when I reached her.

"Uh, hi, Frida, this is Sue Carter." I prattled on. "You don't know me, but I'm a journalism professor, and I saw the article in the NATAS newsletter, and I am really interested in going to the North Pole with you, and can you tell me what you're planning?" Great opening gambit. Blurt it all out like an idiot and she's really going to want to take you with her. I held my breath.

Frida laughed. "Oh, jeez. I didn't know it had appeared yet. Well, here's what I know."

I began to breathe again.

In a voice full of warmth, laced with a Yooper accent from Michigan's Upper Peninsula, she shared with me the plans for the first all-women ski to the North Pole.

"Ann Bancroft, the first woman to ski to the North Pole, is leading this expedition," she said. "It's set for next April."

Hmmm. During school, but at the end of the semester. I certainly could find another professor to cover my classes for something this important.

"It's leaving from Canada, and they're looking for ten women to join Ann and her co-leader. I can give you the name of the contact."

"That's terrific." This was sounding like it might actually be possible.

"Northwest Passage is organizing it, and I think the price is $25,000."

Or maybe it wouldn't be. I hadn't even thought about what this might cost, and certainly not how to pay for it.

"What I'm planning to do," Frida said, "is to shoot the expedition and tell the story on video. That's how I'll pay for my going."

"Do you know if there are still places available?" What could it hurt to be bold, to act as if money were no barrier? This was a chance to be part of a special event.

"There should be. I don't think there are a lot of women signed up yet. The January before we go, there's a training camp in Minnesota. You'll need to be able to run six miles with a twenty-pound backpack, and I think we have to go into the water."

"Why? You mean go swimming?"

Frida paused. "I don't know much about it, but I think they want to prepare us for the possibility of going through the ice. It happened to Ann when she went to the Pole."

What an awful thought. While the water temperature couldn't be too far below freezing, the prospect of jumping into the water in winter—of even putting any part of my body in—sent a shudder through me.

Still, this was going to be the first all-women group to ski to the North Pole. Seldom did a chance like this materialize. So what if I'd be broke and frozen. I'd be nuts not to go for it. I yearned to be part of an event that mattered. To have my time on earth mean something to other women who followed was really important to me. I wanted it for them, and for my daughter, Amanda. And for me.

Frida gave me a contact number to call, and I promised to get back to her after I had more information. There were some huge challenges here, but the idea was still really captivating. Besides, I already knew one of the women. Frida would be there.

. . .

Several days letter, a packet arrived from Illinois with information about the expedition. Ann Bancroft was the headliner, and Susan Eckert, who had an adventure-travel company for women, was co-leading. I called Frida.

"This really does sound exciting. Do you think that maybe I could help with the documentary? After all, I teach broadcast journalism at Michigan State. I could help with some of the interviewing and research—maybe some of the writing."

We talked about products that might come out of an experience like this—documentaries, a book, or lecture possibilities.

"Any chance you might be in Marquette anytime soon?"

I had to chuckle. Louisville, Kentucky, was closer to me than Marquette. "Actually, not in the near future. What about you? Will you be in the Detroit area?" People in the Upper Peninsula are generally loath to travel to the Lower Peninsula, to be south of the Mackinac Bridge. "Below the bridge is where the trolls live," they'll tell you.

"As it turns out, I'm up for an Emmy award for a documentary I did last year. I'm going to be down there with Ron—that's my husband—in May."

That was only a couple of months off. There was a lot to do in the meantime. I could get somewhat organized and put on a presentable front by then.

"That's great. I'll meet you at the NATAS banquet for the Emmys. It'll be wonderful to see you in person, and besides, you'll have another person to cheer you on."

If I really examined my heart, a big part of this desire to ski to the North Pole was due to Kenny McFarland, my next-door neighbor in Xenia, Ohio. My family had lived in Xenia before two devastating tornadoes churned through the heart of the little county seat. Kenny and I were in kindergarten together at Shawnee Elementary School.

One day, when we were five, Kenny and I were sitting on his front steps comparing worldviews, including our own career aspirations. We each articulated our vision of how we would spend our working years before retirement. It was apparent that Kenny had thought carefully about his profession.

"I am going to be a cowboy," he said.

Though media-influenced, it did seem like a fair choice. Besides, he already had the hat and gun. It seemed to me that my professional goals carried just as much excitement, yet with that added frisson of altruism.

"I want to be a fireman."

Kenny pounced immediately, sensing a weakness in my logic. "You can't be a fireman," he proclaimed with some self-satisfaction. "You're a girl!"

The sting of his words and their revelation were devastating. Not even six years old, but already I felt a big part of the world was forever closed to me. A shame seared through me for even having imagined I could be a fireman.

. · .

There was a lot to do before Frida and I met. For openers, my knowledge of the Arctic environment was rather elementary. Peary had been there—along with Henson, who had finally gotten his due. What else? Magnetic north was not the same as true north, but where was magnetic north exactly? The Pole was frozen, though global warming was apparently thinning the ice. Winters were totally dark, and summer—such as it was—consisted of total daylight. And, no, Santa did not live there. But Superman did.

There was also the question of fitness. I had been active, really active, for more than a dozen years with a routine that included running, swimming, biking, and some skiing. There had been three marathons, three triathlons, and a series of 10-K races. Running in the winter evenings with Sophie, my Samoyed, it was hard not to fixate on having to go into the water. Michigan cold was bad enough. Being in Arctic water in full clothing, even for less than a minute, was impossible to imagine. I did start to wear a backpack as we ran our three- and five-mile circuit. I gradually added weights that slowed me down, to Sophie's consternation.

Going to the North Pole on skis meant that I needed to be a reasonably proficient skier. Frida was. Certainly Ann Bancroft was. Anyone else going would need to be, so it was time to pull out the old cross-countries and get stronger.

A lot of people in Michigan ski. For one thing, it's a way to make the winter more enjoyable. It also is a good way to get exercise. The last few winters, though, had been too warm for consistent snow in the Lower Peninsula, so cross-country skiing had been spotty at best. Any real action involving arms and feet in sync took place on a NordicTrack in a gym.

An exercise machine wasn't going to be good enough, though, to prepare for a polar journey. Skiing—in whatever form it took—was what I needed in order to build strength and confidence on the long boards. The most reasonable place was right up the road: Mt. Brighton ski area. It boasted the best manmade snow in the Midwest.

With ski skills that just qualified as intermediate, but with a "whatever it takes" desire to get to the North Pole, I naively presented myself to the Mt. Brighton Ski Patrol and said I wanted to join. This looked like a good way to become a better skier, learn first-aid skills, and get to volunteer in a fun activity all at the same time. Candidate tryouts, I was told, were the first step toward becoming a member of the National Ski Patrol.

I bombed.

It was strikingly obvious that what it took to be a ski patroller was more than I had to offer, at least on the slopes. But determination overcame disappointment, and the senior patrollers were gentle with me.

"Why don't you ski with us for a year, then try out again next February?" they offered.

February was after January, after the Minnesota training camp and the plunge into the water. February was only two months before the expedition to the North Pole!

Still, there was the opportunity to ski with the patrol, even if I didn't officially belong. And after all, wasn't the idea to get experience? Aside from getting a skier's thumb while trying out, about the only injury was to my pride. And pride must be swallowed, because there was a larger quest at hand.

. . .

"You know what you've got, Mary Richards? You've got spunk."

"Gee, thank you, Mr. Grant."

"I hate spunk."

So far, most of those to whom I had explained my crazy notion of skiing to the North Pole liked spunk. I was going to need all the spunk one could muster to get through.

I was a little hesitant to confide my plans to Amanda, though. Earlier in the year, a skydive gone awry had led to a few days in the hospital with a collapsed lung and broken ribs. A late bloomer finally coming into my own as an adventurer, I no longer found bold acts frightening—but they did scare her. At last, several months after first talking with Frida, I told Amanda about the plan. She expressed both the detached excitement of a child hearing about a new adventure, and the worry of a daughter for her slightly mad mother.

"Mom," she said, after turning this all over in her mind, "just how cold is it going to be?"

"Well . . ." How could this information be presented in a way that was reassuring but real? "Remember when you were little, the winter the Super Bowl was in Detroit?" She actually was too young to remember, but she'd heard the story. "And I went out running, and it was 21 degrees below zero?"

She nodded.

"That's about how cold it will be."

Relief. I'd been in that cold. She'd been alive for temperatures that cold, and we'd all survived.

What I didn't tell her was that my facemask had frozen into a hard sheet against my face, and I had wondered at the time how anyone could possibly sustain life for any length of time in that temperature. Now, I was preparing myself to find out.

The challenge of an expedition to the North Pole honestly thrilled me, though. I also wanted to make Amanda proud of her mother, perhaps even encourage her to do exciting things. Maybe a Kenny McFarland hadn't tried to dampen her hopes, but I so wanted her to believe that she could do anything, even if she was a girl.

In May, Frida and Ron arrived—with a wild group of Yoopers—at the Emmy awards banquet in the Detroit area. Frida didn't win, but it didn't matter. As she had promised earlier, she "hugged me around the neck." I was meeting an old friend for the first time. This was going to be a great partnership.

Our talks with Rick Sweitzer of Northwest Passage weren't going so well, though. There was conflict as to who would own what intellectual-property rights from this first all-women expedition. Rick insisted on holding the rights to any documentary. I suggested that was illogical, as we were paying him to provide a service. What wasn't said was that we needed income from a documentary and writings to help cover our costs.

That spring, I flew to Minnesota in search of Ann Bancroft, the leader of the expedition. She and I had spoken on the telephone, mostly exchanging phone messages. It felt important to lay eyes on her, to understand at a deeper level what it meant to be an Arctic expeditioner. My cram-course reading about explorations and expeditions had widened my horizon. It was legitimate to ask if we really could succeed, even though I was becoming confident about our chances.

I had phoned Ann several times just before flying to Minnesota, but was not able to connect. So I figured I'd just show up, and if she was available, that was great. If not, at least I'd tried.

At Minneapolis-St. Paul Airport, I rented a car and drove to the nearby home of two very dear friends from college days. Yes, they knew about Ann Bancroft and knew that she lived in the area. I had an address. Could they tell me how to get there? I'd be back for dinner.

Ann was surprised but gracious when I showed up at her cottage near a lake. Persistence had apparently made an impression, for we talked for a while in her kitchen, sitting in the warmth of a Minnesota spring day. Then we walked around the lake and talked some more. It was apparent that she was feeling disconnected from the expedition plans.

"I haven't been contacted about a lot of this," she said, as I explained what had been written in the brochure. "We don't even have a contract."

It was beginning to look like I might have time to join the ski patrol after all.

CHAPTER THREE

Day One (continued)

The sound of the rotors dies off in the distance, fading beyond the jagged ice pressure ridges around us. We all look around, and at each other, and take in the enormity of our situation.

"Okay, girls," Josée says, pulling us back to the present. We have agreed that we alone can call each other "girls." To the rest of the world, we are women—as in WomenQuest.

"Let's pee and get going," she adds. "It's already four o'clock, but we can go at least four marches before we stop." A march is an hour and fifteen minutes of skiing, followed by a break. The breaks are usually twenty minutes, depending on the time of day and the team's energy level. It really doesn't matter when we stop, at least in relation to the sun. With twenty-four hours of daylight, we could go on until exhaustion. At this point, we can't know that is precisely what lies ahead of us.

Either dropping our pants or using "Herinals" (female urine-collection devices), we all unload our bladders. The bitter cold of the Arctic Ocean makes it important to urinate quickly. Some of us decide not to use the plastic collectors and instead bare our bottoms. It is all the more critical not to tarry. Not trusting the Herinal, I quickly unzip and go. From a stash in my backpack, out comes some precious toilet paper. I am still several days away from using snow as a cleansing wipe.

Training makes the sequence for gearing-up routine: skis on, then backpack. Each of us is attached to our individual sled by a carabiner that links the sled's rope to a loop on our backpack. We can ski along pulling—sometimes dragging—the sled behind. The sleds all have covers so they can tip without spilling the contents all over the ice. It is better to have a sled riding on its bottom, but a sled sometimes flips if it is weighted unevenly, or if it has taken a tumble going over a pressure ridge or a little hummock.

Training at Ice Station Borneo, north of Siberia, has taught us that there are several times we will be warm each day: when we are skiing, when we are in the cook tent eating and preparing meals, and while we are in our sleeping bags. Other than that, we are likely to be cold. That includes while we are setting up and taking down camp, and that takes at least an hour each time. The cold also seeps in at the end of a break following a march. And it will greet us each night in our sleeping bags, before our bodies can warm the down-wrapped space. The one other time when cold is a cruel slap is when ridding the body of wastes. Elimination is not to be lingered over. Reducing caffeine—and liquid overall—cuts down on frequency. Only once have I had to leave the tent and a warm sleeping bag during a sleep session. That was enough to convince a fifty-year-old bladder that it can, and must, do better.

In the helicopter, we wore our black down parkas over our wind suits. When we started out, the air temperature inside the ship fairly matched that of Ice Station Borneo: about –25 Fahrenheit. After getting airborne, the interior warmed up, but we kept our parkas on because there was nowhere to put them, and we would need them once we landed. Now, set to ski on our first march to the Pole, we put the huge down coats away in our sleds or backpacks. Virtually everything we own goes in either our sleds or our backpacks.

At last, with skis on and packs shouldered and cinched, there is a genuine feeling of excitement. Whatever concerns or fears we have encountered—while in the helicopter or after it left us—we have faced them down. We are ready as a team—the WomenQuest's Polar Trek 2001 team—to ski this last distance to the North Pole. Misha Malakhov, co-leader of the Weber-Malakhov Expedition, has helped to train us for this moment. He has also warned us that the publicity we got before leaving is essentially hollow. "You must go off and ski to the North Pole, and then you will be heroes." Given his superb record as an Arctic explorer, it was hard to argue with him. Now we are ready.

. · . ·

Today is bright, clear, and cold, as most of the days on our trek to the North Pole will prove to be. Though the temperatures will moderate all the way to slightly above zero degrees Fahrenheit, the cold is an ever-present consideration. Forget to prepare for it and we risk the consequences. It isn't until later in the trek that we will come to appreciate how dangerous the cold can be. Here, though, on the first march of our journey, we meet the cold squarely and start skiing.

We quickly fall into line on this, our first march. Our training experience at Borneo has made it pretty obvious that we can expect to average about one nautical mile per march. "After this, we'll have only forty-nine marches to go," offers Kerri Finlayson. Kerri, our youngest woman, so far has been the most optimistic and cheery team member.

"Don't start measuring like that," Kathy Braegger replies. An experienced climber, she understands the value of measuring one unit at a time and dealing with only that one. I agree.

At the end of the first march, just about an hour and fifteen minutes later, we stop for a break. First comes the down parka, pulled over the wind jacket to preserve the body warmth built up during the march. Maybe a warmer pair of mitts as well. Then, off with the skis, and out comes the food bag, along with a warm drink from the thermos.

Each of us has a bag of snack food we were given, along with our gear, in Khatanga. The snacks have been carefully calculated to provide a balance of calories from fat, protein, and carbohydrates. Highest in fat content is the smoked, fried bacon that Josée bought from a local butcher in Ottawa. Jen Buck, who is Josée's assistant and chief cook, and Alison Korn, a team member, have fried up nearly two hundred pounds of the thick slabs. "'Porksicles' is what I call them," says Alison. She has written an article about the experience of preparing them for the *Ottawa Citizen*, where she is a reporter.

Besides the fried bacon, the food bags include a very rich pound cake loaded with fruits and nuts, an Italian confection something like divinity fudge, dried fruit, mixed nuts, beef jerky, and specially prepared chocolate from the Rocky Mountain Chocolate Company that Marie-Josée Vasseur (our other French Canadian) has secured. Josée Auclair selected the beef and then turned it into the best beef jerky available. Laced with ginger, it is a terrific protein snack.

On the first break, the porksicles come out. "You must eat food that is very high in fat," Misha has told us, "and the food that is hardest to digest, you must eat first." He has given us his preferred ranking order for break foods, always to be accompanied by warm liquid from the thermos. As we earnestly rip at the frozen pork with our teeth, I wonder if I will ever enjoy a BLT again.

Break over, we stuff our thermoses, food sacks, and down parkas back into our sleds and backpacks. I muscle the strap tight on my sled, anxious that the plastic buckle not break in this cold. It has to be around –25 Fahrenheit at the moment, and the hard plastic can be fragile in these temperatures. So far, through all the training, it has held. The same is true for the two plastic buckles that hold each boot to the ski binding.

The wind is essentially calm, and the sky a deep and immense blue, and we are off on our second march to the North Pole. There is an ebullient feeling up and down the line as we glide forward. Looking at the group of women from my position in the middle brings a smile up from the depths of my being. I have persevered for seven years and gotten myself here. Through long hours of training, false starts, and my own doubts, I have grown into the woman skiing here on the Arctic Ocean. The expedition is no longer a burden. Instead, it is a joy, for we are on our way. Finally, we can put the naysayers behind us. We can do this. We are doing this. It is really happening.

After another hour and a half, we stop for the second break. It is close to six in the evening, Siberian time. That means it is six in the morning back home. Out come the parkas, food, and warm drinks. Off go the skis.

Josée, Jen, and Kathy huddle over the GPS (Global Positioning System), working to figure out our location and our progress. We lost ground on the first march, a fact that was disappointing but not terribly surprising. The swift westerly drift of the ice can affect progress at times. We are, after all, skiing on a floating piece of ice.

But we have lost ground again. This time, something is wrong.

Josée calls me over to explain what has happened. I trust her skills. I also count on her integrity to handle difficult situations, and one is developing right here.

Kathy has a quiet, almost stricken look on her face. Jen is silent.

"What's happening, Josée?" I am not sure what to read from their faces.

Josée is direct and calm. "It seems that we've been going in the wrong direction. Those last three kilometers—they were south."

How could this be? The direction had felt correct, from the moment that we'd gotten out of the helicopter and watched it peel off. There was nothing to indicate that the twelve of us would be skiing in the opposite direction from where we wanted to end up. Less than sixty miles from the North Pole, and we have been going south.

The GPS is measuring position relative to a point, and doing it accurately. The reading at the end of the first march is a hint that we are not making forward progress. The second confirms it. There is no compass needle to show us the way. The GPS needs a change in location to provide direction. We've picked the wrong way.

Using a ski pole and a watch, Josée does as Richard and Misha have taught her. She reckons our position relative to Greenwich on the zero-degree longitude. Knowing the time of day and marking the shadow of the pole, it is clear that north lies exactly where we have come from. About face.

Josée is quietly distressed about the mistake. She has trained for this event, and her first field decision has been an error.

We both know that there is nothing to do but own up and go forward. In the great scheme of things, it is a minor error and not hard to correct. And for the team members who wanted to ski farther, we have just added nearly two miles!

"Let me call everybody together and explain," Josée says, exhaling loudly. She knows she has my sympathy and my support. I have also let her know we need to address this squarely.

She turns back to the rest of the team, most of whom have finished their porksicles and chocolate. Josée has before her the awkward task of telling the eight other women that we have just lost frozen ground, rather then gained it.

"I should have listened to my instincts," she admits, and waits for the criticism.

There is disappointment, yes. But no recriminations, no judging, no blaming. There are not twelve angry women, there is only one: Josée. She is inwardly furious with herself for having made such a mistake, though she displays little emotion about the miscalculation.

The team's reaction is extraordinary, and supportive. We want to reach out to her and let her know that it is all right. "Better to have found out now than three days later," is Alison's view. "Hey," Frida jokes, "we're women. We would have asked for directions, but there's nobody here to ask!"

After those several harrowing days of training on Borneo, when she had come close to a meltdown, Frida is back in good form—and Josée soon will be.

. . .

We ski on, in surprisingly good humor, for another four marches. The minor disaster of the afternoon actually has a salutary effect. The team has pulled together to overcome what others might have registered as a defeat. My confidence in Josée is unshaken. Instead, I am impressed by the way she has handled the miscalculation.

The last march takes us to 11:30 that night. Our new address is N89.22, E85.59. With the sun shining as we kick off skis and shed backpacks, the tents soon go up. As always, the cook tent is first, followed by the smaller tent with "Polar Challenge" and the silhouette of a polar bear right over the door. It is a replacement tent for the one that was stolen in Khatanga.

Over a truly tasty pasta and sauce, made all the more delicious by physical exertion, we talk about our first real day on the trek. No Misha; just the twelve women of Polar Trek 2001. The results are mixed: only four miles of progress that day. To get to the Pole by April 24, we'll have to push harder. Tomorrow is the seventeenth, and that leaves only eight days to cover forty-eight nautical miles—ninety-six kilometers. The day of rest we have been counting on between here and the top of the world is a fading prospect.

The big discussion that night in the tent centers on whether or not to let anyone know we skied in the wrong direction for the first two marches. If we say nothing, only the twelve of us will ever know. The incident is potentially embarrassing to Josée as field leader, and—not surprisingly—the team is protective toward her and unwilling to admit the mistake. It is a hard call, but I know we have to reveal the error. Alison sits quietly, four feet away, waiting to write her story for the next day's edition of the *Ottawa Citizen*.

"I realize this is probably not what you want to hear, but we need to own up that we went in the wrong direction for a short time today." I can feel the groans and protests rising. "But the story doesn't end there. What we did with that bit of adversity is just as important. There's no need to dwell on the mistake, but an honest telling of our story means that it has to be revealed." I am firm that we are going to be honest. We have declared that we are modeling behavior for girls. How can we hide the truth?

I turn toward Alison. "You're a journalist, not a publicist. That was clear when you joined. I can't—and I won't—tell you what to write, but I hope that you do the second stage of the story as well as the first. We dealt with it, actually, pretty easily."

Alison understands her reporter's job thoroughly, but is relieved to have someone—especially the team leader—back her up.

"I do need to put it into my story, but it was actually only part of the day to tell," she says.

Josée understands the decision and feels better with the assurance that the whole story will be told, not just the error.

I make a short satellite phone call to team webmaster Bonnie Bucqueroux, who posts part of my report on the webpage.

"We were like 'Wrong Way Corrigan,'" said Polar Trek leader Sue Carter, whose hearty laugh suggests the diversion did not cause any real problem. They did make progress despite the glitch and are now four miles closer to their goal.

. . . .

"You might want to call NASA and check in," Bonnie says. "The National Naval Ice Center has gotten satellite photos that show a big lead of open water at E116, running about ten to twenty miles south of the Pole."

"Hmm. Not good, though we are south and west of there at the moment. I'll let Josée know."

Either because of the day's miscue, or because there is nothing really to be done about it, Josée is not interested in the information. "Whatever is there, we'll deal with it when we get to it."

I can't argue with the logic. It is 3 A.M., and my brain is fried. Borneo was a long time ago.

CHAPTER FOUR

1994–1995

It was soon clear that conversations with Northwest Passage had permanently stalled. Rick Sweitzer remained firm in his opposition to Frida and me producing a video documentary. A meeting with him in June 1994 at his office north of Chicago had not gone well, and we felt stymied and discouraged.

At the same time, Ann Bancroft and Susan Eckert carefully let us know that plans for the expedition were fading. Ann was turning her attention to the South Pole, planning to complete a transcontinental crossing that had eluded her to date. Susan was moving her travel company from Illinois to Montana— and a home she had designed in the mountains just outside of Bozeman. The dream of a polar trek was on thin ice.

But it hadn't fallen through yet. There had to be a way to pull together a group of women and ski to the North Pole. If you can imagine it, then it must be possible. Frida and I were determined.

"On reflection, dealing with Northwest Passage was pretty silly," I confessed one night on the phone to Frida. "I mean, it's dumb to have an all-women expedition to the North Pole organized by a man."

"Yeah." Frida thought for a moment. "I guess that means it's up to us. It's a pretty tall order for a Yooper chick."

I had to laugh. For all of her sophistication, Frida was, at heart, a Yooper chick. And that was about as good as it got.

So, we began organizing. First step was to contact some of the other women who had expressed an interest in an Arctic trek. Then we faced up to the task itself, which was overwhelming.

The standard route to the Pole was through Canada, starting from Resolute Bay, and the mode of transportation was skis and sled dogs. Dogs and women flown by Twin Otters. At least this provided Frida and me with a template. The problem was, the expedition was still sketchy, and built more on relationships than contracts. The world of polar exploration was, in the main, an old boys' network.

Frida, Ron, and I met with Ann Bancroft in Minneapolis in 1994. She had made it clear that she would not be available to lead us, but she had generously offered to give us some direction.

Ann had been part of the Steger-Schurke expedition that had used dogs, but the animals weren't without their problems. They could be tough to maneuver over pressure ridges, and tending them required a fair amount of energy. And, yes, she had gone partway into the water. It was rather unpleasant, but she'd survived.

As we sat in a downtown Minneapolis restaurant talking extensively over food, I found myself looking at Ann with a sense of curiosity and conviction. Here was a woman who had skied a great distance to the North Pole and was going back to attempt the South Pole. If she could do that much, I certainly could handle a much shorter ski to the North Pole and figure out how to organize it.

The closest exposure I had to sled dogs was Sophie, my Samoyed—a Russian version of a husky. To her way of thinking, she was partly human and had no interest in pulling a sled. There was hope, though. Ron and Frida knew a couple of real mushers who lived near them in the Upper Peninsula, and who were willing to introduce us to dogsledding. Another skill for a résumé: knows how to mush dogs.

By March of 1995, Frida and I figured it was time for some training. We now knew that if the polar journey were to happen, it was in our hands; so we pulled together some of the women who were interested, and decided to learn about handling dogs. Frida's friends Jill and Mark Churchill owned a dog yard, and we would use some of their dogs for an overnight of late-winter camping in near-zero temperatures. Even better, Jill was thinking of joining our team.

We met at Jill's house and headed out back to the dog yard, where some two dozen dogs were tethered. She provided some instruction.

"Before we get the dogs, the sleds need to be fully loaded." She had to project over the sound of the dogs, whose increased yipping let us know they were aware something exciting was going to happen. Really, it could have been anything; after all, they were dogs. "Then, one at a time, we'll bring the dogs over from their houses and hook them up to the gangline."

The gangline is the long chain that the dogs are attached to so they can pull the sled. "Here's the brake," Jill said, pointing to a set of metal rods that dug into the snow when you depressed a pedal. "Make sure you set it whenever you stop. If you don't, they'll take off on you."

Jill had told us that it was critical to get all your talking done before the dogs were hooked to the gangline. Once they were on the chain, their barking would be deafening. Even now, the noise level in the yard nearly overwhelmed us.

"And one more thing," she yelled. "When you're moving, never let go of the sled."

That rumbled through my consciousness for a moment: Never let go of the sled. It wasn't hard to picture the consequences. The dogs depart, and there is the musher—bereft of food, fuel, and shelter—left to walk back in thigh-high snow. I was feeling all the more the neophyte, standing in the yard surrounded by sonic dogs. What was I doing? I'd never even been winter camping, a fact that I hadn't really admitted even to myself.

No, I could do this. I'd show Kenny McFarland.

Once the dogs were hooked up to the sleds, we were going to mush to a large, open tract not far away. We'd need to stay on paths through the woods for a while, and then the trail would open up into a substantial cut area. The woods, ostensibly, would slow the dogs down. I was less convinced of that, as the pressure of them pulling at the brake was mounting. By now, we were communicating with hand gestures.

Finally, the dogs were hooked up. Jill gave me a look I took to mean, "Follow me," and I pulled up the brake from where it had been embedded in the icy snow. I held on with a death grip.

The dogs attached to my sled ripped out of the yard with a speed that stole my breath. I was running behind the sled for the moment, swiftly approaching horizontal, and not quite sure when to jump on the runners. My arm sockets quickly let me know when it was time.

I managed to get my hiking boots, waterproof but apparently not quite up to the task, planted on the rear of the sled. Underneath my gloves, my knuckles were white—as much from tension as the cold. We raced down the lane and right toward the woods. With every couple of yards, I became a little more confident. Jill, Frida, and the others were in front of me. And we were actually traveling in something that resembled a line. I carefully took one hand off the sled handle and readjusted my cap, which had gone a little askew when we first sped away. From deep down inside me came a spontaneous "Yahoo!" This was really fun.

Then we hit the woods.

As the snow-crusted country road suddenly narrowed into an enclosure of northern pine, the dogs slowed down. Marginally. My mushing friends ahead of me were navigating their sleds with a fair degree of coordination through the trees. I was hanging on—a passenger on a train with no engineer. Over the bumps, skirting the trunks and tree roots, I was half running, half riding in a losing effort to control the sled.

The dog team, tearing around the bend in a sadistic game of crack-the-whip, obscured the rut that got me. Onto its side went the sled, body-slamming me to the snow like the loser in a WWF competition. Never let go of the sled. My grip on the handle went from death to rigor mortis. Mashing my knees, half crawling, half running forward, I was desperate to muscle the sled upright. So far, none of the sled contents had fallen out of the bag. Good news, since I had most of the food.

Another turn, and the right runner hit a rock that flipped the sled upright, bouncing it off my shin in the process. "Damn!" I ran to jump back on the sled and finally got my feet planted again. My heart had moved up about a foot and taken residence in my throat. Hanging on for a small eternity, I tried to collect myself. The other sleds had pulled ahead and were entering the open field—mostly snow-covered, but with some bare patches. Yelling for the others to slow down would be useless, except to help me blow off the anxiety the last few minutes had produced. I yelled at the dogs instead.

"You stupid mutts! What are you trying to do, kill me?"

This was not logical, since I was actually the one who had engaged in this suicidal adventure. But logic had no place in this conversation.

"If I ever catch you . . ." Then I had to laugh. Of course I would catch them. We were attached, as long as I didn't let go. What an appropriate metaphor for this whole polar adventure. I controlled the ties that bound me to it.

Up ahead, Frida and the other expeditioners had pulled to a stop. My team must have sensed that this rest meant food, and they slowed down as well. I furtively glanced down the right side of the sled for the brake, hoping it hadn't been torn off during our Disney World Adventureland ride. There it was. As the dogs heeled in, I dragged the anchor in the snow and brought us to a full stop. There was a small tear in my right pant leg, and one of my boots had taken on a little water from a pool of slush, but otherwise the dogs, the sled, the food, and I were intact.

"You okay back there?" Frida asked.

"Oh, yeah, sure." I straightened my cap again. "Just getting the feel of it."

We went on for another three hours until it was time to find a campsite. Jill knew of one that was open enough for our tents and the dogs, but sheltered from the north wind. And it was near a stream that had recently thawed. Instead of having to melt snow, we could just warm up that water over a cook stove and mix in the dogs' food. Only after that was done could we start preparing our own meal.

How close did this resemble a day in the Arctic? It was probably pretty close, except that the Arctic would be colder, water wouldn't be available, there would be no trees, and the winds could be a great deal stronger.

Things didn't go so well with the dogs on the return journey the next day, either. With the camp torn down, the sleds loaded, and the dogs on the gangline, we lifted the brake and yelled, "Hike!" The sled dogs took off, but one of the sleds didn't. The gangline had separated. Of course the dogs didn't look back for an instant. Jill saw the runaway team dash past her and turned her dogs in swift pursuit. The wayward team beat her back to the yard, where she found them lying down and grinning—as if to say, "What took you so long?"

I arrived shortly after Jill. Together, we tethered the dogs in the yard and headed back on the snowmobile to bring in the remaining sled.

Despite the dogs' antics, though, the overnight camp had been very good. It gave our little group a chance to spend time together, learn more about each other, and try things on for size. It was a little like playing "Pretend" in anticipation of a day when reality would replace the imagination. Of course, even Pretend showed how truly far from being ready we actually were. But, we were coming together as a small band. There would be others—I really believed that.

Being ordinary women didn't mean we couldn't do something extraordinary. It just wasn't going to be easy.

CHAPTER FIVE

Day Two

"It is better to spend a long day skiing rather than a short day swimming." These words by our co-leader, Jen Buck, have been hanging around the edges of my brain all day. It is April 17, 2001. A Tuesday. We are facing a thirty-yard stretch of open water, dark and menacing as a shark's eyes. The lead in front of us is a showstopper. There is no way we are going to cross it. We will have to ski to find a narrower location, a place where the lead constricts to a point where we can span it with our skis. Nothing looks promising in either direction.

We began the day by rising at 11 A.M. Already our internal clocks have gotten out of whack. What a tough thing to fight in the Arctic: the desire to sleep longer. The encouraging news in the tent over breakfast was that Kathy, who had mastered the GPS, calculated that we had drifted 1.5 nautical miles to the north while we slept. However, the ocean current had also deposited us 2.0 nautical miles to the west.

After a breakfast of warm granola, sweet hard toast with honey and peanut butter, and coffee, I had joined about half of the women in journaling.

Slept less well—on 10-degree angle. Will make sure to improve tonight. Will take 2nd air sample today. Have a bit of a cough.

Overall, the team's health is good. Alison is still troubled by blisters on her feet left over from the Borneo training, and Diana Ciserella and I have acquired frost nip on our fingertips. Frida's diarrhea, begun during training in Khatanga, has abated. For the second time in two weeks, though, I am having a period. We all find creative ways to deal with such on-ice events, and even manage to laugh about a few of them, but they are, nonetheless, real.

Tents down and gear packed and loaded, we booted up for the second day of our little expedition to the North Pole. It wasn't long before we were stopped short by a yawning lead.

Skiing directly to the North Pole is a myth. In actuality, it is a circuitous path in the best of years, and this isn't one of them. The recent warming has aggravated the problem of open water on the Arctic Ocean. There is little doubt that there are more breaks in the ice this year than even ten years ago.

Like docile donkeys waiting in line, we stand patiently as Josée tests the surface by skipping a piece of ice on the lead's surface. Skim ice has started to form. Sprong. Up and down it undulates—not water, but still not firm ice. Then Josée and Jen ski in opposite directions, looking for some indication that the lead narrows.

The only real possibility for advancing is to ski south and cross about half a mile from where we are. I wonder if this is the lead that NASA spotted from the satellite. In places, it certainly is wide enough to be picked up by satellite. Come to think of it, NASA's resolution is probably good enough to detect our ant-like crawl across the ice. Assessing our situation, we ski south in search of a place where the lead narrows.

Finally, we find a location where the gap tightens enough for the team to cross, though it is nearly four feet across. Slowly, one at a time, we get set to breech-gap with our skis, sleds right at our sides. We use the technique Misha has taught us: first one ski making a bridge, and when that ski is firmly in place, the other ski, tips on one side and tails on the other. Ski poles in front—never behind you—and mash the tips of the poles into the ice on the far side. Steady. Now launch! Once on the other side of the gap, yank the sled along and over the opening in the ice. Ski on. Others are waiting to cross.

We are moving better as a group now. Marie-Josée, Alison, and the other strong skiers are being tested with the heavier loads they are hauling. Phyllis Grummon and Lynn Bartley and I—three of the older team members—are pressing forward, improving our skills, skiing with somewhat lighter loads. I still take my share of tumbles, but am able to negotiate different types of ice that were challenging only a week ago.

In addition to the leads, at midday we find our progress slowed by pressure ridges, those mounds of rubble ice that are formed when the pans of ice floating on the Arctic Ocean melt and freeze up again. Misha's lesson from Ice Station Borneo about forming a human chain is right in front of us. The formula is simple: a few women on the other side, several on top of the rubble, and the rest to pass up the sleds, backpacks, and skis. A new skill to add to my résumé: worked as a baggage handler. Career objective: to load airplanes at Detroit Metro airport. Piece by piece, we haul by hand what the terrain won't allow us to ski. We are quickly reaching the point where everything we need to survive in this environment is in our heads, on our backs, or in our sleds.

Just over halfway through the day, the wind starts to pick up. Wind has been a negligible factor since that afternoon on the bay back in Khatanga. How many years ago was that? I snug down the ruff, thankful for the wolverine that is wrapped around my face. Even though it smells of the dead animal (a scent I will never get used to and can later recall rather too easily), it is welcome. The fur's feathering protects my face from the sharp blast of the wind, but still allows me to see out. The ruff is less appealing when the moisture in my breath freezes it into white strands that scrape my cheeks, but it is still better than being without the barrier.

Despite the distraction of the wind, the landscape—the icescape—is enchanting. In gradations of white, it dazzles, reflecting the eternal sun that graces it. Some patches are stark white; others have a green or a yellow or a brown cast. These are older pieces of ice and rather stable. The ice that is sapphire in color gives me a new appreciation for "ice blue." It is a stunning color. Blue ice in the Arctic, as it turns out, is also the least stable ice because it is the newest.

Beyond the rubble ice, the snow that helps to make up the ice pan has its own set of remarkable qualities. It can be rock-hard or slushy, granular or light powder. It is a white that literally sparkles like so many diamonds cast in front of us. It is never boring. People native to these regions have more than a dozen terms for the word *snow*—hardly enough.

And, the ice sings. Maybe not in the way you and I might normally expect, but the ice and snow make sounds when we ski over it. Occasionally the sounds are a muffled, three-note tune. Sometimes—especially over small, crested ridges—the snow's sound runs up and down the chromatic scale as we ski over domes that remind me of meringues. The Arctic Ocean is showing itself to be a vibrant, engaging environment—one that plays with all of the senses.

. . .

Josée has trained us to carefully observe each other's faces for signs of frostbite: white spots on cheeks and noses. A couple of us, including me, are turning red, but there are no indications of frostbite like that which struck Kerri last week during the ski across the bay in Khatanga. Only Jen exhibits any discoloration on her cheeks, and those are two little starbursts that come from an allergic reaction to the sun.

The highest the sun ever rises today is about 45 degrees above the horizon—not exactly the blazing solar rays of the Equator. But the whole environment acts like a solar reflector. Everywhere, the sun either shines directly or bounces off the ice. I have heard tales of mountain climbers having the insides of their mouths burned from the reflection of the sun off of snow or glaciers. I take great pains to keep my neck gaiter pulled up to my top lip, not wanting to scorch the roof of my mouth.

Keeping the sun from damaging what little skin we do expose is a challenge as well. Every morning, after breakfast in the tent, we pass around tubes or tins of Dermatone, a product we've agreed to accept as a sponsor. The high SPF, coupled with the fact that the cream is free of water, makes for a good combination. The barrier to ultraviolet rays is critical.

The cream isn't perfect, though. Or at least our application of it isn't. While still at Borneo, Marie-Josée acquired a burned nose that is on its way to turning black. Josée has fashioned a "beak protector" from blue foam that hangs from the bridge of her sunglasses and keeps her from burning further. Kathy, Kerri, Alison, and I have picked up a skier's tan, from the top of the chin to the bottom of the forehead. Josée has a deep flush in her cheeks.

. . .

Around ten o'clock at night, Khatanga time, we settle on a flat, firm space to make camp. The wind is still coming at us hard, and it makes for a devilish time setting up the tents. Three of us get one side pegged in, and then the wind comes along and catches the flap, lifts it, and tosses our ski poles in the process. That the ice is rock-solid doesn't help. I struggle to jam the tail of an anchoring ski into the ice pan, with no success. Finally, Kerri and I drag several sleds and lay them on top of the skis that simply refuse to be planted in this frozen field.

Over a supper that is preceded by "Malakhov cocktails"—named after our Russian trainer—and hors d'oeuvres (one must maintain appearances, after all), we review the day.

In five marches, we've gone more than five nautical miles—fair progress for the day, but still not good enough if there is to be any hope of a rest day between here and the North Pole. Josée is encouraging and admonishing at the same time.

"Never forget where you are. You must always, always be aware, and never stop thinking about your survival." She looks around the tent to make sure she has our attention, which she does. "We have to be ready to move at a moment's notice, in case the ice starts to break apart. Keep your boots under your feet, at the bottom of your sleeping bag."

She tugs at her vest. "See what I am wearing? I put everything on at night, so that way—in case I have to jump out of bed and move fast—I will survive. Have your boots and your mittens and your hats right with you."

I'm not sure why she is giving us this lecture. Has she seen something that day that has worried her? I scribble a mental note to speak with her later about it.

After the meal, I call Bonnie, our webmaster and liaison person back home, on the sat phone, but am not able to reach her. She's told me that she'll be away some morning during the middle of the week for a meeting. Is it the middle of the week? Is it midmorning? I leave a voice message and give her our current position: N89.20, E117.24.

Then I call "NASA Mike," our contact at the Goddard Space Flight Center. We talk at length about the site for our webcast hookup that NASA is preparing. Will it be the North Pole or Ice Station Borneo? Based on the terrain, or rather the ice that surrounds us, I am unsure of being able to find a landing strip for the twin-engine Twin Otter from First Air—the plane that will be carrying Mike, Dr. Kathy Clark, and the rest of the crew from NASA to the polar icecap. Having the plane land at Borneo seems like a better choice. It isn't the North Pole, but it is close enough. Besides, we are headed there right after we reach the Pole, and we can meet at the ice station. The Russians can helicopter us from the North Pole, and the First Air Twin Otter can land at Borneo. It is a good place for our webcast to schools in North America. Borneo has a predictable landing strip—much better than one I might find in this environment, pocked with leads and pressure ridges.

Mike indicates that First Air is balking over the Borneo landing and is concerned about being gouged on fuel prices by the Russians. I assure him that Misha reckoned those figures before we left, and that they are reasonable. It isn't clear to me what the real problem of doing a webcast from Borneo is. But it is starting to be apparent that a lot of things aren't especially clear to me, or to most of us on the team. In the back of my mind, Misha's warning dimly sounds: In the Arctic, men are stupid.

After I finish with the satellite telephone, Alison dials the *Ottawa Citizen* and sends along her report:

> *It's weird how little we talk about home and the outside world. There's not a lot of energy left over to think about your family or your friends. Everything you do you have to think about in advance.*

As we shut down the kitchen and head for our sleeping bags, I am thankful that I have leveled the area inside the tent where my bag lies. I am ready for a solid night's sleep.

CHAPTER SIX

1996–1998

One day, many years ago, I looked around my Detroit TV newsroom and realized there were no women over the age of fifty. On the strength of that observation, I decided to go to law school, not intending to practice but more interested in the store of knowledge and the safety net a law degree would provide. After graduation, I found a position in the School of Journalism at Michigan State University. I was out of the daily business of broadcasting, but preparing the next generation. How could I know that this polar dream would occupy a huge part of my life and engage nearly all of my skills and resources, including my legal education?

Frida and I realized early on that we needed an organization to give us some structure and support. We were now women on a mission, and the scope of that mission was one of the things that drew us to the North Pole. It represented a huge challenge. Maybe we could use this personal challenge to encourage other women to take on their own.

"I know not every woman wants to ski to the Pole," Frida said one night on the phone from Marquette. "Jeez, most of them have better sense."

Just back from a cold, hard run, I frankly wished I had some of their good sense. I poured another cup of tea to warm up.

"But, you know," Frida said, "if her task is getting to the bottom of the laundry basket—just finishing the ironing—and she gets some encouragement from what we're doing, then we're successful."

I cast an eye at my own ironing board and the lump of clothes loaded on it. There was no getting to the bottom of this pile. Tomorrow would be another turtleneck day. "Why don't we make that a centerpiece of what we're doing," I said. "Supporting other women in their own challenges. Maybe we should put together an organization focused on that. Frida—what if I explore what's involved in incorporating, and then let's talk about it. I don't know if 'bottom of the laundry basket' is a good legal term, but I think you're really on to something."

My apprehensions about incorporating weren't totally justified. While it required a fair amount of careful reading, talking with friends who were also lawyers, and a tree's worth of paperwork, it was manageable. We called our nonprofit "WomenQuest," and the adventure would be the Polar Trek.

Frida and I ruminated over a mission statement. Encouragement of other women—and girls—remained one of our major goals. A recent report by the American Association of University Women warned that girls were still struggling mightily with self-image, and when it came to math and science, many of their brains apparently calcified once puberty hit. Going to the North Pole would require using math and science, and with an adventure like this, there had to be a way to make it exciting for middle-school girls. They didn't have to trail in math and science "just because they're girls."

Into the mission statement went these ideas—along with an acknowledgment of the women whose sacrifices had preceded ours, and the debt we owed them. We adapted a quote from the first-century poet Lucan to read: "We can see into the future because we stand on the shoulders of giants." Truly we had been lifted high by the previous generation, and now it was our turn to shoulder the burden.

We felt rather official now. An organization in place, a mission statement, and a journey ahead. But . . .

One of the dangers of having a dream is being a dreamer rather than a doer. We had an organization; but we didn't have a date, and we had only the barest elements of a team. This was still no more than a dream, and threatening to slip into a nightmare.

There was a real fear holding back our progress—the fear of failing, having set out to boldly go where not too many women had gone before. If you're still planning and working on it, you haven't really failed, right? And you haven't really had to go, either.

"When are you guys planning to go to the North Pole?" was the question we'd get a lot.

"We're still working on the preparations. These things take time, you know." Especially if one foot is dragging. "We're thinking about next April. Before April, it can be too cold, and after that, the ice can start breaking up. So, we're looking at April." Looking without actually doing.

"Oh," would come the reply. "Well, good luck."

With two more Aprils gone by, I began to feel like a fraud, putting an event on the distant horizon. Overcoming our inertia and actually mounting a polar trek felt beyond my grasp.

Frida was feeling the same way. We talked about it one night on the phone.

"I'm really having trouble with this," I confessed. "I don't know how to let go after all we've put into it so far. But, if we're really going to put together this North Pole ski, I don't know how to make it happen."

"I think about being at the North Pole every day," she said. "Every morning when I get up, it's there. But I just can't seem to make the leap." I hadn't realized that it was still such a compelling force for her, too.

"Frida," I said, "it's been more than four years since we first started talking about skiing to the Pole. Do you still want to do this?" Now was the moment for a truthful assessment.

"Yes. I don't know. I think so."

I waited.

"I just can't get it out of my head. I worry about what it's going to be like in that cold, but you know, I really want to go."

Two things were suddenly very clear. One was that I needed to move this expedition forward—not just for me, or the girls and women that we talked about in our mission statement, but for Frida. The other was that it could really happen.

"Listen, Frida." The energy was rising in me and words came out quickly. "We're smart girls; we can figure this out. So, if you really are in it with me, let's do it!" I laughed. "Besides, I'm definitely starting to feel older. I sure don't want to be freezing my butt on the ice when I'm fifty." And that was less than three years away. "Let me see what I can find out, and I'll get back to you in a couple of days."

Once I had a defined responsibility to my friend, the task of constructing a journey to the North Pole became easier. I was no longer wrestling with my own demons, because there was no space for them. This was for Frida as much as for me, Amanda, and all the women who would follow.

I began to collect information with fervor. Who was currently working the Arctic? What were the likely starting places for a trek to the North Pole? Was it better to go on skis alone, or with dogs? How much would this actually cost? Some of the information was already in hand, but I needed confirmation. I also needed the opinions of some of the top Arctic expeditioners. Most of them had websites, so I proceeded to contact each one and pepper them with questions.

The results were mixed, but helpful. Most of the leading Arctic travelers responded to my requests for information—some of them rather bemusedly. However, Rich Sweitzer—unhappy, I assume, because we had pulled away from him—had said some unflattering things about me within the polar community. It's a very small subset of adventurers, and it's quite porous; the comments got back to me. They certainly aided my decisions when it came to finding an outfitter to affiliate with.

Richard Weber, the owner of Canadian Arctic Holidays, replied to my email inquiry with great depth and thoughtfulness. A land-based departure for the North Pole was probably beyond us, he wrote. It was a more than two-month-long expedition, and would cost many thousands of dollars.

Dogs? Richard had been part of the Steger-Schurke expedition, along with Ann Bancroft, and had found the dogs a hindrance. Humans can move much faster without them. In fact, he and Misha Malakhov, his Russian counterpart, had set the record for an unresupplied expedition to the North Pole and back. Richard knew speed and efficiency.

Point of departure? Leave from a position on the Arctic Ocean north of Russia. The cost would be $15,000 less than going through Canada, principally because of air transport. This could really come together, I thought.

After an exchange of several emails, Richard and I set a time to talk on the telephone. I asked directly if he would help organize a trek to the North Pole for WomenQuest, and if his company would be the outfitter. He certainly had the experience and the contacts to pave the way.

"Richard, there is one point I need to make sure is clear to you," I said very deliberately, hoping that this wouldn't undo what looked like a great relationship. "This is an all-women trek." After a pause, he spoke.

"That's not a problem. I'll train my wife, Josée, to take you."

I couldn't wait to tell Frida. Reviewing my notes from the conversation with Richard, I highlighted the proposal, the cost, and the date.

"We'll go in April of 2000. That's a little less than two years from now. We need a team of ten women"—I was a little breathless now—"and he's going to take his wife Josée with him to the North Pole next April, in '99, to train her to be our guide."

"Why are we going through Russia?" Frida asked.

"For openers, it's less expensive than going through Resolute Bay in Canada. Besides, Richard's expedition partner is a fellow named Misha Malakhov, and he's a Hero of the Soviet Union." In my excitement, I forgot that the Soviet Union was gone. Misha was a Hero of Russia because of his Arctic exploits.

"Now," I added, "all we have to do is to put together a team, and we're going to the North Pole!"

CHAPTER SEVEN

Day Three

It is a short night by design. Enveloped by continual daylight, we need to set a schedule and to stick with it. It helps that the rhythms of skiing during the day and making camp in the evening are smoothing out. We are headed in the right direction at a reasonable rate of speed, and are better balanced as a team. Yesterday's progress of more than six and one-half miles was encouraging. But we still have a lot of distance to cover in a little more than a week.

It is Wednesday, April 18.

Last night, in the message I left for Bonnie, I asked that she post a note on the web that we'll do our best to get in touch with schools we promised to call. She did.

> *"We want to ask our participating schools to understand the need to be flexible in the timing of our phone calls," said Sue. The team uses the satellite telephones provided by the U.S. Navy to make conference calls back to schoolrooms in Michigan that are using the online curriculum. But the priority has to be on making progress toward their goal, so there may be times that phone calls must be delayed until they can reach a point where making the call becomes more easily accomplished.*

Tonight, though, we are determined to get camp set up and dinner underway, if not over, in time to reach morning classes back home. We are still adhering to Khatanga, Siberia, time—a full twelve hours in advance of Eastern Daylight Time, and eight hours ahead of Greenwich.

It is 7:30 A.M. our time when we rise—11:30 P.M. in Greenwich and 7:30 P.M. in East Lansing. It is 23:30 UTC.

If we are going to hit the trail earlier, it means better organization at the front of the day. Josée's waking call of "Good morning, girls, it's time to rise and shine" is the alarm that penetrates our sleeping bags and draws us out of our sacks. The wind has picked up and the cold feels even more penetrating. Jen, who slept right by the door, slides out of her bedroll and rapidly opens the drawstrings of the entrance, crawling out and dragging her mats and bag behind her. Frida, Lynn, and I are far slower to shed our bags, slithering out of our cocoons at the speed of a snake shedding its skin. Diana Ciserella and Marie-Josée are also in our tent, and quicker to leave it once awake. Younger than the three of us by at least a decade, they move faster in the morning. And Diana has already had some experience in the Antarctic.

In the time before breakfast, several of us stuff our sleeping bags and tidy our sleds, readying them for a swift final load. The sleeping mats go into the cook tent to make a temporary flooring; the camp chairs are sent that way too, so there will be seating for all ("I'd like a table away from the kitchen, please"); and the self-inflating air mattresses are unplugged, squeezed flat of air, and stuffed away. Boots, mitts, kit bags are all scooped up. The tent is set to come down. We'll hold off on that until after breakfast, though. Even empty and cold it offers some shelter: a place to put on the final set of liners and the wind suit before strapping on skis in the bitter Arctic cold.

Funny how even the barest micron of nylon can give comfort to humans. In reality, there is no way to keep the outdoors out, but not being able to see it creates the pretense of a break from it. We could sleep outside—even cook outside—with some success. The tents, though, are a haven in the Arctic—in a world that cares not if you live or die.

Breakfast. It is warm, and it is tasty. Even though the menu doesn't vary substantially, the sheer anticipation of it makes the food even better. Sweet, hard Russian bread, similar to Melba toast, loaded with butter, honey, and peanut butter. Oatmeal. Tea, coffee, apple cider from a dehydrated mix that is surprisingly good, or hot chocolate.

Jen, our cook, keeps the Russian stoves going and the pots working to turn snow into water. Our day's ration of hot drink for the trail will come from that. Each of us has a thermos. Initially they were assigned, but that system collapsed fairly quickly. Jen merely fills the thermoses, and they are passed among the women gathered around the stoves in the cook tent. Grab the one you want: tea, cider, or an energy drink that is too sweet for me. I mostly opt for tea—Earl Grey.

. . .

Josée takes great pride in food preparations; they are a hallmark of her and Richard's personal survival in the Arctic, and a distinctive trait of their leadership on the ice. Fresh coffee in carafes for us. Richard is even pickier; he's selected Starbucks for his group.

Josée has told me of encountering a member of another group at the North Pole two years ago. "He was this Norwegian fellow, see," she explained, "and his group had nearly run out of food. He came over to our tent looking for something to eat."

I was surprised that an expedition leader would cut food supplies that closely, but the desire to keep loads light can be overwhelming. She continued: "He wanted to know if he could have something to eat, and if we had anything hot to drink. 'Sure,' I said. 'We've got food, and some tea, too. What kind of tea would you like?'" She laughed a deep laugh. "You could have knocked him over. Our preparations were so much better than his group's."

That story has stuck with me. The food we eat daily is inviting and plentiful, and I have no doubt that there will be some to spare at the end. No way can we go through all of that pasta stuffed in our sleds.

. . .

If we really are going to hit the trail early, it is time to go. Unlike the last two days, the sun is obscured by a gray veil of clouds; the sky is close, and there is a low ceiling and light precipitation. Clouds and snow are not a good forecast for skiing.

At last we clip our sleds onto our backpack ropes—it is nearly 11 A.M. I glance down at the inexpensive thermometer/compass/clock that is hooked onto the bottom zipper of my wind jacket. The thermometer is of no value; it is mostly too cold to register. The compass is worthless at this latitude. Magnetic north is hundreds of miles to the south of us. But the digital clock, so far, has been helpful. Occasionally the face freezes over and the numbers disappear; but on the whole, it works.

At the beginning of each march, I calculate how long we'll be skiing before the next break. It is a little like swimming laps: one-quarter of the way there, now halfway, now two-thirds. Guess what, only one-quarter more to go! The calibrations become fairly significant after about the fourth march of the day—somewhere about the sixth hour of skiing—when the desire to stop becomes stronger. At the moment, that time is far off.

The pressure ridges slow our progress today. Four or five of them rise in front of us as we slog, ski, and sometimes skate forward, scaling ice rubble more than twenty feet high. Each time we summit these devilish peaks, another one looms in front of us. But Misha's fire-brigade training has prepared us for traversing these mounds. It no longer takes fifteen minutes to hoist our equipment and ourselves over the top. We have easily halved the time. He would have no reason now to spit on the ice in disgust at our lack of skill and effort. We are becoming a well-oiled machine.

This third day is one of remarkable contrasts in the environment. It begins overcast and slightly snowing. The sun emerges about halfway through our skiing—not as brilliant as the days before, but still a presence. Marking the sky are thin layers of cirrus clouds, some of them wispy and quite high. The streaks are long blazes connecting one end of the horizon with the other.

Every day, I search for a trace of a jet—a contrail to indicate that there are humans within seven, ten, twenty miles of us, even if above and warm in an airliner. But nothing. There is no sign of any aircraft. The pilots who claim to be taking a "polar route" must be flying over a different pole because it certainly isn't ours.

Around midday—such as we calculate it—we pick up the slight traces of another skier's tracks. Solo. Josée examines them carefully, bending over like an Indian scout. Rising, she makes her pronouncement. "I think it's the French woman." I vaguely remember talk of a French woman and two others dedicated to a long ski to the Pole, and some thought that illness has interrupted their journey. I've been so focused on our trek, though, that others' expeditions are not part of my consideration. The other team members and I look down at the tracks. Then we ski on in a slightly different direction.

Somewhere along the fourth or fifth break, we stop against a pressure ridge, using the icy backdrop as a windbreak—for the winds haven't completely died down. Chiseled into the pile of ice chunks is a little cavern of stark blue ice. Set down in the midst of the rubble, it isn't visible from the open surface of the ice pan. But after turning past two boulders of frozen water, we discover it. It isn't a cavern in the truest sense, but an area hollowed out and hidden—like a blue, backlit living room complete with a natural six-foot-long bench that faces the sun. It is a stunning spot for a break.

The morning's slow and tricky surface is replaced in the afternoon by a smooth pan of ice that stretches on for at least a half mile. Marie-Josée and Alison, used to skating on frozen lakes and rivers in their native Canada, are particularly impressed. Marie-Josée writes in her journal later that it reminds her of the Rideau Canal in Ottawa. Alison likens it to the Gatineau Parkway.

It reminds me of Lake Lansing, a small, overdeveloped lake close to Michigan's capital. I spent hours skiing its frozen surface in January and February, bearing a backpack and dragging a sled. For all of us, though, this particular ice pan is a smooth, fast surface. It is actually possible to pole it—to move forward using only ski poles and keeping the feet together—the ice is that slick. I certainly don't want to fall.

Our advance for the day is solid if not spectacular, and the North Pole is that much closer. With six marches and more than five nautical miles, we have put together a good day of nine hours on the ice. And it still isn't late—at least not as late as it was when we stopped the last two days.

Picking a campsite for the night presents a problem, though. We find ourselves, at the end of the nine hours, right up against a major lead. Josée thinks it makes no sense to try to cross it tonight. With any luck, it might actually freeze before we head out tomorrow, and we can traverse it here, instead of having to ski a distance to find a narrow spot.

Carefully, Josée skies around an area some one hundred yards around. Shed of her sled and backpack, she uses a long metal probe to test the ice for depth and durability. The color looks good, but this close to a large lead, the stability of the ice raises some questions. Finally, with the rest of us cold and our arms flapping like a flock of penguins, she glides back and motions us to a level spot about thirty yards away. As she is strapping on her backpack again, she briefs us.

"It's smooth and pretty firm over there, but you girls need to remember that ice can change rapidly. Be prepared to move quickly if we have to. This is the Arctic Ocean."

By 8:30 P.M. we are camped for the night, and the cook tent is serving piping hot jambalaya as the plat du jour. There will be ample time to make calls back to North America and still get to bed at a reasonable hour. Josée has left us to our preparations—setting up tents, and pulling out food and equipment for dinner—while she skies off to explore the lead that has the potential to bedevil us tomorrow.

Off to the right, and east, she goes. I can see her in the distance climbing a fifteen-foot pile of ice. I am on my knees helping pack snow around the base of a tent. Suddenly, she is back in camp, breathless.

"Any of you want to come and see ice moving?" she asks. Lynn and I look at each other. Our skis are already anchoring the smaller tent, and it will take us a while to walk there in our oversized boots. Marie-Josée and Kathy still have their skis free and quickly strap them on, chasing after Josée as she turns and rips off to the ridge once more. I will just have to wait and hear the tale upon their return.

Josée has spotted a pressure ridge that is moving, and a lead that is about to close. Apparently it is a tributary to the major one facing us. Last night, around the cook stove, Josée shared with us stories of leads closing.

"It sounds just like a big truck," she explained in her French Canadian accent. "It is such a noise that you hope you never hear while you are sleeping in your tent." That concept has stuck in my mind, increasingly numb though it is. That certainly is one noise I do not want to awaken to.

It isn't long before the trio comes skating back, flying over the ice. "We missed it," Kathy says. More words than I've heard her say all day. "But it really is beautiful out there."

Marie-Josée is flushed from the joy of skiing without weight. She is carrying a large amount every day—including the radio that Mike, the Russian ham-radio operator, showed us how to assemble and use back in Solotcha, our staging area near Moscow. She is a graceful skier and enjoys the speed of the sport.

The radio.

Tonight it is critical that we reach Ice Station Borneo using the high-frequency radio we've been dragging around. Last night Marie-Josée and Jen set it up, running the wires according to the diagram that Mike had instructed me to draw. Kerri, who speaks the language better than any of us, called continuously in Russian: "Borneo, Borneo, WomenQuest calling, over"—but with no response. Between the solar flares from the sun during this, the height of an eleven-year cycle, and the antique nature of the set, we had gotten nowhere. Maybe tonight will yield better luck. I really hope so, because the deal we've agreed to is that we'll contact the Russians at Borneo by our fifth day, and that is the day after tomorrow. We have until April 20 to contact them.

If not, they will assume that we are in difficulty and send a helicopter to come rescue us. To wave them off will be a $5,000 charge, one I neither want to face nor pay. Pray for good radio-wave propagation.

Josée reaches Richard at their appointed time of 9 P.M. on the satellite telephone. They too haven't been able to contact Ice Station Borneo. From deep inside me creeps the thought that I should have left one of our two satellite telephones back on Borneo. Misha had pressured me to do that, given that we have two. But the telephones are on loan from the U.S. Navy, and I believed it was out-of-bounds to leave a piece of American military equipment behind at a Russian ice station. Besides, we really do need telephone redundancy, given our heavy commitment to contact schoolchildren and communicate with the media back home.

After dinner, Kerri and Susan Martin pull out their list of schools they have agreed to phone on April 18 and begin dialing. Susan is a middle-school science teacher who has helped Kerri and me create the online curriculum for the expedition. We can only hear the conversation from this end, but the questions sound good and informed. The teachers have done a thorough job of preparing their students for this call from near the North Pole. Sometimes media are present; sometimes the feed goes over the school public-address system. Always, though, the reception is enthusiastic.

The open leads indicated by the NASA photos are posted on our website for the whole world to see—except us. Two of them have required a detour, as I explain that night to Bonnie:

"We look to Josée in these situations, and she quickly found appropriate crossing points," said team leader Sue Carter. In the background, Kathy Braegger could be heard saying, "I didn't even need to unpack my rubber raft."

. . .

There is more.

"You are getting a lot of traffic on the message board that we set up," Bonnie says, "and you're getting some international press coverage." She hesitates. "It has to do with skiing the wrong way."

No surprise there. We knew it would get attention, but reaching our goal will eradicate any negatives about the initial southerly turn.

"Yeah," she adds, "it even made the papers in South Africa. Most of it, though, is really positive. People from all over are following you."

"Bonnie, that is such good news. We are really in an information vacuum up here."

"Did they let them go yet?" Diana mouths in a stage whisper from across the tent. I shrug my shoulders and give her a quizzical look. "The Chinese," she adds.

Oh. Just as we were leaving, an American spy plane had been shot at and forced to land on a Chinese island. The story had ended there—if temporarily—for us. Diana is interested, given that her husband Dave is an Air Force pilot. I explain to Bonnie and get her answer. "No, they're still there, but okay."

I ask Alison if she wants to talk with Bonnie, to debrief her on the trip. Alison nods and I put her on the phone. "I am very task-oriented and would want to keep skiing until I drop," she says. "The team reminds me that I need to take time to appreciate the experience with the other women in this remarkable environment."

. . .

Bonnie suggests I contact NASA about the arrangements for the webcast. I leave a message and then make three more calls for the night: one to WJR, a radio station with a wide reach in Detroit, and another to WILX-TV in Lansing, the hometown crew that has been following us. The final call is to Dan Shine of the *Detroit Free Press*. Done for the evening. This has taken a fair amount of group time—but so, too, have the calls to the schools. It is a mixed blessing: we are in an isolated environment, and highly connected.

Again the high-frequency radio is connected, and again Kerri is calling out into the void, searching for a voice to answer, one to whom she can give our coordinates. There is no answer, though, for the second night in a row.

We turn off the stoves and move to our separate spaces for sleeping. We go to bed at N89.28, E118.19.

CHAPTER EIGHT

1999

The process of putting together a team turned out to be slower and much more challenging than I had expected. My unbridled enthusiasm for going to the North Pole was shared by a few women, but getting a commitment from them was tough.

For openers, there was a sizable price tag attached to the trek, in addition to the time needed to ski to the North Pole. Finally, a prospective teammate was obliged to set aside a week for training in January. Not everyone had a total of five weeks of time ready to pledge.

In the half year since WomenQuest had joined with Canadian Arctic Holidays for our polar trek, Richard, Josée, and I had been in touch frequently. Our conversations were the stuff of expedition planning: gear, itinerary, dates, and the like. And there was always the question about how many women had signed up. By spring of 1999, we were making progress, but barely. Aside from Frida and me as teammates, there were serious inquiries from a half dozen other women, and commitments from two. No cash on the barrelhead yet, but they seemed pretty solid. Plus, I was developing a media campaign that I was confident would get the word out, and then we'd be inundated with applicants. But now, a face-to-face meeting with our guides and outfitters was in order. So in May, I agreed to travel to Richard and Josée's home just outside of Ottawa.

I arrived in late afternoon with a friend, Linda, along for company. After introductions, we settled in over drinks and began to chat. It was heady stuff, being here in the home of a true Arctic explorer. It made our plans all the more real.

Then, Richard caught me off guard.

"I think you should put off the trek for a year. You still don't have a full team," he said, "and there is much more to be done."

"But, Richard, we're starting to get some serious interest, and besides, we've already let it be known that we're planning to go next April."

"Right. And next April is less than a year away. You need a team of ten, and they've got to be trained. You're attempting something extraordinary, and the whole group has to be ready."

I looked at Josée for confirmation. She nodded.

"Richard's right, you know. This isn't an easy job you girls are thinking about. You must have a group that can work together as a team."

My body felt leaden in my chair. I leaned forward, elbows on knees, and rolled the glass of wine between the palms of my hands.

"There may be a problem for me in moving the date," I began slowly. "My sabbatical leave from the university is set for spring semester 2000. Who knows if it can be changed?" It was also distressing to finally arrive at a date, only to have it pushed back.

Sensing my disappointment, Richard said," Don't worry. In the meantime, I'll take Josée with me to the Pole again next spring."

"And," Josée chimed in, "I'll be all the more expert to take you."

What choice was there? It's not as though there were other expeditioners readily available; we'd already checked the field. Besides, I firmly believed that this was the best outfit. Frankly, here was further proof that my choice of Josée, trained by Richard, was the best. It was just that, after several years of marginal progress, the delay tasted bitter.

"I'll go back and see what can be changed at the university," I said, as bravely as possible. But my throat still stung.

Once past the disappointment, we moved on to a wonderful meal. Josée had prepared it along with Jen Buck, who lived nearby. A nursing student and a wilderness guide, Jen would be Josée's assistant on the trek.

The conversation flowed in many directions: past expeditions, characters who inhabit the profession, specific plans for our trek, a tour of the equipment we'd be using. When it came time to take our leave and return to Montreal for a flight home, I was fairly resigned to the new timetable. On the two-hour drive back through a slashing thunderstorm, Linda and I reviewed the visit with Josée and Richard.

"It is a disappointment," I conceded, "but at the end of the day, it's probably for the best."

Linda understood the depth of my feelings. She had tracked my progress for the last four years.

"I know it's not what you were expecting," she said. "But you're still going to the North Pole—just a year later. And you can use that time to really get ready."

I shrugged in silence and drove on through the spikes of lightning of the thunderstorm that enveloped us, wondering if I really could get the date of my sabbatical changed. And I needed to call Bonnie right away to alter the website.

Bonnie Bucqueroux is one of the most talented, independent, and endearing people I know. She is also whimsical. Her choice of a last name, for instance, came out of the opportunity to change surnames following a divorce. A few folks, upon hearing it, think "Buckeroo" and laugh. Bonnie, with a straight face, then spells it out for them, and their amusement turns to shame for having mocked what is an apparently legitimate French family name.

I drove out to her house the next day. It's a sprawling cedar structure set in the woods not far from campus. The dogs—her collection of strays—came out to greet me. The ashes of ones that had preceded them were in a memorial garden off to the side. I took care not to pull the car into the space marked "Parking for Lithuanians only."

Bonnie greeted me at the door. "So, how did it go with Josée and Richard?"

"Think we can change the home page from Polar Trek 2000 to Polar Trek 2001?" I said.

"That good, huh?"

Over a pot of tea, I laid out the conversation we'd had with Richard and Josée.

"Part of me wonders if Richard's desire to do a much longer expedition next spring isn't related to moving ours a year," I said. "Still, he's right. No matter what the reason, our group, such as it is, probably couldn't pull it together for spring of 2000. But I still have to talk with Steve about shifting this forward a year." Steve Lacy directed the School of Journalism and was my supervisor.

"Steve knows this is important to you and may have some value for the university," she said. Bonnie and I had been working on an idea to incorporate a curriculum into the webpage, one targeted at middle-school students, with a focus on math and science. "If there's a way to do this, he'll work it out. And as for the webpage, all we have to do is make a few changes in the text and graphics, and we've got Polar Trek 2001. In fact, we can do it now, if you'd like."

I looked over at the massive monitor and tower in the workspace between the dining area and the living room.

"Probably I should talk with Steve before you change it," I said. "It wouldn't be good for him to read it on the Internet first."

. . . .

Steve listened with great care as I shared the results of my trip to see Richard and Josée.

"Didn't you have the dates for the trek cleared with them?" he said gently. "This has been in the works for a while."

"I did—or at least I thought so. I had sent a letter of agreement laying out costs and a timetable. And I think we could have done this next year." I paused for a moment. "But these events happen in a different world. And I suppose they're right that we can use the extra time to make this expedition really special."

Steve eased back into his chair. "There's another sabbatical application for the next spring, the same time you're now asking for. Folu has also applied for a research grant to continue his field work in Africa." We both taught broadcasting classes; this would mean an instructional void.

"Maybe a graduate student could teach one or more of our sections?" I offered. Not the best solution, but a possible one.

"Let me see what I can do," Steve said. "Oh, and there is one more thing."

I dreaded asking, but needed to know. Whatever the condition was, I was now bound to meet it.

"What is it?"

Steve leaned back even further and smiled. "Tom Hanks gets to play me in the movie."

He ducked the wadded-up paper I threw in his direction.

. . . .

In spite of an unexpected turn in the road, our ski to the North Pole, now officially Polar Trek 2001, was going forward. Problem was, we still had to put together a team. WomenQuest's Polar Trek 2001, we told ourselves, would be different from the standard expedition that was often "every man for himself." We were definitely going as a team, dedicated to a mission. As the idea for a web-based curriculum grew, we envisioned each woman writing a lesson based on some aspect of the trek: environment, history of exploration, the science of navigation, human response to the cold, and so on. Beyond that, we were all going to make it. No one would get left behind.

Armed with a list of about two dozen magazines that centered on women and fitness or women and sports, I sent out news releases announcing Polar Trek 2001 and its mission to encourage women, and especially girls, to challenge themselves—particularly in math and science. By the way, I added, we have openings and we're taking applications.

The inquiries and applications started to come in. Hardly a flood, but enough of a trickle to give encouragement to Frida and me. There would be enough women to assemble a team that would mesh and advance the group's goals. I talked at length with each woman who sent in an application. I mailed several dozen more.

Two women with Ph.D.s in the hard sciences emerged from California, both with impressive credentials in frigid environments, including the Himalayas. A young freelance journalist with solid writing skills and training as a firefighter in Montana also came forward. From Utah, an afternoon disc jockey at a jazz station popped up. Good skiing and outdoor abilities here, too. It was hard for me not to feel outstripped by the women who were applying.

In the interest of local support, I decided to check out another scientist at Michigan State. She led me to a friend of hers. The scientist was on leave and likely to stay out west, but the friend was eager to join the trek to the North Pole. Phyllis, an MSU administrator, was an unlikely candidate, but the chance to have some local support in planning and execution was appealing. Her husband, Dave, was on the faculty, and I knew him from other associations on campus. He collared me one day on a sidewalk near our buildings.

"Why do you want to take my wife to the North Pole?" he said, in a way that was either challenging or humorous—I wasn't sure which.

"Dave, if she wants to be part of our group and can cut it, then I think that's her choice. She's got skills that I think can be an asset."

Dave looked at me, humphed a good-bye, and headed into his building. The next few days, I took a different path from my building to central campus.

Late in the summer, Phyllis approached me about having her fifteen-year-old daughter come aboard as a member of the trek.

"You're reaching out to middle-school girls," she said. "What better than to have one their age go along?"

"Let me ask Josée," I said. "Let's see what she has to say."

I was surprised when Josée didn't see the addition as a problem. "My boys are a lot younger, and they could probably do it. If she wants to come, I'm okay with it."

I reported back to Phyllis that Josée didn't see Katie's age as an obstacle. There was, I agreed, an aspect to connecting with other schoolgirls that was appealing. On that basis, and without an objection from Josée, we added Katie.

Two weeks later, I told my sister. She shook her head. "I think you're making a mistake."

"But if she can hack it, it's a promotable piece. It'll let us forge a link with other girls her age."

"That's understandable, but it takes a lot of maturity, not just physical ability, to go on a journey like this. Remember, you're going to the North Pole." Carol paused. "Would you take Amanda?"

"No, but then she probably wouldn't want to go." She was smarter than her mom.

"Why not have Katie be here as a link? She can be involved, but just not with you out there on the ice. It really is more than a fifteen-year-old can handle."

"You're probably right. But we've already said she could go. We just have to play this one out."

Josée and I kept in regular contact through the summer and into the fall. Her time at the North Pole earlier that year led her to encourage us to have a training session with prospective team members—a trial by fire, as it were. We agreed to hold off asking for a deposit from anyone until after a January 2000 skiing-camping session in Marquette. Frida had generously offered to let her home be the base for a get-together and training.

Come January, Pam and Dana came in from California. Diane flew in from Utah. Carter joined us from Montana. Phyllis and Katie drove up from East Lansing. The core of the team was together at last. I hoped.

CHAPTER NINE

2000

The band of would-be explorers who made their way to Marquette were an interesting lot. Aged fifteen to the midsixties, with skiing ability ranging from stunning to virtually nil, we were women drawn together nonetheless by some common bonds that included a love of adventure, the thrill of life lived out of doors, and a genuine interest in encouraging other women and girls. We also responded to the whiff of adrenaline.

On arrival, we boldly took over the lower level of Frida's house and laid everything out. Then, Josée went from nest to nest, poking through clothing, skis, and sleeping gear, saying, "This is okay. That's all right. Do you have something warmer?" Pam, the Tibetan traveler, got through with flying colors. Several others, including me, were dispatched to the local ski shop for superior mittens, hats, neckovers, and the like. In less than two hours, we must have boosted their weekly till by a third. Even so, our plans for three nights on a snowy, frigid trail were scaled down to two when Josée realized that we all didn't have adequate gear and clothing for even a short stay. It was projected to be at least –20 degrees Fahrenheit, and the wrong equipment could be dangerous, whether you were twenty-five or twenty-five hundred miles from home.

By midafternoon Thursday, we were finally provisioned for our daring two-nighter. Scaling down the scope of the trail time didn't make it feel any less significant, and we were anxious to go. Josée made a final inspection, and bodies and gear were loaded into Frida's van and my truck. I had the skis, backpacks, and sleds; Josée rode shotgun. Frida and the rest of the team piled into the van with the food.

"Frida, remember that all I have is rear-wheel drive," I said. "We flatlanders don't need four-wheel drive that much, so I don't have it."

"Right," she said, waving out the window. And then she was gone.

Happily, I had a map of where we were going. Josée and I caught up with the others a few minutes after they arrived at the head of the McCormick Trail, an hour west of Marquette.

"Hey, Frida," I called out as I clambered out of the truck. "Next time, can you leave some bread crumbs for me? I lost the white plume of your van about four miles ago."

"Oh, sorry." She grinned. "Guess I'm just used to these roads."

We had about two hours of daylight left, so Jen and I quickly unloaded the skis and the rest of the equipment from the back of the truck. Backpacks and gear were rapidly sorted out, and we clipped our toes into our ski bindings. The three-foot-deep snow meant that gaiters were essential. Otherwise, the insides of our boots would soon be wet, and moisture, as Josée kept drilling into us, is the enemy in the cold. Funny—the snow here was deeper than what we'd find in the Arctic. At least that's what the books said.

Because we were planning on camping out only two nights, we had brought sleds for only half of the team. That was plenty to carry tents, sleeping bags, cooking equipment, and fuel, as well as food. Frida had brought along Big Bertha, a sled longer than the ones Josée and Jen had flown in from Canada. Theirs were more like the Kmart plastic toboggans in size than Frida's six-footer. Bertha was home to the video equipment that she would use to begin to document this event. We were definitely in the prequel stage.

Zipping my truck keys into a pants pocket and securing them with a little pat, I joined the line that was headed into the woods, sled attached to my back-pack with a carabiner. There wouldn't be any trees in the Arctic either, I reminded myself. But it would certainly be this cold. It was already 10 degrees Fahrenheit. Below.

Diane, the Salt Lake City disc jockey, took the first turn breaking trail. It wasn't hard to follow the line between the trees, but being the lead skier was hard work—especially for Diane, who was the smallest of the group. She was also, remarkably, one of the strongest.

The first half hour was slow going, partly because the latest snow three days before had obliterated any earlier signs of human passage. Also, some of the women took a few spills, and tumbling into deep snow makes for a real struggle getting upright again. Katie, to her credit, had one of the sleds linked to her backpack with a rope and still managed to keep pace with everyone. Phyllis, without a sled, was finding the going rough. I was feeling it was something I'd have to grow into.

After an hour, we pulled up for a short break. Josée took note of the dimming sky and said that we'd set up camp at the next clear, level space. One hour out, and it was already starting to feel like work. Good work, but work. I was warm from the skiing, and Jen was beginning to pull off a layer of clothing. She would take over from Diane, and that meant she'd burn more energy. The trick was to be warm, but not to sweat while skiing, either here in the Upper Peninsula or on the Arctic Ocean.

It was less than a mile before Jen pointed with her left ski pole at a clearing off to the side, then turned back toward the rest of the team. "That space should be big enough for our tents."

The area she had chosen was some twenty-five feet off the trail, and widened into a fairly flat space that was about thirty by forty feet. Pines lined the northern side of it, and there was scrub around the rest. Once inside the clearing, Jen marked two circles about twelve feet in diameter by skiing around.

"This is where we'll put the cook tent," she said, pointing to one. "And over here, the sleeping tent."

"Okay, who's got the sled with the tents?" Josée said.

Those of us with sleds roped to our backpacks looked around rather blankly. Tents?

They were here somewhere, but we'd have to dig for them.

"It's important to know what's in your sled," Josée said, pausing to let the words soak in. I was starting to get a little bit cold. "What if we have to set up in a hurry? Maybe someone's gone through the ice and gotten hypothermic. We can't waste time searching. Know what's in your sled."

"I've got a tent bag!" Carter called out after a moment. Diane found the other one in her sled.

Before the tents could be laid out on the ground in preparation for raising, the snow had to be tamped down and smoothed. Once snow is pressed down, it hardens fairly quickly, like making a snowball. The trick is to get the snow to harden as a flat surface. Otherwise, sleeping on the ground, even with pads and sleep system as barriers, can be lumpy and rather uncomfortable—downright miserable.

Frida, unhitched from Big Bertha, joined us as we tramped down the tent area as though we were stomping grapes. "This is what we call 'panking,'" she said. It wasn't clear if that was a Yooper word, a Finnish word, or a Frida word. But we all laughed and started into a chorus of "Hanky Panky," that wonderful garage-band hit from 1964. Within minutes, we had hanky-pankied our way through two rather smooth snow circles, ready for tents. I felt at one with the crop-circle makers in southern England.

Next, out came the tents from their bags: first the cook tent, and second the additional sleeping tent. The cook tent would always be the first to go up, so that the meal preparers could begin their work while the others set up the remaining tent.

The tents were the product of Misha Malakhov's experience in the Arctic, along with refinements from Richard Weber, and more recently Josée. These tents are thoroughly ingenious. Each tent has a floor that is entirely separate from the sides and top of the tent. The top half of the tent has two layers of nylon that allow the moisture, for the most part, to escape rather than build up and freeze on the interior. Otherwise, you get a ceiling of little ice chunks. The outer layer is a windproof nylon designed to keep Arctic blasts from roaring through.

Here is the truly special feature of this design: one piece of the top's double layer stays inside at the base, while the other is pulled out and covered with packed snow, keeping it weighted and windproof. At its base, the tent is really more of a snow cave. The advantage of having the top part of the tent separate from the floor is the easy exit from any part of the tent at any time. Imagine a fire or a polar bear, two dangerous propositions in the Arctic. A standard tent has only one way in and one way out. With the Malakhov-Weber tent, all it takes to get out of the tent from any position is to push against the wall. The polar bear is none the wiser.

Once the tent was up, Josée and Jen turned their attention to retrieving cook stoves, food, and fuel from the remaining sleds. That left the rest of us to wrestle with the second tent. The effort was somewhere between the Marx Brothers and the Keystone Cops. Finally, after one or two inadvertent whacks on the back of the head with skis—and I believe Frida caught some of this on tape—the "suburban" tent was ready for occupancy. It had taken half an hour.

"Josée," several of us called out, "what do we do next?"

She poked her head out of the cook tent. "Have you gotten your sleeping bags out?"

Right. Sleeping bags go into the tents, along with the inflatable mattress pads—Therm-a-Rests and Ridge Rests.

"Josée, who sleeps where?" We were in need of guidance.

"I don't care. You girls divide up and figure it out."

This seemed like an awfully important decision to leave up to us.

Diane extracted her pads and sleeping bag from her sled. "I'll sleep in this other tent," she said, pointing to the second one we had erected.

"I'll go there, too," Carter said. Frida and Jen would make it four. That left Josée, Pam, Dana, Phyllis, Katie, and me in the cook tent. It was bigger, and that was fine.

The sun had yielded the sky to an amazing host of stars. It was quite clear that night, and that suggested that the temperature would really take a dive. The clear sky also meant that we would have a good chance to see the first lunar eclipse of the year. I mused for a minute that we wouldn't see one of the prime tools of navigation, the Pole Star, when we were on the Arctic Ocean, for we'd be in full daylight. How very different from this.

The thermometer clipped to my jacket zipper read –20 when I shone my headlamp on it. Most of us had clamped the lights over our caps as we finished the tasks of getting our beds ready. Already, lantern shadows and wonderful smells were coming from the cook tent. I did a final check of my backpack and sled to remind myself where my mats, bag, and personal kit were, then crawled through the entrance of the cook tent. Most of the others were already inside. Several of the women had brought camp chairs and were seated round the sides of the tent. We'd been on the trail less than five hours, and already it felt as though we were days away from any life we knew.

Jen, the chief cook, was sitting cross-legged in front of two Russian cook stoves. It was a posture she could hold for two hours, and it later earned her the name of "Kitchen Buddha."

"Ladies," she said. Jen used the term *ladies* the way that Josée used *girls*. To the rest of the world, we were women.

"Tonight we are having African pork stew."

She and Josée were terrific cooks, as I'd learned on my visit to Canada. The emphasis they put on food was impressive. This evening's meal had been prepared from scratch and then dehydrated. It required only water, in the form of melted snow, to revive.

"But first," she said, "a Malakhov cocktail and some hors d'oeuvres."

The Malakhov cocktail, named for Misha Malakhov, had been described to us by Josée the night before. It was now time to savor this concoction. In other locales it probably wouldn't sell, but in the cold it is delightful. Begin with warm milk made from powder and snow boiled into water. Add maple syrup. Add Crown Royal whiskey. (The latter two ingredients reflect the Canadian influence of Richard Weber on Misha.) Serve in a plastic mug in a warm tent on a very cold evening. It's absolutely just the right touch to pull the mind away from the day's labors and relax the body before the next.

The hors d'oeuvres were equally elegant, consisting of cheese and crackers, smoked oysters, and pâté. All prepared on a plank of plywood and cut with a Swiss Army knife. We took turns cutting and passing the treats around the tent while Jen stirred the pots and Josée helped ready the eating bowls and spoons. First, spoonfuls of rice went into each bowl, followed by stew. Steam leapt from the ladle.

We passed down the bowls until each woman had one. We inhaled the stew in silence, tired as much from anticipation as exertion.

After the stew, there was water for coffee or tea. And there was chocolate.

"Did ya hear the one about Uno and Anna?" Frida said in a heavy Yooper accent. Food had re-energized her. Lingering over the last bit of chocolate, I looked around the tent. Most of the women were shaking their heads. Within minutes, she had us pealing with laughter from the antics of these fabled Finn transplants. How strange this would seem to anyone happening upon us in the Michigan forest. A warm lighted tent, wonderful food smells, and riotous laughter—as if we were the only ones who existed on the planet.

And, at that moment, we were.

CHAPTER TEN

The women around me inside the tents were snoring lightly. Since they were all zipped up inside their sleeping bags with mummy hoods pulled over caps, it was a muffled sound, as if from a dubbed soundtrack of white noise.

I had borrowed my sister's three-season sleeping bag and lined it with a fleece blanket. I had also left all my clothing on, including my jacket and down vest. I was still freezing. Also, my bladder was not yet trained to choose warmth over emptiness. Finally, I found my camp boots and left the tent, gently tumbling over two other bodies that readjusted only slightly in my wake.

The absolute stillness of the Upper Peninsula woods outside the tent was striking. It was somewhere near midnight—my watch face was fuzzy to sleepy eyes—almost time for the lunar eclipse. Sure enough, up in the clear, bitingly crisp sky, the moon was being devoured by the shadow of the Earth. Actually, it was more being nibbled at than devoured, with no trace of the advertised blood-red tinge, but was impressive still. I moved away from the tents to the latrine area and fumbled with my zipper.

Fatal flaw. My ski pants were actually bibs, meaning that I had to take off at least one top layer to get to the straps. In the fogginess of the moment, I couldn't remember if my vest was inside or outside the bib straps. It was inside.

By now, my freezing fingers and toes slowed the process even more. I did have to laugh, because these clothes were of my own choosing. On our polar trek, we would wear the intelligent, stylish clothing that Josée and Jen had modeled for us at Frida's the night before.

"You'll want to have underwear that wicks away the sweat, as well as a bra that doesn't hold moisture. Remember, it's critical not to get wet." As she talked, she demonstrated in her underwear, appearing rather curious with her bra outside of her undershirt. We must have looked puzzled by the street-person couture because she said, "I find that my bra stays drier and doesn't chafe as much if it's on the outside.

"Next, you have fleece pants and top. Two-hundred weight." Whatever it meant, it sounded significant. "Then wrist gaiters and a headover. After that, a wind suit." To demonstrate the impermeability of the suit to the wind, Josée held the red and blue jacket up to her mouth and blew against it. She passed the jacket around the circle for all to test. Nope, Arctic blasts wouldn't penetrate this.

"See the fur around the collar? That's not just for looks. It actually breaks the wind so that it doesn't beat against your face."

Josée slipped her jacket on and flipped up the hood to add emphasis. "And when you tighten the hood like so, it makes a tunnel. You can see out, but the wind can't get to you."

I wondered about inhaling fur.

"There are several kinds of fur, including fox and wolf, but for repelling water, wolverine is the best."

Wolverine! The state animal of Michigan and mascot of the University of Michigan. How could I take a wolverine ruff to the North Pole? Even a dead one. Or especially a dead one. I tucked these thoughts away and turned my attention back to Josée.

"These are the boots we use. They come with two sets of liners that can be used as camp boots."

The white boots were nearly knee-high on Josée.

Josée gazed around the room. "Any questions?"

We all looked back, taking in the Arctic explorer now dressed in full gear. A grace note, and then a peppershot of questions.

"What brand of underwear do you have?"

"Why can't you use a headover that has two layers?"

"How many pairs of liners do you wear with your mittens?"

"What about socks?

One by one, Josée answered our interested, anxious questions. She understood that behind each inquiry was the desperate desire not to be cold.

Now, outside in the freezing night illumed by the eclipse, I realized afresh just how critical clothing was to warmth and survival. There was comfort in knowing that whatever cold we encountered now, we would be better prepared when on the Arctic Ocean. With that thought, I settled my feet into the two foot holes of the fresh air outhouse.

And flopped right on my back, into two-foot-deep snow. I had leaned too far back and lost my balance.

"Shock" is probably the best word for a sudden jolt of snow against my bare backside in −30 degrees Fahrenheit. I flailed to get into some kind of upright position, vaguely aware that thrashing around in the snow like Gregor Samsa diminished my appreciation of the lunar eclipse.

My feet finally got purchase, and I hurled myself forward to almost standing. My reason for venturing outside became secondary to survival.

Doctor: "And how did you happen to get superficial frostbite on your gluteus?"

Patient: "Well, Doctor, I was camping in the Upper Peninsula and I had to go to the bathroom, and I was thinking about warm clothing and then all of a sudden . . ."

The eclipse was still underway as I made my way back to the cook tent, where my bag was waiting. After untying the two cords holding the tent door closed, I slipped in and drew them together behind me. I slid over the same two bodies I had crossed earlier and scrunched down into the bag, still cold in the feet but convinced that there was more sleep to be gained this night.

"Everything okay?" one of the figures said.

"Oh, sure. Just fine. You should see the eclipse."

. ˙ . ˙

Over breakfast the next morning, Jen urged us to eat. "In the Arctic, we'll be going through at least six thousand calories a day," she said, "and you'll probably lose weight."

"Suits me," Frida said. "Maybe I'll get down to one chin."

"Hey, Sue," she yelled over the tent to me, "you can't afford to lose any more weight. Jen, you'd better give her an extra helping."

It was true that my weight had slipped a little during the past few years, due in part to training. I would eat my way back to Arctic-ready trim.

Dana, firm and active in her midsixties, shot a quick glance at Phyllis, who last night had lifted her clothing and exhibited the scar from the delivery of triplets. For Dana, it was a sign of physical softness. I let it pass. There was room for all kinds of women on this trek.

Breakfast finished, we broke down the tents and restowed them in their bags.

"Remember which gear is in your sled," Josée said. "We don't want to be searching around in the dark for things."

With tenderfoot skill, we stuffed our backpacks and sleds—at least those of us who were pulling sleds—and clipped on our skis. Jen took a final tromp through the campground before putting on her skis, poking through the snow with the tip of her ski pole to make sure nothing was left.

Frida slipped into Big Bertha's traces under the critical eye of Josée. Yesterday, Bertha had not maneuvered well over some of the trails and occasionally had yanked Frida to the ground. Josée already had some concerns about our plans to shoot a documentary, and this setup did not help her anxiety. Having been in the Arctic, Josée now knew first hand just how difficult and exhausting shooting video would be, not to mention hauling the equipment. Frida, supported by me, was determined to make this film, and Big Bertha was part of the equation.

Pam, a black-belt with Himalayan trekking experience, took the lead. The plan was to ski the full day, camp, and then trek back to the trailhead the following afternoon. We'd spend that night at Frida's debriefing before heading home.

Carter, our firefighter from Montana, was a little slow and slightly stooped over as the line formed. Jen, a nursing student, pulled up alongside her. "Are you okay?"

"Maybe it's something I ate," Carter said, "but I just didn't sleep that well last night. I felt a little cramped up, but it's not time for my period."

"Well, let's keep an eye on it," Jen said. "And why don't we give your sled to Diane? If it gets worse, let me know."

Diane skied over and turned around so Jen could clip Carter's sled rope to her backpack. Carter, a quiet and gentle woman, nodded and readjusted her pack. We were ready to head out.

Pristine, wind-driven snow in a rich environment. We broke trail through a landscape that was breathtaking, and not just because of the temperature, now at fifteen below. I had to remind myself that the landscape we'd be seeing a year from April would be hostile, bleak, and barren.

About midmorning, the pristine, untouched environment revealed three other skiers. While on a break, we spotted them on a lake we were intent on traversing—distant figures also pulling sleds. Probably campers like us. I wondered if we would see others on our trek to the North Pole. No women, though, were doing what we were doing. Certainly not ordinary women.

The fifteen-minute rest was over, and Josée was up and ready.

"Here's what we're going to do." We were on the edge of the lake, and she had to raise her voice to be heard over the wind. "We'll ski one behind the other. It looks a little soft out there, so be very careful."

I remembered the cold of last night. "You mean we all could break through?"

"The ice is plenty thick, but because there's been a little warming recently, and some snow, it may be wet on top. Don't forget, water is the enemy, so don't let the bottom of your skis get wet."

The puzzled look on my face must have been echoed on others.

"If your ski bottom gets wet, ice builds up, and it becomes very difficult to ski. It can get several inches thick, and you don't want that."

Frida squirmed in Bertha's harness. Carter was emotionless. Pam asked if she should stay in the lead.

"No, I'll go first, and Jen will bring up the rear."

The warmth of the last hour of skiing had nearly worn off by now, and several of us were starting to chill, windmilling arms and stamping feet. With a quick look back at the line that was forming behind her, Josée put one ski tip and then another onto the ice of the lake, gracefully gliding several yards ahead of the rest of us.

In single file, we slipped off the shore and onto the frozen lake, some a little more gingerly than others. According to Frida's map, the lake was some two miles long. We'd ski it and then pull up on the other side, and continue on a few miles until the light began to fade. Then camp and dinner. That was the carrot in front of me at the moment as I skied to get the cold out of my bones—and my feet.

The lake's flat surface made for smoother going than the snow-packed trail, but the surface was still pocked with wet spots. Despite extra wax, our skis started to stick. Soon the bottoms of the sleds were clogged with ice.

Jen dropped her pack and skied effortlessly out to the middle of the lake, looking for firmer ice. She sped back to Josée. "It's not much better out there," she said. "I think we ought to either turn around or head to a clear trail on the shore."

"Frida," Josée called out over the tops of our heads, "does your map show a trail along this shore?" She pointed with her ski pole to the north shore of the lake, the closest side.

Frida tugged off her mitts, strung with a cord around her neck, and reached around into the pack on her back. After a moment of studying the chart, she looked up. "Nope. At least not an easy one. It starts to get steep there." She folded the map back for another view. "If we can't go ahead, then we're better off turning back."

Dana moved forward. "Josey." (Dana had been steadfast in calling her "Josey" rather than by her French Canadian name, Josée. Dana either didn't grasp the cultural difference or chose not to.) "I don't see any real reason why we can't go on. We're out here to get some experience, and this ought to be part of it. It doesn't make any sense to go back."

Josée bristled. "Listen, Dana. I'm telling you that it's not good to get your skis wet. We cannot let that happen in the Arctic, and we are not going to let it happen here."

"Well, I think you're wrong," Dana said. She started to ski off in the direction we had been headed.

Josée turned to the rest of us. "We need to turn around and get back on the trail. There's lots more to ski around here without getting our skis wet."

"What about Dana?" Frida asked.

"Do you see anyone following her?" Josée said. "She'll be back."

Pam, Dana's friend from California, hung back, clearly torn by the decision. She waited, then turned to join us. Dana went about a hundred yards before circling back to the group. The incident left me shaken. I'd already known that organizing and physically preparing for our trek to the North Pole was going to be a challenge. I'd just gotten a hint that the human face of this adventure could prove just as difficult.

CHAPTER ELEVEN

We were tired and more than a little frazzled when we settled on a spot to make camp that evening, the second of our two days on the trail. By now, the tension between Dana and Josée was palpable. Phyllis had fallen a number of times and had yet to pull a sled. Frida was struggling with Big Bertha. Carter worked hard to keep up, but something was wrong. The rest of us were quiet.

The end of skiing and the prospect of a warm dinner revived spirits. And the temperature didn't seem as cold as the night before, though the thermometers registered about the same: twenty below and falling off the bottom.

"How are you holding up, Katie?" Frida asked. The girl had pulled her share of sled that day, and skied adequately for a teenager with little experience.

"Oh, I'm okay," she said as she dug into her backpack for some warmer clothing. "I'm pretty hungry, though." My sister's doubts about Katie—doubts echoed by Dana and Pam—came back to me. Perhaps they were right, but based on the day's performance, Katie was stronger and more capable than her mother.

We identified the contents of our sleds much more quickly this evening. Food, utensils, stoves, and fuel rapidly emerged and were hustled into the cook tent for Jen's use.

We were famished. It's not that we hadn't eaten well during the day's ski. We had consumed the better part of the food bags Jen and Josée had prepared for us. If this was the routine we were facing on the Arctic Ocean, we'd certainly be the first team to put on weight.

We would be ready to hit the sack, literally, after dinner. I dug through the sleds looking for my Therm-a-Rest, but wasn't able to locate it at the moment. No matter. I stopped rummaging when the smell of pasta from the cook tent called me. It was time to move inside, out of the cold.

From the outside, in the gathering dark of the far-north woods, the tent looked eerie: silhouettes and sounds emanating from a cocoon. Once within, it was hard to remember that the walls were thin nylon and presented virtually no barrier to the outside, at least when it came to sound. Everything said inside the tent was clarion clear outside. Any pretense of privacy was simply that.

Diane and I were the last to crawl into the cook tent. She had been tidying up her gear and, I suspected, needed some time alone. I was just slow. I tumbled through the tent entrance on her heels, tapping my feet together as I crawled through to get the last bit of snow off my camp boots.

"That's good," Josée said. "Remember, girls, to brush the snow off of you before you come in the tent. Down jackets stay outside because they bring in moisture. If moisture gets into the tent, we can't dry off what's in here."

She nodded her head toward the center of the tent where mittens, gloves, and even some boot liners were dangling from a makeshift clothesline. The center of the tent was held high by one of the tallest skis, this one belonging to Pam. From it hung the Coleman lantern.

Snow from the snow bag, a small nylon duffle bag that was filled, and emptied, for every meal, was now boiling in one pot, while the pasta was coming to life in the other.

"You know," Frida said, after she had taken a sip of her Malakhov cocktail of powdered milk, maple syrup, and whiskey. "I'm not as cold as I thought I was going to be."

It was a relief to hear her say that because Frida worried a lot about being cold. She had read nearly two dozen books about the Arctic, and each one seemed to deepen her fears about the environment and its capacity to administer painful cold.

"But that Big Bertha, I gotta do something about it."

"You're right, Frida," Josée said. "That sled just won't work. It's too big. You'll never be able to get it over the pressure ridges."

Josée was a firm believer in a smaller, more compact, and highly agile sled. The larger sleds, or sledges, were too unwieldy and potentially unsafe. In one instance, a Japanese expeditioner fell into Arctic water harnessed to a larger sled. His body was discovered days later, still lashed to his sled.

"I know you don't like it, Josée," Frida said. "It's just that I need space for the video equipment, and it has to be sturdy space." Besides, Ron had gotten the sled for her for Christmas in a show of support. Despite his doubts, he was doing his best to back her up.

There was nowhere for the discussion to go. Josée wisely let it drop.

"Carter," she said, "how are you feeling?"

"I think I'm better now," Carter said. "At least it doesn't hurt so much."

"Think you want something to eat?" Jen said.

"As good as your cooking smells, how could I pass it up?" Carter's smile was a little too brave, but we all joined in. "Yeah, it smells great, Jen. Is it ready yet?"

. . .

Dishes done and put away, and the last Yooper joke told, we all began to sort out things and pull together our bedding for the tents. The same women were headed to the smaller tent: Carter, Diane, Frida, and Jen. The rest of us would bed down once more in the larger cook tent. There was a problem, however. My Therm-a-Rest mattress was still missing. I was a little concerned about being even colder this night than I had been the night before. The extra layer underneath was important. Besides, the mattress wasn't mine; my sister had loaned it to me.

. . .

"Josée, I can't find my Therm-a-Rest. I've checked through all the sleds and my backpack, and I can't seem to find it. Any suggestions?"

"We need to find it, because you'll need it tonight. It's going to be cold."

We agreed that it hadn't been left behind at the last camp, and it was unlikely that it had fallen out during the day's ski. The Therm-a-Rest had to be around the camp somewhere. Josée and I switched on our headlamps for one more check of sleds and all the backpacks. Nothing.

The others had completed their final preparations for the evening and were mostly snuggled down in their sleeping bags. Josée poked her head in first one tent and then another. "Has anybody seen Sue's mattress?"

"What color is it?"

Josée turned to me, standing outside the tent. "Green," I told her.

"It's green," Josée said. I could sense her irritation growing as the others made sympathetic noises, checked the color of their mattresses, and then said they hadn't seen it. The more annoyed she got, the higher Josée's voice pitched and the thicker the French Canadian accent became.

"Listen, everyone." The women in both tents could now hear her. "If this happens on the Arctic Ocean, it's serious. Someone loses a piece of equipment and it means that we share. If you don't want Sue with you in your sleeping bag tonight, I suggest you get out here and help her look for her mattress."

I wasn't sure how I felt about that. Having to bunk with me wasn't the worst thing that could happen.

Frida, Diane, and several others immediately slid out of their bags and pulled on their boots.

Dana stayed inside.

After a few minutes of searching, the Therm-a-Rest appeared in Josée's hands. We had overlooked it somehow. Appreciative, but embarrassed at having been the cause of the disruption, I thanked the searchers, dragged the mattress into the tent, and quickly slid it under my sleeping bag. Determined to put the day to rest, I burrowed deeply into my bag and was swiftly asleep.

. . .

Jen rousted the cook-tent inhabitants out early so she could start breakfast. As we emptied the interior of sleeping gear and cleaned up for the morning, we were greeted by the sight of Pam doing sit-ups and push-ups. This was going to be some kind of ride.

Carter emerged from the other tent. It was evident that she had not spent the best of nights. Her face was drawn and she moved slowly. But no complaining.

Once we all gathered inside the cook tent, we reviewed the day's plans.

"What we'll do is ski back to the trailhead, but spend some time working on ski techniques," Josée said. "I want everyone to take a turn at pulling a sled. That includes you, Phyllis." Phyllis winced. "Your daughter Katie has done such a good job. Now the mother needs to do well also."

. . .

We had about seven miles of trail in front of us. It hadn't snowed since we'd broken it the day before yesterday, so the return should be easier. I reflexively reached down and patted the sole pocket in my ski bib, the one I had zipped my truck keys into almost forty-eight hours ago. Still there.

The tents went down, and camp was struck even faster this morning, the result of experience and a little urging from Josée.

"When we're skiing to the North Pole, we can't spend all day getting ready, or else we'll never arrive," Josée said as she prowled the remnants of camp, checking the site and adjusting backpacks. "You know, we're going to be skiing seven or eight hours a day, so you'll have to be faster."

Silence as we all took in the information. It wasn't that we didn't know before how much skiing we'd be doing. It's just that now it meant something. Especially if we skied the last two degrees as planned, from the eighty-eighth to the ninetieth parallel—a distance of 120 nautical miles. Clearly we'd have to move faster to cover that distance.

On the way back to the trailhead, we went through ski drills. Transfer weight from one ski to another. Use your arms. Stake the ski pole ahead and pull as well as push. Do it again. In a Nordic version of a conga line, we went through the drill. For some it was merely a refresher, for others a first impression. There were some hard tumbles and tender bruises.

By midafternoon we arrived at the road. To my relief, Frida's van and my truck were there and unscathed. Both vehicles started right away. People in the van; skis, sleds, and equipment in the truck bed. And away we drove—Frida leaving me fishtailing in her snow dust.

This time, though, I knew the way.

. . .

Josée again rode with me. As we began the thirty miles back to Marquette, she was quiet. Being the field leader of this small band had pulled a lot of energy from her.

"I want to thank you," she said after a while.

"What for?" I asked.

"For giving me a chance to lead this group, for organizing and making this happen."

I was completely caught off-guard. After two days with her as my taskmaster, a debriefing or a critique was more what I had anticipated.

"You see, for so many years, I was Richard's wife. I was always preparing him, supporting him, getting him ready for an expedition. Now it's my turn, and it's because of you."

"Josée, we couldn't ask for a better leader." I really meant that. "You are thorough and well prepared. And someday, Richard will be known as Josée's husband."

We both laughed as I raced to keep Frida's taillights in sight.

. . .

That evening, after showers and dinner at Frida's, we did go through a debriefing, led by Josée and supported by me as the organizer of the trek. We talked about the experience and what we had learned, about the absolute necessity of teamwork—especially if equipment turns up missing, as it had last night. I suspected Josée had contrived the situation and hidden my mattress to make a point. No matter; the moment had been real enough and allowed for some insights into the women.

Josée ended by saying, "I'd like to meet with each one of you, one at a time."

Surprised looks.

"It will be a chance to make some suggestions for the coming year and to hear from each one of you." She gestured around the room. "How about a short break, and then let's start with Diane."

The group shuffled around, a little uncomfortable for a moment at this unexpected turn. It had been a stressful two days, and everyone was ready to relax. But not yet.

As the rest chatted, loosening up again, Josée pulled me to the side.

"Dana cannot be part of the team," she said.

I was a bit surprised and searched her face for more. Certainly, Dana had taken Josée on, but this kind of adventure attracted strong women who weren't afraid to challenge. If Josée was being petty, I was not sympathetic.

"Tell me why you feel that way," I said.

"Did you see how she didn't help look for your Therm-a-Rest when it was missing last night? She's used to looking out for herself, and to being with a group of men who take care of her. I don't think she's ready to be a part of this team."

I saw the wisdom of this, but Dana brought some other skills and connections to the effort that could be very helpful. Besides, given how tough it had been to get even this many women, I was concerned about cutting any loose. If Dana wasn't going to the North Pole, Pam might back out as well. Down two.

"Josée," I said, "I trust your judgment, but are you sure she won't fit in?" Even as I said this, I remembered how Dana had pushed me hard on several issues, harder than I like to be pushed.

"No," I said before Josée could answer, "you're right. Better to decide now than later down the line." I paused for a moment. "Is there anyone else?"

"Katie's got a big heart, but she's just not ready to go. She's still a little young."

I didn't disagree, but I found it interesting that Katie had outperformed her mother. And, with Katie out of the picture, the mother-daughter dynamic would be gone.

"Everybody else is solid, then?" I ventured.

"Oh, yes. This is the beginning of a really good team. Carter and Diane are strong. Frida's certainly good, though I worry about this film. You'll get stronger, and I think that Phyllis should be able to make it, if she works really hard."

Well, I thought, at least we're halfway there. Five out of the ten that we need.

As expected, Pam demurred, but wished us well. Diane headed off, figuring ways to raise money to pay her share of the trek. On returning to Montana,

Carter went almost immediately to the emergency room, then straight into surgery to have her gallbladder removed. Phyllis had a fender-bender on the way home and got a ticket.

CHAPTER TWELVE

Now we were five. And it was about to get worse.

Within weeks, I got a letter from Diane, writing that she wasn't going to be able to join us. I called her right away.

"Diane here."

"Diane, I just got your letter."

"Hold on. I have to go into a break. Be right back."

I had dialed her work number. Work for Diane was being a disc jockey—a "jock," as it's called—at a radio station out West. When she put me on hold, I could hear the program feed.

"You're listening to the Smooth One. It's seventeen minutes after two. Cloudy tonight with some light snow and clearing tomorrow. Up next, Kenny G."

Nice. I rather liked Kenny G. Diane came back on the line.

"Yeah, this is Diane."

"Diane, I got your letter today that you're not going to join us." I thought carefully about what to say next. "I know you're concerned about money. What can I do to help?"

"Hang on. I gotta read a tag line."

Back on hold. "Available at all local SuperMaster stores. Right off his latest album—Kenny G."

"Okay, I'm back."

"Right. Like I was saying, maybe there's a way we can help support you."

"Thanks, but I thought a lot about this. I may be changing jobs, and being a jock doesn't pay that much anyway. Besides, it'll probably be tough for me to get the time off if I start at a new station."

That was likely the case. But a small part of me was also piqued that she'd gotten my hopes up. She would have made a great team member.

"Diane," the adult in me responded, "I really understand. I think you're terrific, and if you change your mind, there will be a place for you."

"Hey, I really appreciate it. Thanks for a great time in the U.P., and say 'hi' to Frida."

"Will do, and you take care. Bye."

I hung up the phone. Never did get to hear Kenny G.

.   .   .

Now we were four.

An earlier mailing to women's health and sport magazines had turned up most of the interest. Maybe it was time for another round. What would it say?

Got an interest in freezing your butt, exhausting yourself, using up all of your vacation time for the next five years, and running through at least $10,000? Do we have the adventure for you!

I laughed. Guess I was feeling a little sorry for myself that four dozen other women didn't feel the same way about my nonsensical quest. Too bad Don Quixote was a man. And dead. And fiction. Maybe a little tea with Bonnie in the woods was needed. I called.

Bonnie was home and would be there the rest of the day. It was already nearly five, and I could be there in about twenty minutes.

I shut down the computer, threw some things in my briefcase, and pulled my office door closed. Elevator or stairs? Come on, polar explorer, there's a choice here? I opened the door to the stairwell.

"Professor Carter?"

Behind me stood one of the myriad thin, six-foot-three freshman males who populated my mass-media introductory class. I sent up a short prayer, thankful that I didn't have to feed him.

"Are you leaving?" he said tentatively.

It seemed like a question that didn't need an answer, but I answered it anyway. "Yes, I was actually heading out."

"I was just wondering if I could get my test from last week. I couldn't make it to class today."

I dipped my chin and smiled as I fished my keys out of my purse. "Sure. Let me get it out of my office."

It was the second of four exams in the class, and the first had been a wake-up call for a number of these first-year, second-semester students. One had told me in deep earnest, "College is a lot harder than high school." For that one, I had hope.

I dug Sean's exam out of the pile and handed it to him, glancing quickly at the B-minus grade. He looked at it, flipped through the pages. With a measure of relief, he looked up from underneath the bill of his baseball cap, which was, surprisingly, not on backwards.

"Thanks," he said. "See you in class Wednesday."

Right.

Door shut and briefcase in hand, I was out the building and into my truck.

. . . .

No one was parked in the spot marked "Lithuanians Only" at Bonnie's, but I still didn't chance it.

She held on to one of the dogs—nameless to me—by the collar, and opened the door. "Welcome. I've got some water on for tea."

Those were about the best words of the day. February was dreary enough, and the events of the past few weeks hadn't been inspiring. Physical training for an Arctic trek was challenge enough in the face of a full-time job. Organizing the bloody thing was all but impossible. I stamped my boots on the mat, took off my coat, and jumped right in.

"Diane sent me a letter that she's not coming." There it was. "We're down to four: Frida, me, Phyllis, and Carter."

"Ooh." Bonnie scrunched up her face. "What happened?"

"She said that it's a combination of money and the possibility of moving to a new job. I suspect there's a little boyfriend factor mixed in." In the tent, in the Upper Peninsula, I had gotten the impression that her relationship with her boyfriend needed some shoring up.

"So, what now?"

"At minimum, we need to pull her picture and bio off the website. Then, look for new members."

"Something we haven't tried yet are web rings," Bonnie said.

I was clueless.

"There are groupings of similar-interest websites. We can also ask permission to link to some of the other websites that active women visit." Bonnie grinned. "We call it 'trolling' for applicants."

As only the best web wizards can, Bonnie spent the next hour darting and searching in and out of JavaScript, turning what looked like Klingon verse into hot links. Three cups of tea later, it was finished. She sat back finally and swirled the last bit of honey-laced tea in her mug.

"With these links and a downloadable application form, we ought to see more action," she said. "Let's also put up pictures and bios of Josée and Jen. That'll make six on the home page and give it a fuller look."

We scrolled through the few webpages we had, reviewed and critiqued, and decided that was a fair day's work.

I thanked Bonnie and half patted the nameless dogs that had roused from slumber to send me off with a chorus of barks. It was getting late, and I still had a date at the "Y." Tonight it was weights and cardio machines.

. . .

"Y-M-C-A." I hummed the Village People song as I bounced out of Bonnie's driveway onto the road. I took a general delight in being a gym rat—either at the "Y" or in the intramural buildings on campus. Several years ago I'd gotten my lifeguard certification, and now I volunteered. Watching toddlers take to the water, and keeping overactive teenagers from generating tsunamis that would swamp them, was something I enjoyed.

It hadn't always been that way. Reared in an era when girls were not encouraged to participate in sports, I started out as a wallflower in the world of athletics. The desire was there, and occasionally I bought the equipment that made my fantasies seem possible, but I was sidelined, along with thousands of other women. I've often joked that because I'm a pre–Title IX baby, I still have my knees.

The truth is, I do still have my knees, though it may be as much the result of Mendel's law as legislation. I even smoked until I was twenty-nine, a fact that continues to embarrass me. It took the death of Jesse Owens in July of 1980 to get my attention and persuade me to quit. Jesse was one of my heroes, a man of firm principle. As a young radio reporter, I had interviewed Jesse on several occasions and was struck by the graceful way he shared himself. Here was a man who had seen Hitler with his own eyes. And bested him.

I still remember asking him what it had been like to win four gold medals at the 1936 Olympics in Berlin. Even though he must have answered the question a thousand times, he gave me a response that came from deep inside him, as if for the very first time:

"It was an honor to win those medals and to show up the Nazi idea of superiority. But, you know, when I came back to this country, I still had to ride in the back of the bus."

I wanted to weep.

When the news hit that July morning that Jesse had died in Arizona of lung cancer, I was so angry. I knew he smoked a pipe; he had one when I had interviewed him, and I think he was holding it in the picture taken of the two of us. He had also owned up to smoking a pack of cigarettes a day. How could he? How could I?

I started running that night.

Since then, there had been marathons, triathlons, ski races, and bike races. Ahead lay the North Pole.

. . . .

The Parkwood YMCA was a hive of intense activity when I got there. In the locker room, I began to peel off my day clothes and trade them for workout clothes. Blue shorts and a white T-shirt with some blue in it (color coordination counts), along with white socks and shoes. I felt a little like a refugee from a ninth-grade gym class. Then, the somewhat laughable weight gloves. With leather pads and cut-off fingers, they looked a bit silly on my small hands and thin arms—okay, a lot silly—but they produced the right mood.

A tour through the Nautilus machines, free weights, the dreaded sit-ups, and on to the StairMaster. It was a little more than an hour's workout, but enough to get the endorphins coursing through the veins, enough to settle my thoughts about being one of a team of four when we needed a team of ten to go to the North Pole. Tomorrow, Scarlett, was another day.

Later at home, showered and refreshed from the workout, I finished a bowl of soup and some salad. There was still class to prepare for tomorrow—an undergraduate course on media law—and I wanted to make a quick call to my daughter, Amanda.

She was a junior, living on campus. I tried not to play Mom too much, but it was tough as I was right in the neighborhood. In fact, I was sometimes in front of the class, as she was a journalism major. (Teaching your daughter was within university rules as long as another faculty member graded her materials.) Frankly, in a large lecture hall, I didn't always spot her right away, though I could always pick out her laugh. Something along the lines of the "mommy-baby sniff test" that demonstrates blindfolded mothers can identify their children by smell alone.

No one answered the phone in Amanda's room.

In bed that night, I replayed the tape of the day once more. Was there anything I could have done differently to convince Diane to stay? No, probably not. She'd evidently given her decision full consideration. Was the web going to give us enough of a presence to attract potential team members? Who knew. Would I have enough money to keep this going? That remained to be seen. But the last thing I was going to do was let Frida down, having gotten both of us committed this far.

Have to call Frida tomorrow.

. . .

I called Frida three days later, waiting for a more positive mood. No sense in two of us feeling discouraged.

Ron answered the phone. He was trying to support Frida, but my voice was a reminder that his wife was part of a crazy scheme to ski to the North Pole, leaving two young kids at home. Our conversations were always polite, but brief.

He called Frida to the phone.

"Hiya, Suzy Q.," she sang into the receiver.

"Hi, Frida. How's it going up there—still have good snow?" A second warm winter meant spotty, slushy snow in the Lower Peninsula. It was hardly an auspicious time to be training for a polar trek.

"Yep. Ron and the kids and I just got back from Marquette Mountain. He came in second tonight, and I was third in the geezer division."

She and Ron were terrific downhill skiers and raced in the local adult leagues. Eryka and Ian were equally skilled on snowboards. Ian was near the top of his age group nationally.

"Well, I don't want to keep you," I said. "Just thought I'd check in. I also wanted to let you know that . . . I got a letter from Diane saying that she isn't coming."

"Why?" Frida asked, stretching out the word to a near diphthong.

I filled her in. I also told her what Bonnie and I had done to get more team members.

"Have you talked with Josée?" she asked. "I heard her say something about knowing a couple of women that might be interested."

"Hmm. Good idea. I'll see if I can reach her tomorrow."

Frida then described her latest equipment discoveries. A chief worry was the video equipment: which maker, which model, how many batteries for two weeks in the Arctic cold. Richard had offered to loan a solar charger, but Frida was still unconvinced it would be enough. I just listened to her talk, knowing she needed an ear.

We hung up, promising to check back in a week. Maybe I'd have more news about prospective team members then.

. . .

The following day, I called Josée at her home near Ottawa.

"Allo."

"Hi, Josée. How are you and your boys?" Her boys included not only her two sons but also her husband, Richard.

"They are all well, thank you."

We traded pleasantries a bit; then I told Josée of the latest team-member departure. She was sad about Diane's leaving and concerned about our dwindling numbers. I quizzed her about possible candidates.

"Yes, I do know some strong skiers who might be interested. One of them lives not too far from us. I will talk with her about the polar trek. Perhaps it is something she would like to do."

"That'd be terrific. In the meantime, Bonnie and I—you remember the webmaster?—will put out more information from this end."

What a roller-coaster ride this was. There was a piece of me that longed to be on the other side of the trek. There was a lot of snow, though, between here and the North Pole.

. ˙ . ˙

Actually, it was Carter who found the next applicant: Anne, a friend of hers in Montana who was a freelance photographer. I arranged to call her when Carter was going to be at Anne's home.

Anne was forthright and a bit brusque, questioning me about the trek, the distance, the planning, the clothing, and three dozen other things. I was patient, but wondered who was in charge here. Let it go. We needed another team member, and if she was with Carter, she had to be pretty sound.

"Have you thought about the kind of clothing you're going to have?" she said. "On my last mountaineering trip, it got to 20 degrees below. You've got to go with good equipment. And what about sleeping bags?"

Okay, this was a little more than I was willing to let go. "Didn't Carter tell you about our relationship with Josée and Canadian Arctic Holidays, the company she and Richard own? For a set fee, we are completely taken care of: food, gear, equipment, transportation once we arrive in Moscow."

"Moscow?"

I took a deep breath and explained why we were going through Russia, and Richard's relationship with Misha. "They have great experience in the Arctic, Anne," I said. "I think we've hired the best outfitter, and Josée is experienced. She's as much a team member as the rest of us." I could hear Carter on the other phone, wanting to break in. "Didn't you get that sense of it, Carter, when we were in the U.P.?"

"Oh, yes. It's just that we want to be sure."

Where was this "we" coming from?

Carter hesitated for a moment. Then, "It's a lot of money, and if there are suppliers who can help us cut the costs, then maybe we ought to look at them."

Suddenly, I wanted to tread lightly. We couldn't afford to lose another one. Or alienate Josée.

"The cost is already set, and in reality it's a good price; but why don't you call Josée and talk with her about equipment. It's her decision, so run it by her."

We hung up, and I reviewed the call in my mind. Anne had pushed a little hard, but shy women aren't drawn to this kind of adventure. Also, Carter had a substantial portion of her expense already covered. Of course she would stay.

Along with setting up the nonprofit corporation, I also filed papers to copyright our logo—a woman dressed in classical Grecian clothing, gazing down on the globe she was cradling in her arms. I had worked with a local artist on the design. We had started with my idea of a woman holding a globe, a takeoff of DaVinci's man with arms and legs spread. Unfortunately, the frontal view made her look ten months pregnant, and that wasn't the image we were going for. The artist thoughtfully tilted the woman a quarter turn and softened her up. It made for a graceful yet strong image.

Phyllis had agreed to be the organization's treasurer, Frida was the secretary, and I was the president. Carter and Bonnie were added as board members. We were moving forward. Now, where were those other team members?

CHAPTER THIRTEEN

A centerpiece of our trek planning was to share the experience with young women and girls, in hopes of giving them more encouragement to explore broader horizons than we'd been able to. Some progress had been made, but math, science, physical fitness were still seen too often as "boy things."

So, in the previous fall of 1999, we had brought some seventy girls, fourth through eighth grade, to campus on a Saturday.

I greeted the rambunctious throng and detailed the plans for Polar Trek 2001. There were lots of questions about the event: How cold would it be? What would we eat? How would we go to the bathroom? Then I delivered their assignment.

"Here's your task: Come up with a list of things you'd like to know and some small experiments that possibly we could perform while we're in the Arctic."

From their presentations later that day, it was clear that each of the seven groups had worked really hard at framing intriguing questions and coming up with interesting, and slightly devious, experiments they wanted us to perform. I mentally tossed out the ones that required needles.

I was struck with the earnest effort these girls had made. Some of the groups had designated one of their members to report to the rest of the students. Other groups let each girl speak. They weren't abashed, and they weren't shallow in talking about their ideas. Imagine what our sharing a trek to the North Pole might do for them.

The materials we gathered that day helped provide the core of a curriculum for middle-school students that several of the team members wrote and posted on the web. Bonnie and I carefully considered the look and the potential reach of the lesson plans. We wanted to create a curriculum that could/would be adapted for classrooms, using model curriculum frameworks.

. . .

Our website started to generate inquiries. Nothing more than a trickle, but enough to offer some hope. A phone call or an email would come in, an application form would go out—complete with patch designed for our trek—and I'd wait. And wait. Follow-up calls and emails tended to lead nowhere.

February turned to May, and I was headed to Europe for a month in July 2000 to co-instruct a course in telecommunications. Did I mention I needed more money? Frankly, I also needed a break from the intensity of trek preparation. Email would still connect me, but an ocean's distance would ratchet down the volume.

About six weeks before departing, I got a phone message from a young woman who was an instructor at a community college in northern Michigan. Kerri sounded energetic and all business. I called her back.

We decided to meet the following week. I wasn't positive, but based on Kerri's intellect and obvious enthusiasm, I figured that by the end of the afternoon we might have another team member. So I brought along a camera in case I needed to take a photo for the webpage.

It was a smart move to bring the camera. Kerri was enchanting—just the right combination of seriousness and abandon. Her questions were sharp and well considered. It was a task to supply equally thoughtful answers.

Kerri took it all in, mentally calculating how this would mesh with the academic year and her teaching commitments.

"What do we have to provide?"

"The outfitter we've hired is presenting a full package." I detailed what was included in the $10,000 fee.

She sat back for a minute. We had run through two cups of coffee and finished the pie we had shared.

"So, what do you think?" I said.

"Sounds good," she said finally. "I'm in."

Now we were six.

. . . .

Fundraising was still a bugaboo. Dammit Jim, I'm a professor, not a financier. It was clear that my meager efforts to attract money had produced just that—meager money. Thanks to Carter's stepfather, we had some operating cash, but without that and money out of my pocket, we existed mostly on paper.

Phyllis had a friend with marketing and development skills who was willing to lend a hand. "We'll need to identify potential sponsors," Ann Marie said when we met, "and then put a media kit in their hands. I can follow up with phone calls. We ought to get some interest."

"I can write another news release like the one I sent to magazines last year. And we've got some team bios and pictures we can add, as well as information for potential sponsors. What's missing?"

"We could use more information about the trek," she said. "Maybe a time-line, or a description of what you all plan to do. I personally can't imagine being in that cold, but I really admire what you're planning."

"Thanks, but I'll feel a whole lot more comfortable once we've stopped talking about it and start doing it. In the meantime, these are really helpful ideas."

"Where can we get a list of folks to send the kit to?"

I thought for a moment. "I have a graduate student who could probably use a little extra money. I'll hire him to generate a list of women-owned and women-targeted companies. That ought to be fruitful."

"It's a deal." She gathered up her materials from the table. "Just let me know as soon as you have the list, and we'll get them in the mail."

. ˙ . .

July found me sitting in one of the few Internet cafés in Paris. It felt strange to log on and read ongoing chatter from a world that was six time zones away.

Leading a study-abroad program covering five countries in four weeks had accomplished part of what I wanted to happen: I was thoroughly occupied with the present, and a bit removed from the pressure of mounting an interna-tional expedition.

For instance, there was the Korean student who had developed an eye infection on the eve of our departure for London from Paris, requiring a visit to the emergency room in the shadow of Notre Dame. There were also two lost passports, and two purses stolen in a Parisian bar. Then, there was the student on the Eurostar who discovered the bar car at 10 A.M. and proceeded to get fairly potted on champagne.

So it felt like a return to normality when I opened email in Paris. There on the screen was an email whose sender was unknown to me, but the subject was Polar Trek 2001.

Kathy was an outdoor enthusiast with mountaineering experience who wanted to know more about the trek. She was vitally interested, and was there still space? I emailed delight to learn of her interest, and promised to send her an application as soon as I returned at the end of the month. And, yes, there was still a position open. I did not mention that she could have a whole tent to herself. If she had questions, I'd be checking email every couple of days. Please feel free to stay in touch.

The proprietors of the Internet café, immigrants from some former French colony, weren't quite sure what to make of it when one of their patrons exploded into yips of joy. They wrote it off to crazy Americans and turned back to the espresso machine.

Now, maybe, we were seven.

CHAPTER FOURTEEN

Day Four

April 19, and the beginning of the fourth day of the trek. It is nine days since we left Siberia—nine days on the Arctic Ocean. And each one is more impressive than the last. Even the strong winds that we wake to are not a discouragement. They simply reinforce where we are—near the top of the world, in a truly rarified atmosphere.

The message at breakfast is "Stoke up, girls; it's going to be a long ski today." Jen dishes up ample helpings of bacon and eggs mixed together with tomatoes and mushrooms, served along with sweet, hard bread—a delivery mechanism for butter, peanut butter, and honey.

Kathy checks the GPS. We have gained about a quarter mile overnight due to the Greenland Drift. But we have also moved two degrees to the west. That makes our position N89.29 and E116.39. There is still some margin for a westerly drift before the ski to the North Pole will be out of reach, but we are sliding quickly to the west, and that concerns Josée.

It is strange to imagine skiing north, but on a moving pan of ice that pulls so hard to the west that it becomes virtually impossible to overcome the drift. But if the Greenland tug is too strong, the expedition must end. This is a dark thought in the back of Josée's mind. More than one group has been evacuated because the drift was too rapid and closed the polar window.

Our 7 A.M. rising means that we'll be on the trail before eleven o'clock. Eight or nine hours of skiing, with breaks, should get us into camp, settled in, and on the satellite phone by 9 P.M. After a week and a half on the ice, the days are starting to feel less random and more routine.

I am worried that Frida is withdrawing. We have all talked about "polar moments," those times when we feel overwhelmed to the point of melting down. I had my own polar moment back on Ice Station Borneo, when I was forced to confront the fact that my physical preparation was subpar. Frida experienced a polar moment as well, and Phyllis had a rough go back in Siberia. Even Alison, among the strongest, encountered her polar moment the first day of our training, when she cried over the weight of her sled and pack.

Frida, though, is drawing inward and needs to be brought back.

"It's just that Jen and Josée seem to jump on me for the littlest things," she explains to me when I find a quiet time to talk with her in our sleeping tent. Frida can be a little taxing with her constant desire to have explanations and answers, but Josée, and particularly Jen, have been brusque in return. Theirs is a heavy burden, but Ernest Hemingway's nostrum is still true: Grace under pressure is class. There are some sharp edges developing here.

"Frida, it might help to remember Richard's operating rule that Josée shared with us: 'Will it matter in six months?' If it won't, then let it go. If you think it will, then there's something to talk about."

"Yeah, I know. It's just that I miss my family so much. I don't think I should have come."

"Frida, you'll look back on this as a terrific experience. You're shooting great tape, and it's something you'll always remember."

Actually, I know that she hasn't shot any tape, outside of the tent, for the last two days. She is really a bit overwhelmed. The cold is sapping all of us.

"Yeah, I guess so," is her half-hearted answer. Maybe I can stick closer to her today.

. . .

The team equipment is showing some signs of fatigue. One of the buckles on my skis has broken, and I am reduced to tying the strap to secure my boot. Yesterday, another team member's binding split. Josée managed to drill holes and stitch the two pieces back together. There is also a quick repair required this morning for the basket of one of the skis. With no flourish, but a lot of skill, Josée pulls out a glue stick, warms the tip in the flame of the Russian stove, and sticks the two broken pieces together. Field repairs will get us to the Pole.

My seamstress abilities are coming up short. The right side of my ruff is pulling away from my hood where I had laboriously stitched it when we were still in Khatanga. There are dental floss and needles available to repair it. However, I find a safety pin in my kit bag and settle for that as a fix. Everything takes so much more energy in the Arctic.

The lead that halted our progress last night hasn't frozen over while we slept. It lies right in our path, some twenty yards wide and covered only partially with skim ice and little frozen chunks. A more advanced group could cross it, creating a snow bridge, but that is well beyond our experience.

For more than three hours we track the lead, forced to ski to the west along its southern border, looking for a spot narrow enough to support a crossing. It is discouraging. We are on our fourth day out, we have four more days in which to reach the Pole, and we aren't even going in the right direction. This time, though, it is no fault of our own.

Sometime after the third march, Josée picks a segment of lead that is narrow enough, and just stable enough, to support us. She could have crossed much sooner, but the rest of us are less adept. She has wisely chosen a long ski instead of a short swim.

The spot features several large slabs of ice that have lifted up and collapsed together in a postmodern sculpture. It is beautiful—and accessible, if we go very carefully from the ice to the mush beneath it. We are ready to attempt a crossing.

"Come here; everybody come here and let me explain to you," Josée calls out. She then describes how we will traverse this partially frozen stretch.

"I want you to unbuckle your backpacks and your skis, but keep them on," she instructs, "and to go by twos—but only two on the ice at a time." I look over at the lead. If Josée is this serious in her instruction, then she is worried.

"Don't cross until I tell you. I will go over, and Jen will stay here on this side. Take your sleds off your backpacks. We'll bring them over after."

Skis and backpacks are loosened and ready to discard if necessary. How awful it would be to be trapped in the water, weighted down by a pack, with feet trapped by skis. There is no good way to stage a rescue here. If hypothermia didn't do in the skier, the weight of the equipment would.

. ˙ .

Josée pairs us up in twos, making sure that the stronger skiers are helping the weaker ones. Diana and I are sent over together. Half of the team has already gone ahead of us. Then Diana and I set out, feeling as though we could break through the surface at any moment. Shuffle, slide, don't look down on this thinnest of ice.

Beneath our skis, the slush wobbles, almost like Jell-O. It is better to look ahead than down. Our eyes are pinned on the other side. This is not the place to lose balance and fall—and go through.

"Remember to shuffle," Josée calls over to us. "Don't lift your skis! And keep going when you get to the other side. Don't stop at the edge."

We reach the other side and gingerly step up onto the bank of the lead. Skis forward, no sidestepping. Keep going on. Don't stop here. Move onto firmer ice.

By twos, everyone completes the traverse. On the other side, with the remaining equipment ferried after us, we stop for a break.

"You girls did really well," Josée says as we pour hot tea and cider into frozen thermos cups. We nod, each of us thinking about what we have just done. Here, on the other side of the barely frozen lead, we can relax a little and congratulate ourselves on a successful crossing. In candor, it has been a series of harried and tense moments. Skiing on a slightly undulating piece of ice that could open at any moment and draw us in is an unsettling experience. We can afford to be cavalier on the north side of the slushy river. It required a lot of trust to be on the south side, contemplating crossing.

We quickly cool down, and the break ends. It is time to ski another march—another hour and fifteen or twenty minutes over ice that can change from minute to minute in texture and quality and beauty.

We leave that lead, but end up skiing along a branch of it for part of the next march. Segments of it are frozen, but large stretches are open—dark and murky. Again, the shark's eyes. I keep looking for a seal, remembering that the day before we arrived at Ice Station Borneo, some of the Russian crewmembers spotted a seal right near their plowed airstrip. Misha, who had captured and killed a seal during his record expedition to the North Pole and back with Richard, detailed for me how he would have trapped the seal at Borneo. His use of line and hooks was ingenious. Killing the seal, however, held no interest for me. I just wanted to see the creature in its natural environment. None were around, though.

Music gets stuck in one's brains at the most interesting times. The continual motion of gliding over extended stretches of ice puts several tunes into my head. Ski, ski, note, note. What most frequently creeps up on me is Beethoven's Ninth Symphony and the "Ode to Joy." Beethoven and I go on for stretches, skiing and shuffling along in 4/4 time. It isn't just the music, which is compelling, but the tenor of the symphony itself. It is a riotous cacophony of sheer happiness, and there are moments skiing, buried in my clothing and solitude, when I think my heart will burst from incredible joy. Here, in God's absolute wilderness, we are coping, succeeding, and sharing. What a privilege to be here.

Those are the high moments. There are more difficult ones. Challenges with group dynamics are opening small fissures and have the potential to create some larger cracks. We are asking a lot of ourselves, twelve women struggling toward a goal in a harsh environment. Even the Disciples had their moments. Maybe I need to be softer in my expectation of this group, or any group, to exist in constant harmony. I put those thoughts aside as I ski, accompanied by Beethoven here on the Arctic Ocean.

We ski six marches before stopping to set up camp for the night. Increasingly we call it the "sleep session," for there is no real night as we know it. It is 7:30 P.M. by our reckoning—waking-up time back home.

Over stew that evening, we agree that this has been the best day so far, even given that we were delayed crossing the lead. Skiing has been good; our ability to cross the lead has given us confidence, as has the speed with which we have crossed piles of rubble ice. Still, it looks like we aren't going to be able to stop for a day and have an extended rest. But with this steady pace, we are on a good track to make the North Pole.

It is also getting warmer. The temperature has risen more than five degrees to –20 Fahrenheit, taking some of the sting out of the brutally cold air. We can perform some tasks outside, reloading sleds and the like, with a little less discomfort.

That night in the tent, we make our regular series of phone calls. Kerri and Susan connect with schools for a conversation with classes, and Alison files her story with the *Ottawa Citizen*. I talk with Bonnie and give her information to post about the day's ski, including crossing the lead that could have doubled for a Slurpee.

> "A lead isn't just open water—there is always some skim ice on top," said Sue. "A lead seems more like a river than an opening in the ice. The strategy is to travel alongside the lead until you find a place where the ice is thick enough or the distance short enough that it is safe to cross. There is a tactic where you can throw snow on the water and it can freeze solid enough for a minute or so that you can get across, but we aren't skilled enough for that."

. ˙ . ˙

There is one small victory added to the day. Diana's notebook has turned up. It has been missing for two days, and we have all been afraid that it had somehow been left at a campsite, though how didn't appear possible. This is an uncluttered environment—no trees, no leaves, no rocks—and objects that aren't white tend to really stand out. It was unlikely that her diary had stayed behind, but it has taken several days to surface from the depths of her own pack.

Base communication is still a concern. Despite our dedicated efforts, we have not been successful in contacting Ice Station Borneo to let them know that we are all right. According to the diagram, the antenna is properly strung, there is power, we can tell the signal is going out, but there is no response.

Perhaps spotty propagation, or maybe calling when the radio shack isn't staffed are the explanations for no response. Whatever the cause, though, it is reason to worry. If there is no message from us by tomorrow night, April 20, a helicopter will be dispatched, only to be sent back to base at a cost of $5,000. We have twenty-four hours left before the real worrying begins.

I have enough to fret over, though, without borrowing trouble from tomorrow. Bonnie and I are continuing efforts by satellite telephone to arrange a meeting at the Pole with the team from NASA. The current plan is to try for Borneo, but Mike and I haven't been able to talk tonight. His group is on the way to Resolute Bay, Canada, to be in position to catch a First Air charter north.

. . . .

At the halfway point of our journey, Alison does a group interview—a round-robin with the team members about their feelings. Each of us presents our reactions to where we are, and to all that has happened so far.

Kerri Finlayson: "I had all these questions coming in and was worried about the cold. The first two days did freak me out as far as keeping my hands warm was concerned. Now I know no one will let you freeze to death."

Diana Ciserella: "Today I gained more confidence on my skis. I crossed several areas that were intimidating and I didn't fall once. Crossing the lead was thrilling for me. My snow bath was great" (*she rinsed herself off in the snow*).

Susan Martin: "I feel more confident than before. I'm less worried about things like open water, but the cold is still an issue."

Frida Waara: "I've been wanting to do this for seven years. For eight years I've been studying Arctic literature. I cannot imagine the polar explorers ahead of us. I am overwhelmed by what they endured, and that has put my discomfort in perspective."

Josée Auclair: "It's funny how all you girls said you had a heck of a good day. I finished and I was upset because we did a lot of zigzag. I feel like we're halfway through the race and I can't say we've won it yet."

Phyllis Grummon: "What a difference Josée has made in my life by believing in me. I appreciate how people let me be selfish and ski behind Josée because that's the best place to be."

Jen Buck: "Four down and four to go."

Kathy Braegger: "This is a very beautiful, magical place, and it will always be a part of me."

Marie-Josée Vasseur: "I think the hardest thing is I am not able to speak English very well. It takes a lot more energy."

Sue Carter: "It seems real to me for the first time today. It was an epiphany. Today I believed, and now I thoroughly understand what's happening here."

Lynn Bartley: "I feel fine, and I wonder what's ahead as I keep counting our blessings."

CHAPTER FIFTEEN

2000

The student reporters at the *State News* had been pressing for a story about the ski expedition to the North Pole for several months. Many of them had been my students, and we had talked occasionally about it in class. As my sabbatical project, it was generally available for inquiries by them. Indeed, many of them had heard about the expedition through their college years—it had taken so blasted long to plan.

In order to get the best play for the story of a team of women skiing the last distance to the North Pole, it needed to be presented and managed properly. Our team had just one chance at our fifteen minutes of fame, and this required careful thought. Years earlier, as press secretary to a Michigan governor, I had seen how critical the play of a story was. Bad timing or poor placement could substantially reduce a story's significance.

The student reporters were insistent on writing about their professor. I mulled it over. We could either get a big press pop at a major media level—and that seemed unlikely at the moment—or we could build it from the grass roots. One TV station runs with a story and other media suddenly look at it in a different light as a legitimate news story after all. Along comes the bandwagon around the corner, and soon they're piling on.

A few years earlier, I had had the opportunity to experience this process firsthand and share it with students. They watched as a story unfolded at higher and higher levels before their eyes, a remarkable case study in the making.

It was 1997, and I was doing the radio color commentary for the Michigan State University women's basketball team. Things were going well that year. The team was headed for the Big Ten title and a berth in the NCAA tournament.

Fortunately, it worked out that my teaching schedule allowed me to do home and away games. This experience provided wonderful insights into the remarkable discipline it takes to be a student athlete at a major university. The traveling also made me eternally thankful that I was a faculty member at MSU and not elsewhere. Consider Penn State in February. You can barely get there from here in good weather.

In fact, it was to Penn State that we were headed when the story, which would become a news story, began.

Running late from class, but never one to miss a meal—especially the training table—I had dashed to the buffet, loaded a plate, and proceeded to inhale quantities of food. The team bus was about to leave for the airport.

The word "inhale" has particular meaning here. I literally got a partially cooked red potato lodged in my windpipe. Not just sort of stuck. Not just uncomfortable going down. Lodged. As in: not going anywhere. This required immediate attention, for all of a sudden it was clear that I had no air exchange. How much time?

Not much. The room suddenly seemed to get very big and filled my field of vision. I swung my head from left to right. There were a few players and staff left in the room, but it was rapidly emptying. No one had seen my distress, so it was time for me to get some attention.

Sitting next to me on my right, talking to a player across the table, was the head basketball coach, Karen. This was my shot. I made a fist with my right hand and banged against her left thigh, getting her attention. As she turned, I put my hands up to my throat, crossing them, to make the universal sign for choking.

"You're kidding," she said, eyes widening.

Like hell I am. I vigorously shook my head back and forth. Recognition flashed across her face. There must have been relief on mine. I immediately stood, my back to her and my arms up in the air. I was starting to feel a little oxygen-deprived, and the world at the edge of my vision was closing in, but conscious I still was.

With a couple of thrusts of her fists into my diaphragm, she dislodged the offending tuber, and I choked in some air. It was a minute before I could speak.

"Thanks, Karen." I felt sheepish, and more than a little foolish.

"Not a problem. You're okay?"

I nodded, shaken.

"Good. Better go get cleaned up. We leave for Penn State in ten minutes."

. · .

That next evening, in the brand-new arena in State College during the post-game wrap-up, I gave special thanks to the coach. In thirty seconds, I recounted what had happened the night before.

"I don't want to be overly dramatic about it," I added, "but what she did may have saved my life." End of message. Story over.

But not really.

We headed from Happy Valley to Minnesota for another game. When we returned to campus Sunday evening, several local reporters were there to cover the team's return. One of the reporters, a former student, also wanted to talk with me about the coach's heroics. I told the tale again. The next morning, waiting for me in the office, were calls from several news outlets around the state.

The story ended up above the fold on the front page of a Detroit daily newspaper. I had become an object lesson for (a) Chew your food carefully, (b) Don't take too big a bite, and (c) Here's what to do if "a" and "b" are violated. There was a little sketch of one woman applying the Heimlich maneuver to another, along with our pictures. (In a twist of irony, I had interviewed Dr. Heimlich nearly twenty years before, in a public service piece to share his life-saving procedure with my Detroit radio audience.)

Back in my introductory-level journalism class, I shared the event and its unfolding with my students. Each day, the story was played at a higher level, as some new twist was given to the story.

"Just watch," I told them on day 3 of the coverage—five days after I nearly bought it over a red potato at the training table. "It's not over yet." Sure enough, "Coach Saves Broadcaster" made *USA Today* and ESPN. It was a real-time case study.

The choking episode came back to me as I wondered how to promote our trek to the North Pole. It was okay to start little. You must trust that the story you have is a good one. Go with your instincts.

So, in mid-November, the *State News* ran a front-page story on Polar Trek 2001 and our desire to use the Internet to involve girls and young women. The wire service picked up the story, it went around the state, and the calls from other media came in. This was working.

The first week of December, an article appeared in the *Lansing State Journal*. The following week I got a letter from Lynn, an assistant principal at a local high school. She skied, she had climbed Mt. Rainier, and she wanted very much to go with us to the North Pole.

With the earlier addition of Susan Martin, a middle school science teacher, this could be number nine.

We met over coffee, and I was struck by her enthusiasm and honesty.

"I had a riding accident when I was a young woman, and part of my spine is fused." Medical information that was important to share, but Lynn knew it might work against her. "But I've since done a lot of things, including the climb up Rainier." She was advocating her case by putting it all on the table. No surprises here. "I'm also fifty-one, soon to be fifty-two." That would make her the oldest woman on the team by more than a year. She was a little nervous and had some doubts about her capacity to make the trek herself, but not many. I liked her drive and maturity.

"Tell you what. Why don't you and I go out skiing and just get comfortable." It would give me a chance to describe her skills to Josée, who would want a full report. This approach had worked with Susan Martin, our latest addition to the team, and seemed worth doing again.

We met several days later at a local park. The fresh snowfall earlier in the week had settled into a nice, thick layer on the ski trail. With the snow came all manner of skiers, from the chisel-legged skate skiers to the shufflers chug-chugging along on their twenty-year-old boards dug out from the back of the closet at home.

Lynn and I met at the trailhead, checked the map, and picked a five-mile course that was moderately challenging and would ensure we'd be back before twilight.

Lynn led and I followed, pleasantly surprised to find her a stronger skier than I had expected. In her business attire when we first met, she hadn't presented as a particularly athletic woman. But what she might physically lack, she certainly made up in determination. A very high spunk factor. I knew it wasn't going to be a cakewalk for Lynn, but success was certainly as much mental as physical. For instance, neither Phyllis nor I were great skiers. But as older members of the team, we probably had the capacity to endure more, and hopefully to do it with grace.

The conversation after we reached our cars at the end of the trail was warm but short.

"Lynn, if you want to join us, we'd like to have you be part of the team."

A big hug.

"We'll be getting together after the first of the year, in late January, for a training session in Marquette." A reprise of the previous one, with a real team and better results. "If this sounds good to you, we need a deposit of a thousand dollars. There's another payment due in January and one in March, for a total of ten thousand."

"I'll get it to you right away." Lynn was brimming with excitement. I felt particularly good about this teammate.

Now we were nine.

CHAPTER SIXTEEN

The third week in January of 2001, the year that we were actually going to ski to the North Pole, the team was meeting for our last North American training session. The next preparations would be in Siberia. By then, it would be too late to turn back.

The nine of us, plus Josée and Jen, planned to meet in Marquette. Frida again graciously allowed her home to be our staging area for a three- or four-day trek into the Porcupine Mountains—more "porcupine" than "mountain."

Late in 2000, Josée and I had frequently been on the phone or trading e-mails: clothing sizes, visa requirements for Russia, airline schedules, payments. There were monumental details to be worked out, in addition to my ongoing training that couldn't be neglected. Josée had the extra burden of food preparation, plus readying Richard for the Polar Light expedition he and Misha were leading in April. Then there were a growing number of inquiries from schools that wanted more information about the trek, as well as from suppliers who had "just the right sleeping bag," and from the media.

One of the local Lansing TV stations was quite taken with the idea of the trek, and Kevin, the news director, asked if I would mind if he assigned a reporter to cover us.

"That would be terrific," I said. "Any coverage you can give us will help get the message out. We particularly want girls and young women to feel there aren't barriers to becoming, or doing, whatever they want." I could feel myself starting to wind up and took a breath. I was already preaching to the converted. Kevin laid out his plan.

"What I'd like to do is send a reporter and photographer to Marquette to cover your training. Maybe go on the trail and shoot a piece with you."

I sucked in my breath. This was more than I had envisioned.

"Kevin, I'm impressed. That's a big commitment for you, and we're really honored."

"Listen," Kevin said. "We're awfully proud of you women from Michigan, especially the three of you from around here. If you're willing to freeze, we're willing to cover you."

"Thanks, Kevin . . . I think." We closed with an agreement that we'd talk details next week. That *State News* article was really paying off.

. ˙ .

"Misha wants to come to Marquette in January," Josée told me one night after Christmas.

I sensed something behind her calm delivery of this news. Misha Malakhov, Hero of Russia, had been Richard's partner on their record-setting expedition. Unresupplied. Except for that seal. His experience in the Arctic and his willingness to train us was a huge benefit in my mind.

"He's got business here in Canada. He and Richard are looking for a new boot manufacturer because the one they've been using is going out of business." Boots were critical to any adventure in the Arctic, and Richard and Misha prided themselves on a foot system that maintained warmth and blocked water, should a heel go in. "The problem is, they haven't come up with a replacement manufacturer yet."

Back to Misha's desire to be with us for training here in the United States. He wasn't making the detour for frequent-flyer miles.

"Is he concerned about us?" I was struck by this unexpected visit.

"No, not really. Misha just wants to get a head start. After all, you're just now putting together the team, and it's important that it works."

I was still unconvinced, but knew that Josée wasn't going to reveal any more in this phone conversation. The ice experts had made a decision and decided to keep the reasons to themselves.

Josée and Misha had not always been close. A Russian male and a chauvinist in his earlier days, he had rubbed Josée the wrong way during a visit to Ottawa. Josée, in response, had bundled up all of his clothing and gear and tossed it outside. She had made her point about not being treated as secondrate in her own home, and Misha made the proper corrections. He was a bright and adaptable man. That he was putting the political and economic changes in Russia to his best use was prime evidence of that.

I changed the subject. "Some good news on the team front. One of the Detroit papers, the *Detroit Free Press*, wants to send a photographer and a reporter to Marquette to join us." Josée already knew about the crew from Channel 10 in Lansing. "The photographer is a woman who really wants to come along to the North Pole. I met with her last week, and she's putting together a plan to sell her bosses on the idea."

The *Free Press* reporter had gotten information about the trek from his dad. Neal Shine, just retired as the newspaper's publisher, had given his son Dan the information. Neal and I had been together recently on an educational mission to Cuba, and sitting at a breakfast table in the Hotel Nacional in Havana, I had pitched the expedition to him. That promotional packet had gone a lot of miles to the south to announce a ski to the North Pole.

"Also, I got a call from a CBC station in Toronto that's looking to talk with one of the Canadians going. I gave them your name, of course. And I returned the call from *Dateline*, but haven't heard back yet."

"Well, it all sounds really good. You are getting a lot of media attention. But remember to keep training."

Yes, mother. I know.

"With the recent snow," I said, "we've really been able to get out on skis and not just hike around with a backpack, dragging a sled."

"That's good. *Au revoir.*"

"*Au revoir,* Josée." I knew we'd talk more about Misha's visit soon.

CHAPTER SEVENTEEN

January 2001

The snow cover was holding, the temperatures were still cold in the heart of January, and it looked like Polar Trek 2001's last training camp in Michigan's Upper Peninsula would be successful. Twelve of us would be descending on Frida: the entire rest of the team, along with Josée, Jen, and Misha, plus Mandi from the *Detroit Free Press*. Happily, Frida's house is huge, as is her hospitality. Nor would we lack for sleeping space. Josée was bringing tents as well. We could always pitch them in the backyard. This wasn't about the comforts of home.

E-mails raced back and forth along the information superhighway: equipment to bring, directions to Frida's, airplane arrivals for those flying in. The form of the training and camping trip was emerging from this minor chaos, and I was truly thankful that my sabbatical had started at the beginning of the new year. Running this operation was becoming a full-time business.

. · .

The November 2000 election, only two months before, had brought a host of surprises, including a phone call from Carter. It came the week after I returned from the Cuba trip.

"Hi, Sue. This is Carter." There was no mistaking her voice. It carried in it the gentleness of her personality.

"Hello, Carter. What's going on?"

"Well, you know how committed I am to this trek, and I'd understand if it's not okay, but I'd really like to get to Marquette on Sunday." There was a real nervousness in her question. We had been firm about insisting that all of the team members arrive at Frida's by Friday evening, January 19. Our time together was critical, and we needed to be focused, with no distractions. At this point, on the verge of the actual trek, there was scant margin for wasting time. This was one of the lessons from last year's event that had stuck with me.

"Well," I began slowly, not knowing what was coming next, "tell me what's going on." I couldn't have been prepared for her reply.

"See, my cousin is getting inaugurated on the twentieth, and that's the Saturday after we're supposed to be there. Actually he's not my first cousin, he's, like, my second cousin because our grandparents were siblings, and the whole family is going to be there, and my dad's got a suite of rooms, and we were there when his dad was inaugurated, and I can get there on Sunday because there's a flight in the evening, and I've checked it out and there's space." A breath.

Of course. Carter Walker. George Herbert Walker Bush. George W. (read "Walker") Bush. The "Carter" had thrown me off the scent.

"Carter, that's absolutely fine. What a terrific opportunity to be there, and for the second time. The only thing I ask is that you come back and tell us lots of stories."

"Oh, yes. I will!" She was so happy, and so relieved. What a delightful young woman, and a good team member.

. . . .

Our countdown to Marquette, and to the polar trek that lay beyond it, continued. Phyllis and I met to go over the accounts and ascertain where the team members were with their deposits. Frida had gotten maps and information about permits to camp in the Porcupine Mountains.

Josée kept in touch with regard to equipment she was bringing, as well as keeping tabs on travel plans. And, Misha needed a letter from our organization inviting him to come to the United States, in order to get a visa. I faxed one to his office, Centre Pole, not quite sure that the numbers I punched into the fax machine were the right ones, nor in the correct sequence. Apparently they worked. Misha was off the next day on a 120-mile trip from his home in Ryazan to the U.S. embassy in Moscow to get his documents.

I still didn't have a full sense of why Misha felt it so critical to come all the way to Michigan to meet the team. After all, he was going to see us in less than three months in Russia. The answer came from Josée, in one of our planning conversations.

"I think he wants to meet all of you because he wants to make sure that you can do it."

I was a little taken aback. Maybe we were babes in the woods, or tenderfeet on the ice, but we were preparing and training, and we were smart.

"Does he really have doubts about our abilities to do this trek?" I needed to understand his view because he was one of the keys to our chance at success, and he was our host in Russia.

"He's a Russian male, after all. And he thinks that you may be trying to cover more ice than is wise. Two degrees is a lot of skiing. Remember, it's sixty miles to a degree. And," she added, "none of you girls have any experience skiing in the Arctic."

. · . ·

According to our printed schedule, the women would be arriving all day long Friday. Most of the planes were on time—last night's snow had moved on—and Frida and I shuttled trucks and vans full of people and gear from the airport.

Misha's presence was an exciting prospect. As exotic as he was celebrated, his arrival filled us all with anticipation. He did not disappoint us.

Among our first tasks was to lay out our equipment and skis, to show him what we had brought. He and Josée inspected and probed. "Ahhh," he would occasionally remark. "And what is this?" was his comment directed at some article of gear that he had not seen before. He would listen to the explanation, and when it was seemingly finished, would continue, "And . . . ?"—drawing out the vowel as though extruding something extra, all the while looking the examinee directly in the face.

This might be followed by an awkward silence on the part of the team member, not knowing exactly what to say next. Eventually, Misha got the additional information he was seeking. I wasn't sure if this was Misha the Russian, or Misha the doctor coming through. But the style was certainly different from what we were used to.

Once all had been checked, Misha and Josée asked Frida if there was a park or a trail nearby where we could go skiing. It was Friday night. It was past evening, and we hadn't eaten.

But, it was into our ski clothing and out to the van and truck, with skis and headlamps in hand. Twenty minutes later, we were at the trail on the point by the harbor west of town, and climbing into skis. The moon had passed its last quarter a few days before and offered a minimal glow. The chief light was from our headlamps and the city of Marquette, whose illumination spread across the snow and the harbor that separated us from it.

Single file, around the course we went. A few flakes spat gently at us, but the night was mostly calm.

"Good, good. You must continue to attack," Misha exhorted. Attack what? I wondered. "Now, you must turn off your headlamps. It is not good to waste energy. You must ski without light. Learn to trust your skis!"

After a couple of tumbles, and working to be more "at one" with our skis, we successfully glided our way around the trail the second time. Then it was back to the vehicles, out of the skis, and on to Frida's.

A quick buffet meal, and Misha pulled out a bottle of champagne he'd brought with him from Russia. There was enough for a sip for all. Misha offered a toast to the women of the polar trek: "And remember, you must continue to attack." He turned to me. "Sue Carter, can you give a toast?"

I thought for a minute. "To a good training, and a successful attack. To the women of Polar Trek!"

It was the most interesting champagne I had ever tasted. Now I understand why Russians drink vodka.

CHAPTER EIGHTEEN

New morning, big breakfast, and lots of energy about the day's coming events. The team plan was to leave shortly after noon for the trail. After some consultation, we had switched locations from the Porcupine Mountains to Pictured Rocks National Lakeshore, along the southern edge of Lake Superior. For one thing, it was closer than the "Porkies." In addition, the snow conditions there were quite good, and there would be the opportunity to ski on ice rubble on the lake's shore. A reasonable simulation of Arctic pressure ridges.

A few last-minute errands in Marquette to get final bits of food, fuel, and gear, and we were ready to go. It was, however, later than early afternoon by the time we were packed and on our way. We had all that we needed to sustain us, and good weather as well—though a bit warmer than last year's –30 degrees Fahrenheit.

In fact, night was closing in by the time we arrived at a trailhead in the park on Lake Superior. Part of the trail had been groomed, but the tracks rapidly disappeared. The path through the trees was clear, though, and there was no question as to which direction to take.

Not long into the ski, we spotted a clearing off to the right which was fairly flat and level, and large enough for our two tents of fourteen people—the eleven women of the team, Misha, and Mandi and Dan of the *Detroit Free Press.*

With headlamps dancing all around like fireflies in the dark, we set up the tents, and Jen fired up the Russian stoves in the cook tent to get dinner ready.

There was a Malakhov cocktail (named after our esteemed trainer), hors d'oeuvres served à la plywood with a Swiss Army knife, and stew was on the way.

Later, over coffee and chocolate for desert, Misha took the opportunity to instruct us in Russian.

"You will need to know some words in Russian, and I will teach them to you. Repeat after me: *Doh-bray-OO-dra.*"

He waved his hand like a maestro conducting a chorus. "*Doh-bray-OO-dra. Doh-bray-OO-dra. Doh-bray-OO-dra.*"

"Good morning."

"Good morning," we replied.

The lesson continued. "*Spa-SEE-bah.*"

The chorus came back in triplicate.

"Thank you," Misha said, indicating the word's meaning.

"Thank *you*," we giggled.

The lesson went on until we had learned—or at least repeated—ten segments of phrases. There would be more tomorrow, and an expectation that we would know some two dozen by the time we landed in Russia in a little more than two months.

Fluent in French and comfortable in several other languages, I didn't find Russian too daunting. It occurred to me that learning the Cyrillic alphabet was one of the keys. Knowing the "secret code," *pectopah* suddenly becomes *restaurant*.

After extended skiing together, we had a pretty good idea of each others' skills. The best way to ensure that a group will move at roughly the same pace and not string out is to put the slowest people up front. Phyllis, Lynn with her knee brace, and I hung out at the head of the pack. Lynn had twisted her knee earlier in the month skiing and was being very cautious and protective of it.

What we learned was that our pace was about two miles an hour. Most of us had fallen at least once and struggled to get up, weighed down as we were by backpacks that tied us to uncooperative sleds.

Several marches and several breaks into the second day of training, we came to the shore of Lake Superior. The wind was out of the northwest and the sky was layered with stratus clouds, with an opening between sky and lake for the reddening sun. This is where we could camp, though not quite yet.

Our progress through the woods on the narrow trail had been slow, and consequently we hadn't gotten in more than five miles total for the day, which wasn't enough for Misha and Josée.

"We are going to ski this way along the ice"—Misha motioned east along the lake shore with his ski pole—"and then, we will ski back to this place. Then, we will make a camp."

Two miles along the ice-laden shore, with the second leg right into the teeth of a wind that must now be near twenty knots. I knew that I had gotten the best people I could find to lead us. Why did they think that we had to be the best as well? As a team, we just wanted to get there.

Over coffee that night, we made Misha an Honorary Woman by acclamation. It was gleefully done, but with full respect for the WomenQuest team.

Puzzlement crossed his face on receiving the accolade, and he turned to me. "Sue Carter, is this a good thing, to be Honorary Woman?"

"Misha, it is a very good thing."

. ˙ . ˙

We didn't make breakfast the following morning, but just bundled out of camp, pleased with ourselves and anxious to get going. We were headed for a local breakfast joint down the road.

Misha climbed into the truck cab with me. How very strange it must seem to him, all the different ways that women in this country act. He probably didn't know too many women back in Russia who drove a pickup. In the States, though, I was just another mom with a truck.

During the half hour it took us to get to the restaurant, we talked about the team, its performance, his plans, his life in the former Soviet Union. I asked him about his family.

"I have a brother who is a colonel in the army, and my mother lives near me. But my father is no longer alive. He died several years ago."

I glanced out the corner of my eye and measured him up. Misha had to be close to my age.

"Did your father fight during the Second World War?" I gently probed. It was somehow important for me to know. Perhaps I was looking for connections to a life led on the opposite side of the Cold War.

"Yes, my father was a soldier in the Russian army. He was captured by the Germans and put in Dachau, but he escaped."

Dachau, the notorious concentration and prisoner-of-war camp just to the northwest of Munich.

"Misha"—I turned full face to him for a moment—"my father was among the troops who helped liberate Dachau."

We were very quiet for a moment. We had found an unexpected point of connection.

. ˙ . ˙

Later at the airport, Misha and I drew off to the side. On my mind was his view of our performance.

"Misha, what do you think about this group of American women now?" I found myself starting to slip into his speech patterns after several days together.

"You are good and brave American women," he began, "and I think that you will be able to make this march to the North Pole. But you must continue to train and work hard, Sue Carter. You must continue to attack."

My heart welled up with feelings for this complex and strange man. I reached up and gave him a peck on the cheek. "*Da-svee-DA-neeya*, Misha."

"Good-bye, Sue Carter."

Coda

The Noquemanon Ski Race in Marquette on Saturday was challenging, but great fun. We all chose the half marathon of just over thirteen miles.

Ron, Frida, and Kathy all finished well in their age and gender categories. Kerri took third in her age group, and Susan claimed first. I made it to the finish line before they had taken the last banners down.

CHAPTER NINETEEN

On the drive back home from several days of training in the Upper Peninsula, I was filled with relief and a sense of accomplishment.

We were also two months shy of departing for Moscow, though, and payments from some of the team members were slow in arriving. The initial deposit was $1,500, and all the team members had paid. There was a schedule for paying off the balance that divided the remainder roughly into two parts. With a couple of the team members, I needed to be more direct in getting their accounts current. Josée required, quite rightly, money to pay her suppliers. Anne, in particular, was behind in coming up with the cash.

She and Carter had headed off to Salt Lake City right after the training, and had enthusiastically approached potential sponsors about the polar trek. However, Anne and Josée had had a pointed conversation about sponsorship and gear before we separated in Marquette. It was Anne's idea to substitute, or possibly augment, Josée's gear with contributions from other manufacturers. Josée made it clear that her selections stood, and she firmly told Anne so.

I called Josée to share the news and to check in on several items, including some late payments.

"You've got to be tough, Sue," Josée said. "The bottom line is, if the money's not there, they can't go."

"Of course, you're absolutely right." I guess I had been a bit naive in thinking that this part would go like clockwork. After all, I'd already put in double what we were asking team members to pay. The start-up costs had fallen to me, a burden I had willingly assumed. With some of the other team members, however, more firmness was required.

"Well, I actually have some good news for you," Josée said from her end. "I think I have two more women who might be interested in going. One is Marie-Josée, the sister-in-law of a woman who went with Richard and me last year. She doesn't speak much English."

"We will do everything to welcome her," I said in my best French.

"*C'est bon,*" Josée replied. "It would be good if you called her. I'll give you her number."

"Who's the other woman?"

"Her name is Alison. She's a former Olympian—rowing—and she and her team got a silver medal in Atlanta and a bronze in Sydney. Canadian, of course."

Young, strong women. This was a good thing.

"I haven't been skiing with her yet, but we're going out tomorrow. And, she's a reporter with the *Ottawa Citizen*. If you decide to take her on, it looks like the paper will pay her way. She'll report on the trek."

This was coming together nicely.

. · . ·

News of Polar Trek 2001 was now circulating in the "women-who-do-wild-things-outdoors" community. Several emails arrived, including one from a woman in Germany, an American whose Air Force husband was stationed there. Diana had been signed up for another ski to the North Pole, but the expedition hadn't filled and was subsequently cancelled. She was actively looking for a replacement expedition.

It was late in the planning, but I emailed an application, and she filled it out and sent it back along with a resumé jammed with cold-weather experience, including a stint in Antarctica dispatching air freight.

We talked several times, and she and Josée talked as well. Diana was also willing to come to the States to meet me and others of the team. She was eager to join us, and seemed to genuinely like the aspect of being part of an all-women team.

After Josée and Diana had spoken on the phone, I called.

"What do you think, Josée?"

"Well, this Diana, she's sharp. I also like the photo she sent to me of her skiing in Switzerland. She's got the right equipment."

Equipment was critical to Josée. The hallmark of an experienced skier was being properly outfitted, and Diana had been that.

"This will put us at fourteen. Does that make the team too unwieldy?"

Josée thought for a minute. "No, I don't think so. The tents can handle fourteen, but probably no more. If you like Diana, she's fine with me."

Fourteen women did make for a big contingent. But Diana struck me as a really good addition, even if a late one. With her track record in the Arctic, she should have no problem fitting in, at least physically. I was betting that she'd blend in with the team as well.

. · . ·

Visas, clothing sizes, ruffs. Frida had found a firm in Canada that would cut pelts to our specifications. I had settled on wolverine, given the pelt's properties—namely, that it dries quickly and frost shakes out of it fairly easily.

Immunizations, too. The campus travel clinic had researched the region and determined the protection we needed. Hepatitis A and Hepatitis B were good to have, along with polio, diphtheria, and tetanus boosters. Remember, the clinician cautioned, tuberculosis was resurgent in Russia. Try to keep a three-foot distance from the residents there. I'd do my best.

. · . ·

We were still stymied in our search for a satellite telephone. The financial demise of the Iridium system left the North Pole effectively without any commercially available satellite connection. The system was still operating, and the U.S. military was managing it, but the likelihood of us civilians having access to it was pretty small.

Word was that the successor system to Iridium would be back on line at the end of the first quarter of the year. But the end of March was perilously close to April, the time we were scheduled to fly to Moscow. Besides, I couldn't get anyone connected with Iridium to actually confirm the rumor about the company's resurrection.

Kathy was able to acquire the use of a satellite phone through her company, but the footprint went only as far north as Siberia. That phone would be tremendously helpful while we were in Solotcha, several miles from Ryazan, the ancient capital of Moscow. However, the phones would be inoperable once we were on the Arctic Ocean as the company had no satellite coverage there.

The use of a satellite telephone was important to our mission for several reasons. Kerri and Susan had set up a schedule of calls to middle schools back in Michigan. As students became involved with our plans for the trek and the curriculum we were posting, this would allow them to have a real-time conversation with a team of women on the ice. Not as glamorous as the Space Shuttle, but not bad.

There was more. Now that Alison was a team member, she hoped to file regular daily reports with the *Ottawa Citizen*. After all, her paper was paying for her to go. I also would be making calls to media in the States, and wanted to be in touch daily with Bonnie to give her information she could put up on our webpage. This was not a client-based ski to the North Pole. Rather, Polar Trek 2001 had a mission to communicate, and I was determined to see it fulfilled.

Tom, Lynn's husband, had volunteered to lend a hand in the search for a satellite telephone. He sensed that I was approaching maximum capacity in my ability to accomplish tasks. Tom had run errands for us, picked up deliveries, and cheerfully done whatever we needed. It was he who suggested contacting one of Michigan's U.S. senators for help in getting a satellite phone. That Senator Stabenow was a woman and from our part of the state couldn't hurt.

At the same time, Phyllis mentioned to one of the university vice presidents that we were still searching for a satellite telephone. He happened to have an in-law of considerable rank in the U.S. Navy, and another door opened. She got in touch right away.

Phyllis called me later. "Good news. We've got two satellite telephones the Navy is willing to loan us."

"That's fantastic." This was a tremendous boost. Now we could communicate with the world beyond our tent on the ice.

"There's a slight complication, but it shouldn't be a big one," she continued. "We need to pick up the phones and batteries in San Diego."

She and I both laughed. Kathy Braegger lived right there. Picking up the phones in San Diego couldn't have been more convenient. The satellite telephones were being loaned to us by SPAWAR (Space and Naval Warfare Systems), a naval command center in San Diego. They were interested in testing their phones in all kinds of conditions, including extreme ones. Seems that our trek qualified.

Kathy was glad to meet with the officials from the Navy and get directions on the sat-phone use. The two Navy instruments, along with the other handset, now gave us three satellite telephones—and a new role for Kathy. She was now Official in Charge of Communications for Polar Trek 2001. Kathy methodically organized the phones, labeled the batteries, and took responsibility for keeping them charged—no small task in the cold, as it would turn out.

.   .   .

The call I didn't expect came from NASA, and a man who identified himself as "NASA Mike." He'd gotten word that Senator Stabenow's staff was helping us locate a satellite telephone. Yes, NASA had a phone, but he had another idea.

"Why don't we fly to the North Pole and meet you for a webcast. We've got a satellite that orbits the poles, and we should be able to clear access and do a live 'cast."

I was flabbergasted. NASA meet us at the North Pole? For a live webcast? There were no words coming out of me. Finally I found my voice.

"Mike, how much is this going to cost?" At least I had sense to ask the one basic question that would determine the answer to any others that might follow.

"We can probably do it for, let's see . . . If you can cover, say, $75,000, we can get in-kind contributions from this end and make it go. We do a lot of educational stuff in this unit, and it would fit right in."

I was fixating on two things. One, this would be so cool, and two, where was I going to get $75,000?

Mike outlined what the webcast might look like, adding that we should be able to get weather briefings from NOAA and Environment Canada as well. And maybe there would be postings on our website and a link to theirs.

Seventy-five thousand dollars.

"Mike, that's a big chunk of money, and we're a bake-sale operation with only three weeks left before we ship out." Still, I didn't want to foreclose anything, at least not yet. "Let me get back to you."

. ˙ . ˙

I dreaded calling Mike. My efforts to come up with anything approaching the amount he needed from our end had fallen way short of the mark. It was just too late in the day to get that kind of contribution, and I wasn't willing to raid my retirement for that sum.

"Mike," I began, "I'm really sorry, but there's just not that kind of cash available to us. You've outlined a marvelous plan, and we really appreciate it, but we've got to let it go."

"No, wait. I think there's a way to do this. If you can come up with $45,000, then we can make it happen."

I was beginning to see from his enthusiasm why he was called NASA Mike. But I'd checked the sources where funding might have come from, and the money—at this late date—wasn't there.

He was not about to let go. "Let's get your friend Kathy Clark on the line and see if she can join us, and if she's got some travel money in her budget." Kathy Clark, Ph.D. was a friend of mine from Ann Arbor who had taken a position with NASA as chief scientist for Human Exploration and Development of Space. Kathy was in charge of experiments on the space station.

She picked up the phone on a conference call and listened to Mike's outline.

"I do space, Mike." But the idea of going to the North Pole still intrigued her.

Kathy continued. "Let me check my calendar. I don't even know if I'm free then. What are the dates again?"

I laid out the schedule for Kathy. We were due to arrive at the North Pole on April 24. The twenty-fifth was the backup date in case there were—as Richard had put it—any "Arctic surprises."

Mike and I talked a little more while Kathy reviewed her extensive travel plans.

"I can't believe this, but I'm actually free those days." This was highly unusual, as Kathy's travel schedule was extensive and took her all over the world. We'd tried on several occasions to get together—either in Washington or Ann Arbor—but without success.

The conversation continued, and I listened while they talked budgets.

"That will work," Mike concluded. "Sue, if you can come up with about $20,000 to cover our airfares to Resolute Bay and the charter from there to the North Pole, we can go ahead and plan.

"Mike, I can handle the travel," I said, though I wasn't sure exactly how. I just knew that it was a more manageable figure. The chance to join with their resources and reach middle-school youngsters was certainly too good to let pass.

"Hey, Kathy, see you at the North Pole," I bubbled.

"It's a deal."

CHAPTER TWENTY

Day Five

Somewhere in the world it is Friday.

We sleep later than we planned to—until 8:30 in the morning. It will be a struggle to stay on track all day as a result, and to not let ourselves ski too late in the day. We are hooked on the horns of a dilemma: ski a sizeable distance, but not overly long. We still have calls to make to students and others back home, and we have to fight the urge to move to a twenty-seven-hour day.

I slept only moderately well during the night, the "sleep session." Josée moved Phyllis out of her tent and into mine to get her to settle down and sleep more. The cook tent quiets later than the second tent, and Phyllis, in Josée's view, needed more rest. The level of snoring in our tent subsequently rose.

Hot liquid and a Cream of Wheat breakfast, and then we strain to get our sleds and backpacks stuffed and ready for the day's ski. No matter how hard we push, we are still slow. Steady, but slow.

The section of ice we polar trekkers are on is still moving too rapidly to the west. Kathy's morning calculations of our position put us at N89.39, E104.51. We've experienced a nine-degree shift to the west over a twenty-four hour period, and traveled less than six miles north. The shutters on our window of opportunity are starting to close. Making solid progress today is critical, and that isn't going to be easy. Just to the north of us lies a major lead that will force us to ski along it until we find a narrow crossing, or it closes.

Having come off yesterday's ski feeling so good, we begin this day, April 20, feeling a bit discouraged. We are forced to ski west—and we are already drifting west—when we want to go north. Compounding the challenge is a wind that has kicked up. The −25 Fahrenheit feels much colder. No one knows or really cares what the wind-chill factor is at this point. Cold, colder, and damned cold. We are registering damned cold.

The wind has also blown the sun from the sky. For the first time since we came to the Arctic Ocean, the world is flat, and the sky is indistinguishable from ice terrain. For the several of us who are less than confident on mostly ice, it is harrowing. I take several spills, and my sled launches itself toward me at one point in what must be an act of retribution for being dragged around a cold, slippery place. The bruise on my calf is going to be colorful.

Josée sees my distress and skis up to lend a hand. She has been riding herd at the back of the pack.

"Sue, what you need to do is repack your sled," she diagnoses as she takes the top off and starts shuffling things inside to more secure places. "And this big thing," she says, pointing to the Styrofoam picnic chest that contains my air samples, "this thing we may have to leave behind."

I can feel my defenses rising. "No," I insist. "At least not yet. Let's see how the day goes. We don't have to decide now." I'm not willing to ditch the vacuum tubes yet. I can ski better—and I will.

. · . ·

It is about halfway through our third march when we see it. Actually, when we see them. Two seals are swimming in the lead that keeps forcing us westward. First one head and then another pop up from the green-black water, some forty yards from the team—the first form of life we have encountered. It's likely that the noise from our skis and sleds has gotten their attention, and they are curious about who is making such a racket. They swim along a short distance separately and then submerge. One resurfaces another twenty yards farther along. Then, just as swiftly and silently as they appeared, they disappear. We never see them again, though they may well have been tracking us from a distance, or under the ice.

As exciting as it is to see the seals, it raises my level of vigilance. Seals are a polar bear food source, I remind myself as I shuffle along. If there are seals here, there could be a polar bear, a mammal that definitely deserves wide berth. If you see it in time. This region is not typically polar bear territory, though it isn't unknown for bears to travel here. I keep a weather eye out the rest of the afternoon.

It takes a long time for the sky to clear up, leaving an invitation to think. Burrowed down inside my wolverine-lined parka, there is no other person to talk with but me. I do a lot of intrapersonal communication in between movements of Beethoven's symphony.

I am thankful to God that this amazing event has come together. There are pieces of it that I am worried about, though. It still isn't clear how exactly we are going to hook up with NASA at the North Pole or Borneo, and I have $20,000 of my own money riding on that. I am distressed with the way things turned out with Carter and Anne, though there is nothing to be done at the moment, or perhaps at all. Phyllis is starting to drain my batteries. She is high maintenance and apparently needs to challenge me, though I'm not sure why. I am confronted with an example at the next break.

We have just crossed another pressure ridge, and it isn't clear whether or not we are going to stop there for a rest or press on. If we are continuing, then I'll buckle everything back into place. If not, I am ready to move my sled over and rummage around for my thermos and a hot drink.

"Jen, do you think we'll head on, or do you want us to stay here?" I ask.

Phyllis jumps in. "Josée said we were going to stop here before the next march."

This is getting tiresome. Slowly, I turn. "Phyllis, I didn't ask you, I asked Jen. It would be helpful if you stopped answering for other people." An icy reply in the Arctic.

"Oh, but I . . ." Phyllis begins. I never hear the rest of what she says. I have already walked away.

. ˙ .

We carry what we need on our backs, in our heads, and on our sleds. That phrase keeps rattling through my brain as I haul and hoist bags and sleds over the frozen icescape. Life has gotten stunningly simple since we arrived on the Arctic Ocean ten days and an eon ago. Our work, eat, sleep patterns are reasonably well established, though the desire to lengthen the day is strong. Our hygiene is routine and the required minimum: a once-a-day quick wash, and tooth brushing twice a day (flossing once). Some still brush their hair, but I stopped three days ago. A close cut before I left East Lansing is my solution to a neat, groomed look. I know it will grow out, and I don't want to mess with it while skiing north.

Toilet paper is becoming precious. My mother was a Peace Corps volunteer in Belize during the late 1970s, and she instructed me on the finer points of t.p. in the wild. One, make sure you have plenty of it. Two, get the kind that's packed with as many sheets to the roll as possible. Three, share, but do so wisely. Four, make doubly sure you have enough. The alternative to using toilet paper is to grab and apply a chunk of ice.

There is lots of time for random thoughts because we are slogging on, though not making much forward progress—as Alison describes later to her editor at the *Ottawa Citizen:* "We picked our way across. We detoured around. We weren't covering very much distance."

It is late in the afternoon—still, as always, in full daylight—that we experience what we have dreaded, but secretly wanted to see. It comes without warning, but with full sound. Josée cautioned us that it was possible, but not one woman has fully appreciated what it might mean. The ice moves.

It doesn't just shift or slip a little. It moves. With an eerie mechanical sound that belongs more to a huge combine in the field than a chunk of ice, it starts with a growl that catapults into a mild roar—continuous and ominous.

Almost all of the team have just skied across a pressure ridge formed by two plates of ice coming together over a small lead. I am on the far side, having crossed as Diana was working her way over the bridge that spans the lead. Suddenly, off to the right, less than twenty feet away, the fearsome sound of two masses of ice butting heads grows instantly loud.

"Get back. Get away from the edge," Josée yells from the other side. I am momentarily transfixed, rabbit-still, trying to take in what is happening and utterly fascinated that it is occurring right in front of me. It is mesmerizing. Only for a moment, though. The intensity of the sound leaps forward, seemingly assailing us. As Frida and I and the rest of the team rapidly draw back from the edge, Jen reaches up on the ice rubble and yanks Diana back. From a distance, we watch as ice chunk heaves upon ice chunk, coming together to form another, higher pressure ridge. This must be what it's like to see mountains being formed, in the fast-forward mode. Two plates come together in an uplift and—voilà!—the Alps.

The rumbling stops, and the ice settles into a new ridge. Josée, Jen, and Diana find a crossing less than fifty feet away. Josée skis up to us and launches into it.

"When I tell you to get back, you have to move!" she begins. I feel shamefaced because I had lagged in responding. But it was an incredible moment, one I might never experience again. "Don't just stand there, because the whole piece of ice may be unstable." No excuses justify standing there to witness the astonishing ice formation. Josée is absolutely right; we had stayed in harm's way. But I probably never will see the likes of ice moving in that way again.

. . . .

But the biggest Arctic surprise—and scare—is yet to come.

Our late start hasn't helped us mentally. Our agonizing progress, coupled with the pressure ridge going active on us, has left us flagging. Even with the clouds finally out of the sky, the day's prospects aren't bright. We have been skiing for five marches and are barely moving a mile north an hour. There is lots of side movement, but little in the desired direction. We seem to be skiing two miles to go forward one.

Coming out of the sixth march of the day, we are all tired. I collapse on my sled, having yanked my down parka out of my backpack along with my thermos and food bag. I've made it through the porksicle and beef jerky for the day. The pound cake I put into my vest pocket earlier still hasn't warmed up enough so it won't break my molars. Instead, I dig out a handful of nuts. I am off to the side watching the group, trying to restore myself for the round of phone calls later that day, when it begins.

Near the center of the group, Susan is starting to move around. She tends to cool off faster than the rest of us and usually doesn't want to rest as long. She appears to be chilled now, but isn't doing anything about it. Her down jacket is still in her backpack. Kerri gets up from where she is sitting on the top of her sled and goes over to Susan. They had become good friends during their training together in northern Michigan, and Kerri often looks out for Susan.

I watch and then realize that something is wrong. Kerri is trying to get Susan to put her down jacket on, but without much success. She is resisting. Susan isn't cold—in her mind—and doesn't need to bother with the extra layer. She is swiftly becoming hypothermic. Her confusion is a sign that the cold is settling in deeply and rapidly. Several of us quickly move around her; Kerri and I find her jacket, and I zip it on. We surround her as a windbreak and insulating layer of humans, while Marie-Josée hands over a cup of warm drink. Josée quickly comes to the same diagnosis that the others and I have made. In her hypothermic state, Susan needs to be placed in a heated space and quickly warmed up.

It is earlier in the day than we had planned to stop, but that no longer matters. There is an emergency at hand. Susan has stopped shivering, which is a bad sign. She is also pale and somewhat confused. If we don't stop now and set up camp, Susan could easily degrade further.

Jen grabs a long pole from Josée's backpack and heads off around the edge of a pressure ridge to test the ice. If it is old enough and thick enough, we will halt here, swiftly raise a tent, and then put Susan into it with stoves at full blast.

Jen returns and motions in the direction she has just scouted.

"It's okay over there. The ice is solid, as long as we stay away from this part near the lead. Ladies, let's move over there and make camp."

The rest of us rapidly strap on our gear and ski a couple of hundred yards to the site Jen has marked off. Just as quickly, we stake out the tent.

"Anybody have any warm drink left?" Josée shouts from inside the tent. Kerri passes in her thermos. It is vital to rewarm Susan and to give her ample liquid. While Susan's status is serious, she hasn't been too badly compromised, but her condition can't be allowed to worsen.

From this point forward, though, we'll have to keep a closer watch on her. She is inclined to be cold, especially given the relatively small amount of body fat she has, but she also has a habit of not dressing as warmly as she needs to. Misha noted that in January when he pointed out that her inner layers of clothing weren't tucked into her pants. She needs to be responsible for herself as well, if she is going to be with us all the way to the Pole.

. ˙ . ˙

With Susan's emergency addressed, the second tent goes up speedily. We arrange our sleds, pull our sleeping bags from their stuff sacks to fluff up—hopefully to lose some of the accumulated moisture—and then slide into the cook tent for dinner. Pasta. It is preceded by a Malakhov cocktail, and followed by tea and some chocolate for dessert.

Susan, by now, has revived. Her temperature has risen; she is alert and a bit sheepish about having allowed herself to get into a hypothermic state. We talk and agree to shorten the breaks to reduce the harsh effects of chilling down. It would feel better if a thousand needles weren't embedded in my own hands each time we begin a new march.

Marie-Josée and Jen have strung up the antenna for the radio so we can call Ice Station Borneo. It is the fifth day of travel and they need to hear from us, or we can expect a pickup tomorrow. Again, the dollar signs loom. That's what an expedition leader has to worry about, in addition to the actual event.

The mic is plugged in, and Kerri again keys the radio and calls in Russian: "Borneo, Borneo. WomenQuest calling." Again, and a third and fourth time. Nothing. The solar flares must be really active. Phyllis tries. I try. And still there is no sound coming back.

Kerri gets back on. "Borneo, Amerikansky WomenQuest. Over."

A sound that is staticky, but not static, comes back. It isn't clear, but it sounds as though we have gotten through. "Borneo," Kerri continues, and then gives our coordinates in Russian. We all nod in relief, for it appears that we have been heard. We will be spared a visit and a false alarm tomorrow. We have managed to contact Borneo on the fifth day.

. ˙ . ˙

Tonight, Alison begins her story with "Mom, don't read this." And Bonnie starts off the day's entry for our webpage with: "NOTE TO FAMILY AND

FRIENDS—Despite the problems detailed below, all is well, so read on knowing that everyone is safe and warm tonight." The scare of Susan's hypothermia is distributed worldwide.

We go to bed having skied only a little more than five and a half miles, and we still have twenty-one miles left to get to the Pole. Twenty-one miles in four days. And that's if we go in a straight line.

CHAPTER TWENTY-ONE

March 2001

For the girl in me who had wanted to be an astronaut and could still name the Mercury Seven, the week before departing Michigan was a heady experience. Multiple conversations with folks at NASA, including Mike, along with emails and letters—it was a tremendous tonic, and a terrific energy drain.

I still hadn't figured out how to pay for the NASA webcast, but I knew how to cover it. The Steger-Schurke expedition in 1986 had been cash-poor at one point and used credit cards. Such action is not for the faint-hearted nor the foolish; it can be a rather expensive "bridge loan" in urgent times. I designated this an urgent time.

Bonnie was impressed with my chutzpah at laying the money on the line. She was also thrilled at the opportunity to work with NASA's webmasters, whom she deemed "absolutely the best." Bonnie, as our link back home, would build webpages and coordinate charts of our progress, including satellite images of the area we'd be skiing. The irony was that we, the women of Polar Trek 2001—who needed the images the most—wouldn't be able to see them. It would end up making a difference.

Bonnie and I went over the details of how we'd communicate, using the U.S. Navy's SPAWAR satellite telephones. "I imagine that the Navy will see that we have plenty of power. The last thing they need is a headline that reads: 'American Women Lost at North Pole—Not Enough Batteries.'"

We laughed.

. ˙ .

To make sure the deposits were in, I'd sent around a reminder via email to all team members. The last payment had been due March 15, and a few women were still short of the full amount. Finally, with about two weeks left before departure, all the money was in, except for Anne's. I was concerned, and I talked with Phyllis about it when I dropped off the last of the checks that had been mailed in.

"She told me that she was having trouble coming up with the money," Phyllis said.

"Better she should have told me." I was irritated with the situation all around. Anne had paid only her initial deposit, and had not responded to my calls or emails during the last week. Josée and I were clear on the matter. Only fully paid team members could go.

Anne had put energy into contacting suppliers and coming up with additional clothing, but the operating premise had been clear. This trek could go forward because was it was self-funded. In-kind contributions would not substitute for payment, for our reserves were precious little as it stood.

I finally reached Anne a week before we were to fly out. It was a hard conversation.

"Anne, you must remember that everyone has to pay the $10,000 fee before they can go. Josée and I agree that anyone who hasn't paid will have to turn around and leave Moscow—"

Anne jumped right in. "But look at all I've done. I went out and got all of this stuff. If I had known, I would have spent my time raising money."

"Anne, we've been clear from the beginning. It's the fact that we all pay that allows this trek to take place. Anything beyond that is great, but it is an add-on."

"Still, I think I should be given some kind of credit for what I've done."

"And where do you think that money will come from?"

"It isn't fair that this doesn't count."

"There never was a separate deal, Anne, only the one that all of us have. It's really important for you to get the rest of the money in, or you can't go."

. ˙ . ˙

It was now a little less than two weeks before departure for Moscow. Some, including Carter and Anne, Marie-Josée, and Diana, were planning on arriving in Russia before April 3. The majority of us were leaving Detroit on April 2, heading to Russia with connections in Amsterdam—loaded with bags, skis, and several boxes of extra gear, including one with scientific supplies for gathering air samples. We'd all meet in Moscow.

. ˙ . ˙

Russia is, in many ways, a cash economy. Credit cards, traveler's checks, other typical instruments of conveying money aren't readily accepted there. You *can* leave home without it, except for U.S. dollars.

The week before we were set to leave, Josée asked me if we could bring the balance owing—more than $20,000—in cash. It would be used to pay the Russians who were supplying us and transporting us to the Arctic Ocean.

"Why can't we transfer the money to you? After all, you and Canadian Arctic Holidays are making the arrangements. We are paying you, not others."

"Ah, yes, that's true. But our lawyer is concerned that if we have too much money moving into our account here in Canada and going out as cash, that the government might get suspicious." I was silent, and Josée filled in the blank. "You know, drug money."

That was the furthest thing from my mind. Josée and drugs didn't even belong in the same paragraph. But, governments bent on crime busting don't necessarily work along the same lines.

"Josée, let me check to see how much we can legally take out of the United States. We'll bring that amount, but I can't go above that. It's not worth losing my law license. Not to mention jail."

Among the four of us flying out of Detroit, we could each carry $5,000. So I let Josée know that the rest would be sent to their bank in Canada.

But what kind of bills to get? What do Russians like? Mr. Hamilton on the twenty, or maybe a fifty, or a hundred-dollar bill? The greater the denomination, the easier to carry, and to shelter from potential pickpockets. But I was without a clue here.

I went with twenties.

Josée did tell me that the Russians like their bills crisp and new, so I stipulated that to the bank when I put in an order for the money. Maybe the bank had $20,000 in small bills lying around, but it was a small bank—two steps above a mom-and-pop operation—and it didn't seem likely. They would acquire fresh twenty-dollar bills for us that would be ready for pickup the morning of our departure.

I asked my daughter, Amanda, to join me on the trip to the (only) downtown branch of the bank. I'd go in and get the cash, and she'd stay in the car, ready to drive away. The fact that this was a totally legit operation didn't detract from the sense of intrigue. When you've raised cash by bake sales most of your life, anything above fifteen dollars seems like a fair piece of change.

I was in the bank shortly after it opened, and the cashier counted out stacks of twenties totaling $20,000. The pile was actually smaller than I had imagined, not being used to transactions of this sort. Amanda, waiting in the truck with the engine running, pulled away as soon as I climbed into the cab, earnest in her duty to get me home quickly and safely.

Lynn had gotten money belts for us to wear, and we'd divide the cash up at the airport, for security as well as legal reasons. No box to add to the pile here.

. . . .

Because NASA's invitation for a North Pole webcast came late in the planning, there were still some questions regarding the NASA team's flight to the Arctic. And Misha was expressing concern about this latest activity as well. Through the veil of different languages and cultures, I gathered he was worried about the hasty planning, the burden of a distracting event, and perhaps that it wasn't his idea.

NASA Mike, after talking with the flight personnel of First Air in Resolute Bay, Canada, said that they could land at the Pole, but would need me to identify a close landing strip of at least 2,500 feet—almost half a mile. It didn't sound terribly hard. We'd be on the Arctic Ocean, on a flat pan of ice. As a pilot, I know what a suitable runway looks like, even when there isn't one apparent.

Once an airstrip was identified, I'd call in the coordinates via the satellite telephone. That way, the plane would be able to touch down, using information from the ground. Maybe a little tricky, but absolutely feasible. Planes had landed at the North Pole before. Not all the time, but they did land there.

Working through which "clock" we'd be on was a bit trickier. We'd communicate based on UTC, Coordinated Universal Time. Our group's reference would be to time where we were in Siberia, while NASA would use Eastern Daylight Time. We had several hours of satellite time available for the webcast that would coincide with evening-news programs in Michigan. NASA's circumpolar satellite would be ready with a footprint over the North Pole.

Mike and I talked in terms of UTC, or Zulu, always trying to remember that we moved into daylight-saving time at the beginning of April. And, what time was Resolute Bay on? While there were more logistics we'd have to figure out, it seemed like the arrangements were close to being set. Thank heavens Bonnie was there to shepherd details not completed before we left.

One big piece of the Arctic expedition was still unresolved. Anne had yet to send in the balance of her trek payment.

Josée was adamant about the condition of participation being a fully paid share. Cash on the barrelhead would make it go; there was no room to make an exception. Other women had made contributions as well as Anne: Kerri and Susan helped with the schools and the curriculum, Phyllis handled the books, and Frida was preparing to shoot the video. As team leader, I had given substantially to the effort.

E-mails and phone messages the week before we left didn't get a response from Anne. I understood the tender nature of her situation, but not being able to talk about it made it all the tougher.

By Thursday, four days before the last of us were flying to Moscow, we had to confirm participation with Josée. It was three days after the final deadline for getting the money to us—to be certain all checks would clear. There had been no word from her. Anne was out. The deadline had come and gone.

I was heartsick, as much for Anne as for my failure to avoid this. If I had been firmer and clearer, more Top Kick than sidekick, this probably wouldn't have happened. It was a flawed exercise in leadership, and a painful one.

. . . .

It didn't take Anne long to circulate the word that she wasn't going. In fact, it was less than twelve hours. I was home when the call came in from Alison Korn, in her capacity as reporter for the *Ottawa Citizen*.

Having a reporter as a team member was a double-edged sword. The publicity was great, but the truth telling would also be hard to bear. I had been very clear with Alison right from the beginning: she had free rein to report. The only exceptions would be very personal moments that were identified, up front, as "off the record." Otherwise, everything was public. And this was one of those public moments.

"Hallo, Sue, it's Alison," said the voice at the other end of the line. "I've talked with Anne and I understand that she's not going. I need to get a quote from you."

My job was to protect the organization and its mission, not to make Alison's easier. The quote was direct, and somewhat terse.

"Sometimes what individuals think and hope will happen doesn't come to pass,"
WomenQuest founder Sue Carter said before our team left for Russia last night.

"Anne made the choice not to pay the $10,000 (fee)," said Sue, who decided
Saturday that time had run out for Anne.

It wasn't perfect, but it never is. The essence of the story was true, though. Anne hadn't made the payment in time to allow her to be a part of the group. It hadn't turned out as any of us had wanted it to.

While Anne's situation wasn't unexpected, what happened next absolutely stunned me.

I had been out Sunday afternoon, running last-minute errands, and returned to a phone message from Carter. In a strained and trembling voice, she said that the decision not to take Anne left her no choice but to bow out herself. She was leaving, and not available by telephone.

I immediately grabbed the phone and punched in her number in Montana. It was unlikely that she would be there, but she might be checking messages.

"Carter, this is Sue. I just got home and heard your message. I really encourage you to reconsider. You've worked hard to get to this point, and it would be a shame to toss it out." What to say next that might get her to call? "The team really wants you to be with us"—which was true. Carter was a precious sparkplug in our group. "I'll be home the rest of the evening and until tomorrow afternoon. Please give me a call."

I knew she wouldn't.

Anne's departure was not nearly so troubling as Carter's. I had privately questioned Anne's ability to be a full member of the team if the chips were down. Carter was the opposite. She was solid and reliable to the core. And while she was being loyal to her friend, the loyalty to Anne felt misguided and one-way. But, not mine to decipher. I had to work to keep the polar trek on track. It couldn't be derailed or even distracted at this point. Tomorrow we were flying to Moscow.

. . .

When I got to the office later that morning, there was an email from Carter in my mailbox. Subject: My intentions regarding Polar Trek. Something had just reached inside my chest and squeezed.

In it, she shared her sorrow at not being able to join us, but underscored how important Anne was to her, and how in Anne's absence she couldn't go forward. "So, I wish you all the very best," she closed. "I will be with you in spirit, to be sure."

I hit the print function and just slumped back in my chair. Better to get my crying finished now. Tears will freeze at the North Pole.

CHAPTER TWENTY-TWO

Day Six

We wake up closer to our goal. The winds that whipped through our camp and our tents during the sleep session have also worked in our favor. We are at N89.46 and E99.21. The Greenland Drift is still carrying us farther west than we want to be, but we have gained slightly more than two nautical miles to the north. More than two hours' worth of skiing; it is a welcome gift.

Some of the women have been bothered by the relentless wind that batters the tents while we sleep. Marie-Josée writes in her diary that she feels anxious watching the tents billow in and out. For some reason, I find the wind comforting. It is dynamic, and it blocks out other noises. Like a lullaby, it cradles me into a deep sleep. My log reads: "Slept well. Lots of wind but it was actually comforting. Sack felt really good."

Yesterday's overcast is replaced by today's near whiteout. Visibility is poor when we rise at 7 A.M., and it is no better when we wrangle up our gear for a day of skiing. The upside is that it is warmer—considerably warmer than it has been, even in Siberia. I am getting a reading of +3 degrees Fahrenheit. The conditions are adequate for lengthy skiing.

That's what Josée has in mind. She has made it clear that we are going to have a long day of skiing, because we need one. Actually, we need four. Today's progress will have to be made in spite of obstacles presented by leads and pressure ridges. Somehow, Mother Nature hasn't gotten the message that this is a team of all women. Or, if she has, she is showing no favoritism toward those of her gender.

The leads we have encountered the past two days are still there as we ski off. During the first few marches of the day, we often find ourselves skiing around or scampering over a pressure ridge, only to be confronted with a lead.

Jen urges us on, giving more guidance to some of the team who are having trouble crossing.

"Follow the person in front of you—or swim," she says. "Plant the picks of your poles on chunks of ice." Because if you jam them on snow, you can find yourself face down in the Arctic Ocean.

Yesterday's crossing of one of the leads turned out to be a bit problematic. Both Phyllis and Lynn put a boot into the water. Not fully, but enough to dampen socks. The socks quickly froze on their feet and later were warmed by their bodies, but it was a reminder that anything more than a quick dip could be dangerous.

The snow conditions are also devilish—and sometimes it isn't even snow, but sheer ice that makes it very difficult. Our progress slows considerably. I plant a pole, or try to drive in a pick of the pole, only to have my ski slide out, the edge lost. Our skis are backcountry skis, made for off-trail conditions and equipped with metal edges. The makers probably didn't contemplate that the users would go this far off-trail. Whether it is the ski or operator error, I am getting banged up in the knees, my right one especially. My right triceps is also complaining. I take some ibuprofen after the third march.

Given the challenging conditions of the morning, it is a good thing that I got a sound sleep during the last session; this skiing is really taxing work. I am not overwhelmed, though. Part of my relief is probably due to the fact that we communicated yesterday—through much static—with the Russians back at Ice Station Borneo. The prospect of having to wave off a rescue, at no small fee, had been distressing. Now we're in the clear. The next task is to get to the North Pole.

Beethoven and his Ninth Symphony still pound in my head, though today it is less of a joy and more of a mantra. I measure my steps and my glides by it, trying to stay focused in the moment and on the skier in front of me. I am mid-pack, a location in the conga line to the Pole that seems to work fairly well for me. By watching the skier in front of me—often Diana, Frida, or Kerri—I can assess the ice just ahead. Smooth, slushy, or snow-covered, it helps to see another go over it first. Usually it gives direction where to ski. Sometimes it is just an indicator of where I am going to fall.

It is critical that we stay in line and not let ourselves get too spread out. Another's tracks indicate that the ice is firm, something we can't tell if we are spread out. A short line, head to tail, also guarantees that another team member will be there very quickly if a problem develops.

To date, we have been free of any real accidents or medical emergencies, though Susan's brush with hypothermia yesterday was a bit close for comfort. Skiing along, I roll through my mind a possible scenario, had she required

In Solotcha, Alison Korn begins sorting gear for the expedition.

Diana Ciserella

One of the two tents at Ice Station Borneo on the Arctic Ocean.

Diana Ciserella

WOMENQUEST
POLAR TREK 2001

The assembled team just before liftoff from Ice Station Borneo. *Top:* Diana, Alison, Kathy, Frida, Lynn, Jen, Josee. *Bottom:* Susan, Kerri, Phyllis, Sue, Marie-Josee.

Diana Ciserella

Moments after the helicopter deposited
the team at its starting point.

Alison Korn, Canadian
Olympian, team reporter,
and "big, sweaty girl."

Lynn (*left*) and Sue during a rest break.

One of the many leads—streams of open, partially frozen water—that diverted the team on its way north.

The beauty of blue ice, the newest and the most dangerous.

The Russian helicopter crew takes off, after having checked
in on their "women," leaving a bottle of vodka behind.

Josee, bottle of vodka in hand, watches the Russian helicopter depart.

With sleds hitched to backpacks, the team follows Josee north.

Team members tug sleds over chunks of ice.

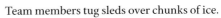

While the team rests, Josee climbs a pressure ridge to scout the next march.

Phyllis digs her down parka out of her backpack as Josee climbs yet another pressure ridge to survey the route.

Jen Buck, team cook
and Josee's assistant.

Diana Ciserella

Diana's backpack
with the American
flag attached.

Diana Ciserella

The American contingent —Kathy, Susan, Sue, Lynn,
Diana, Phyllis, Kerri, and Frida—at the North Pole.

Diana Ciserella

The Russian helicopter lands at the North Pole behind
schedule to take the team to meet the crew from NASA.

Dr. Kathy Clark interviewing Sue with the assistance of the
NASA crew near the North Pole. NASA Mike is in the center.

medical treatment. It would have meant some or all of us camping until she could be evacuated, and that could take time—given our difficulties in contacting Borneo, and the current weather outside the tunnel of my parka hood.

Keeping an eye on Susan has become even more critical. I should have picked up on an earlier sign when, two days ago, her hands got so cold that she had to warm them on Jen's belly. We can't risk our goal of the North Pole through inattention to Susan's condition. Kerri, Lynn, the others, and I make a point of checking Susan regularly for any signs of cold. She will make it, but it is important that neither she nor the team be compromised in the meantime.

The ceiling is lifting, and it turns out to be a fairly clear day. Off to the southwest are long streaks of stratus clouds, but in a configuration I have never seen before. It looks as though someone, maybe God, has raked a hand across the sky and left a stream of white marks. I can also see up to infinity. There are no longer dense clouds overhead; the stiff winds have blown them away.

It is the fourth march of the day, and we are making good progress. Suddenly, from off in the distance, a tremendous roar comes racing up to our ears. Heads wrench around, and a freezing jolt goes down my spine. We are on a flat pan of ice, and more than half of the team stretches out in front of me. Each of us instinctively stops and pulls our sleds in tightly behind us, an Arctic gesture akin to preparing to circle the wagons. Even the fur on my wolverine ruff seems to bristle.

We aren't near a lead at the moment, and the ice we are on looks to be old and solid. But ice can shift, and in an environment where there is little to block sound, the noise can travel fully, and with great speed.

In a bizarre flash, I wonder if it is a submarine underneath us. I've seen *Ice Station Zebra*, though admittedly not as many times as Howard Hughes. No, a submarine is too far-fetched. But what is it? As I consider and discard the possibilities, the thundering grows louder. Then, a helicopter bursts over the horizon. An orange and blue helicopter. A Russian helicopter that is supposed to pick us up—*only if they haven't heard from us.*

What has happened? My mind races with concern and calculations. Didn't they get our transmission last night? Surely, they must have heard and known that we are okay. *We don't need a pickup.*

The heat my body is now generating is almost overwhelming. Stock-still in my tracks, I watch the huge chopper with Aeroflot markings pass over and swoop down in front of us. The downdraft from the blades pushes my body temperature back down. But I am still soldered into my slot on the ice.

Whatever it is, it will be okay—I try to calm myself. If we have to send them back, then so be it. A little $5,000 charge, but we'll deal with it. We are not getting on board. My team is fine, and we're going forward to the North Pole, dammit.

The helicopter settles to the ground ahead and to the right of the team. In a series of amazing events, this is yet another remarkable tableau. A line of a dozen women in red and blue wind suits patiently standing by, somewhat in awe, as one of the biggest choppers on the planet lands within fifty yards. *Deus ex machina.*

Josée is in front of the line, and she sheds backpack and unstraps her skis to walk over and discover the reason for the helicopter landing. I hold back and watch, knowing that she has more experience negotiating with the Russian crews. From inside the belly of the craft, red-jacketed people are peering out. None of this makes any sense to me. But I need to be patient and to quell my anxiety.

It is Igor's helicopter and crew. Sprightly Anatoli, the dear Dolgan navigator, comes bounding out of the chopper. No, they didn't receive our message yesterday. But, no, they aren't here to evacuate us either. The helicopter is on a North Pole flight with a group from Britain. The Russian crew has asked the passengers if they mind if the helicopter takes a small detour and goes to check on the American women. Anatoli had carefully plotted out what he believed to be our course, and he has been remarkably accurate. They found us without much difficulty.

Our scruffy Russian guardian angels. They were worried whether or not we were all right and on target for the Pole. In the face of other expeditioners' derision, the Russian crewmen truly believed that we were going to make it to the North Pole, though they weren't above checking up on their bet.

In a firm gesture of friendship, Igor pulls out a half-liter bottle of Parliament vodka and places it in Josée's hands, along with a big hug.

"They were very sweet," she tells us as the helicopter is rising to make its way to the North Pole for the tourist visit. "They gave me a big hug and asked if we were okay, and wanted to know when we were going to be at the Pole." We are actually wondering the same thing ourselves.

Still holding the bottle, Josée adds, "The Russian men really want us to make it."

In the course of ten minutes, I have run through a complete range of emotions—from abject concern to immense feelings of warmth for these gruff, yet gentle men. The Arctic is not a boring place.

. . .

With ceiling and spirits lifted, we push on. The next few pressure ridges don't seem nearly so daunting. The slow speed of earlier in the day is erased, and we end up in camp at 9 P.M. Khatanga time—9 A.M. back home in Michigan—with more than five nautical miles of progress. But we still have more than thirteen to cover.

Before we gather for the evening meal of chili and Indian lentils called *dahl*, Josée approaches Alison and me.

"Some of the other girls are saying that the time that the two of you are spending on the telephone is cutting into their time to relax and socialize."

I wonder where this is going.

"It would be easier, I think," Josée continues, "if you did your calls from the other tent. Jen will put a stove in there so it'll be warm."

Josée is carefully watching for my reaction. I'm not sure if this is going to matter or not in six months, but it isn't a ditch worth dying in. Alison follows my lead.

"That'll be fine," I reply. "We will make the accommodation. But I want the tent warm. We won't make the calls we need to if we're cold."

I feel undermined, though not by Josée. She was just carrying ice water. In my tired and somewhat depleted state, I am coldly furious that it is all right for others to make calls to schools and not be seen as disruptive, but that the significant, far-reaching work that Alison and I are doing is denigrated. Interestingly, Phyllis, who had pointedly declined to make calls back home because she didn't want to be distracted from the purpose of the trek, has arranged to call her children's schools when they and their father will be there.

Alison is distressed and irritated along with me. Her important role as a journalist chronicling the trek has been made clear from the beginning. And this certainly is not a client-based expedition. This is a team event, and two of us have been, even if temporarily, voted out. I am frustrated, knowing that the phone work I do makes the rest of the team heroes back home. It frankly is taxing work and I, too, would prefer not to spend rest time in cajoling camaraderie with media back home. Or trying to track down NASA to figure out where the hell we are going to meet so that everyone can be on a worldwide webcast and have their faces on ABC's *Good Morning America*. I feel unappreciated and am deeply hurt. By the time I talk with Bonnie, I have calmed down, but the hurt is tattooed in.

"The others are getting a bit tired of us (Sue and Alison) keeping them up with our telephone calls—or, as Alison says, when we are plying our trade," said Sue. "So we

set up a separate tent tonight so that we could make our calls without disturbing them." The tent is warmed by a Russian stove, and Sue would periodically take a moment to check on the flame to make sure it wasn't touching anything in the tent.

. · . ·

I am not able to raise the NASA crew on their Iridium sat phone. I still don't know where we're going to meet—and it is scheduled for fifty-four hours from now.

CHAPTER TWENTY-THREE

April 2001

Khatanga, Siberia. A training stop for my team and a launching pad for North Pole expeditioners.

We piled our bags and gear onto a stake truck that pulled up next to the Aeroflot airplane that had flown us from Moscow. The team had already been in Russia several days, sorting gear and making last minute food purchases in Solotcha and Ryazan. Lynn and I had also accompanied Misha to his son's high school for a cultural visit. I dug the piece of paper with hash marks out of my pocket and counted thirty-six bags. Whether or not there were that many items of baggage would remain to be seen. Right now, they were part of a jumble that was moving fast in the brilliant, cold morning.

The hotel—the only one in this city of eight thousand—was a short walk from the landing field and its corrugated terminal. Slightly dazed from the flight and the stunning cold, Josée headed us in the direction of the five-story brick building. Off we clomped to get our next set of instructions.

The lobby of what passed for the hotel reflected the unusual character of Khatanga, eclectic as it was. The town traces its founding to 1626, and has been host to unusual foreigners of all sorts and from various ports—the latest crop of expeditioners to be counted among them. Pasted on the glass that separated the receptionist from the rabble were stickers representing previous polar expeditions, various sky-diving attempts, and balloon launches. Khatanga is a gathering place for postmodern type A's, who have marked the territory to show they were there. In earlier centuries there might have been cairns.

The center area of the first-floor lobby is rimmed with fake ficus and firs and a collection of local wildlife that had made a visit to the taxidermist before taking up residence here. A rather large Arctic hare occupied the middle and was overflown by Arctic terns and various gulls, including what looked like a kittiwake. We sat on a low brick ledge around the edge of the exhibit while we waited for our room assignments and keys.

Frida and I drew a room on the third floor and joined the crowd hauling the baggage that had been deposited outside up the stairs. In the land of few toilets, there certainly wasn't an elevator. But the team was ready for any kind of physical activity, and this would do for the moment.

With gear stowed and faces washed, the team regrouped in the main lobby for a short while before heading off to the restaurant, some five minutes away. We'd put our personal baggage in our rooms, but left the food, tents, and sleds in the third-floor lobby, shoved off to the side. Our team wasn't the only one on that level, but we occupied most of the rooms.

The restaurant, one of two in Khatanga, lay on the other side of two streets. North Dakota towns must have looked like this at the turn of the last century. The building's outer and inner doors opened into a vestibule and cloak room, where fur-rimmed parkas covered pegs on the wall. The vestibule led through yet another door to a darkened dining room with three long tables, a bar at one end, and a disco-era stage at the other. It wasn't clear who, or when, the entertainment would be. As the twelve of us stomped in, wearing our knee-high white Arctic boots, light bounced faintly off the mirrored ball that hung above.

The food took on a new twist: reindeer, and lots of it. At a long table, we relaxed and ate. When we finished, we had a full afternoon of work ahead of us: sorting equipment, repacking and labeling food, and dividing up everything among the team members.

Back up on the third floor, a mild chaos ensued. Weight assignments for the sleds were being made, and bulk food was distributed into meal-sized portions. Pasta for one night in one bag, drinks for one morning in another.

Josée had superintending control. "Okay, girls," she chirped in a voice that belied her size and strength. "You need to make sure you have enough for your personal food bags. We haven't packed them for you. It's your responsibility." A French Canadian, she rolled her r's.

The individual food bags were very important. They held the nourishment that we'd consume as we skied during the day. Dried fruit and nuts, smoked bacon, beef jerky, chocolate, pound cake loaded with fatty ingredients, an Italian confection reminiscent of divinity fudge—these were the items that would carry us over between breakfast and the evening meal. They were the team's critical source of energy while on the trail. We'd go through nearly six thousand calories a day. And many of us would still lose weight.

We each picked a sled and a top to go along with it. Frida had brought paint pens, someone else had colored masking tape, and we named and marked our sleds. On the side of my black sled top, I wrote in pink, "Hi Amanda!" and then took a picture.

There were messages to the world, to other teammates, and to family written on our sleds that day. Frida marked off the distance to Marquette: 2,500 miles. The number wasn't right, but I liked the sentiment.

By now, Josée had an idea of the relative physical strength of the women. That was critical to distributing the weight of gear, cooking equipment, tents, the radio equipment, and fuel. The fuel was heavy, and essential. The Russian stoves required naphthalene, white gas, and we needed a supply that exceeded the days we planned to be on the ice. The heavier sleds would be pulled by the younger, stronger women, a reality of age and capacity that was tough for all of us to accept at times.

Finally, the sleds and backpacks were loaded, and the bindings fitted on the skis for the final time. We shoved the afternoon's work against the lobby wall and washed up for dinner.

Back to the same restaurant and essentially the same offering of reindeer, complemented by fish. The fresh fruit, including grapes and strawberries, was surprising and most welcome. Josée had advised us that food would taste really different, and better, upon our return from the North Pole. It was pretty delicious at the moment.

. ˙ . ˙

The hotel residents were among the wildest I've ever encountered. That evening, a Saturday, gave me a chance to see all in full blossom. The best description is to think of the intergalactic bar in the *Star Wars* movies. A creature from here, a different life form from there. The hotel at Khatanga rivaled that.

There was a tall, lithe Swiss woman who had just completed three skydives over the North Pole and was seriously celebrating with her crew and photographer. An Italian duke was there with a video crew, hoping to retrace part of the journey his great-grandfather had taken shortly after the turn of the last century. A French team was on hand and anxious to go. As it turned out, there were balloonists from Kalamazoo, Michigan, staying as well. We met them later when one of the men popped his head into our tent and said, "I hear you gals are from Michigan." Not a particularly remarkable event, unless one is on the Arctic Ocean.

And, there were the Norwegians. I hadn't seen them, but they are among the preeminent polar trekkers and some of them must have been close by.

Most of the expeditioners there were jockeying for flights to Ice Station

Borneo. Given that my team had arrived later than some of the others, it was reasonable that they should leave before us, but not assured. Money and connections entered into the discussions as to who would fly out first. There was also the weather to consider. Would it be a direct four-hour flight, or would there be a layover in Sredny en route? The questioning was cagey, and multilingual.

"*Buon giorno*, Valerio. *Stai bene?*"

"*Si. Et tu?* And do you have a time you will be leaving here?"

"No, but I think it will be after you and the duke go. I hear that the weather is bad and may delay us all."

The rumors were rife, and the cause for the delay in getting flights was ascribed to a crack in the runway at Borneo, as well as weather and greased palms. Who knew for sure?

. . . .

After dinner, we returned to our gear for some final adjustments.

Josée gathered us around. She and I were in an interesting exchange of roles at the moment. Her authority was clear on the ice, and in the physical preparations for being there. I was the leader and organizer of Polar Trek 2001, and asked to be consulted on major items, and kept informed.

"Well, it looks like we will be leaving tomorrow morning at ten o'clock." This was sooner than we had expected. "Misha has talked with the pilots, and the chances are good." There was a buzz among the group. We were all ticking off things that needed to be taken care of before we hit Borneo. I still hadn't finished sewing my ruff to my hood.

"What time do you want us ready to go?" Kerri asked.

"I tell you what," Josée replied. "Because these things can change on a moment's notice, don't set your alarms. We'll get you up in time to have breakfast in our rooms. The hotel will give us a samovar for coffee and tea."

"Josée, are there any last-minute items we need to take care of?" I asked, wanting as much information as possible.

"No, we're in good shape, and it's already about midnight. If the hot water is turned on in the showers, you might want to take one now. It'll be your last one for a couple of weeks. Otherwise, we'll see you in the morning."

. . . .

Ice Station Borneo is a wonderful example of repurposing. Originally a Soviet military listening post begun in the late 1930s, it existed as an annually-created station that floated with the drift and housed both soldiers and scientists.

Early on, work at Ice Station Borneo centered on charting the ocean bottom and currents, as well as gathering meteorological data. When the Cold War was in full force, it tracked foreign submarine movements as well.

The ice station is established annually near 89 degrees north, and remains primarily at that latitude, though the longitude alters markedly during the time that it's staffed, which is now about a month out of the year.

Since the fall of Communism in 1991, the post has been given over to commercial interests. It's a staging area for expeditions to the North Pole, hosting many of the same intergalactic folks who inhabited the hotel in Khatanga. It all takes place for a fee.

When fully operational, Ice Station Borneo has a landing strip made by a snowplow smoothing the ice, plus inflatable huts for a crew of about 20 for two helicopters, along with their supplies and a radio shack. The temporary buildings resemble nothing so much as orange Quonset huts.

The Russian helicopter crews were once the Soviet military personnel who remade the ice station annually. They come with a wealth of experience and a great attitude. The pay for working here is substantially more than their monthly salaries. Picture a deer camp—with a bonus check to boot!

In a concession to the tourist trade, there is even a temporary post office, with a stamp that records a trip to the North Pole.

. . .

It was after 9 A.M. when I woke up the next morning. It was Sunday, April 8, my mother's seventy-third birthday. I wish I could have given her a better present than worries about her daughter on some harebrained trek to the North Pole. But remember, Jane, you were the one who quoted Auntie Mame to me when I was a child: "Darling, the water buffalo are waiting at the gate."

Frida and I had stayed up for a little while, talking about what we were going to face and how she was feeling about being here. I wondered if I had pushed her into an experience she didn't need. She struck me as distracted, and it's tough to begin an expedition like this unfocused.

After a quick wash in the room's small basin, I went out into the hall to find the others, and the room where breakfast was being created out of bread, honey, butter, and peanut butter, accompanied by tea, coffee, or hot chocolate. Outside, the sky was fierce and the wind was blowing in hard. The runway was visible from our hotel window, but not the windsock—though it had to be straight out in this blast. No doubt the weather was grounding us.

In the surrounding rooms, the hotel had been a little quieter overnight. One of the teams—was it the Italians?—had left. Misha confirmed.

"Yes, there was a team that was able to leave last night. But they did not go to Borneo," he said matter-of-factly. "They were sent to Sredny instead. The weather at Borneo was bad, too."

Josée jumped in, as if to mitigate our disappointment at being left grounded in Khatanga. "They do not have as nice a place to stay as this one." Slight snickers around. "You know what I mean," she added. "Better to stay here for a day or two than get stuck on the way."

That made sense to me. Besides, Frida and I had both raised a concern with Misha about pushing too hard to get to Borneo if we could stay here and train. The team, including us, needed some rest before the huge physical challenge that lay in front of us. Looking at Frida, I saw sunken eyes, and knew I had made the right point. Here, at least, we could have a small measure of rest.

"So"—Misha took the floor once more—"today we go for a small ski to test out equipment and get some exercise."

Out for the first time on our skis in an environment something like the one we'd soon be in, we hoped. The temperature was −5 Fahrenheit, fairly mild. But the wind was enough to stand us up straight. It was a revealing first look at ourselves, and it took only an hour and a half to appreciate where some of the flaws were. Marie-Josée discovered she needed some longer ties on her windbreaker so she could use the zippers without taking her mittens off. Susan needed to be careful in the cold—something she knew and that Misha had stressed to her. I had to better adjust the straps on my backpack.

. ˙ . ˙

Let's go out for dinner tonight.

Great, where should we go?

I know this cozy little Russian restaurant with good food and interesting people . . .

. ˙ . ˙

We had been in Khatanga slightly more than twenty-four hours, but news of this unusual all-women team had captured the imagination of some of the others who were also North Pole bound. Apparently there were side bets taking place as to whether or not this fairly ordinary band of women would survive in the Arctic and make it to 90 degrees north. Smart money was against us.

In the dining room of the restaurant that night was the French team as well. They had arrived earlier and were well into their meal and their drink by the time we were seated and served. In joyous fashion, they sent a splendid fruit plate over to our table. We reciprocated with a bottle of vodka. They toasted us with champagne. We responded with mineral water, thanking them for their good wishes and saying that we would reserve the champagne for when we returned.

The final treat came when their Russian translator, with a great mustache and spirit to match, demonstrated how Hussars toast their women. Standing right beside us at our table, he took a shot glass, filled it, and then rolled it across his cheek from his ear to his mouth, tipping the contents down his throat when the drink met his lips. *Za-drov-ye!*

. · . ·

That night I called Bonnie, using one of the satellite telephones. The disadvantage to the phones is that they will not operate inside of a building. No big problem if the assignment is in Key West. Big problem if one is in Siberia.

Standing under a lamppost outside the hotel, I fumbled with the numbers, jammed mittens back on my hands, and tried to tuck the phone inside my hood. The batteries last longer if they're kept warm. I had no idea if this would be warm enough.

"Bonnie." Name as statement. "We're in Siberia."

"Fantastic! I figured when I didn't hear from you yesterday that you were traveling."

Ouch. I realized that I should have taken time last night to call. I had gotten too wrapped up in preparations to remember. That wouldn't happen again.

"Yeah, we were on the road. Flew all Friday night and got here Saturday morning. We thought that we might fly out today, but the weather is grounding us. We're getting gear ready, though—resting, and eating well. Reindeer, and some caribou mixed in. And, you know what?" I was feeling playful for the first time in a couple of days. "They don't taste like chicken."

We chatted on for a few minutes. I told her about the flight from Moscow and some of the people at the hotel. The phone was starting to beep, and I knew I had only a few minutes left before the battery went dead.

"I don't know if we're leaving tomorrow, but either way, I'll find a way to call you, okay?"

"Sounds good. You're twelve hours ahead of me, right?"

"That's right. And, Bonnie, could you do me a favor? Would you call my mom for me and wish her a happy birthday?"

I went inside the hotel and across the lobby to the hole-in-the-wall bar with two tables. The sign outside read "Pilot Café," in Russian and English. I ordered a Polar Bear beer.

. ˙ . ˙

Monday, April 9. The sky was still menacing, and prospects for leaving Khatanga were no brighter. As we were going through our gear in the third-floor lobby to get ready for a long ski, I heard Marie-Josée say that her bag was missing.

"I had it here last night, right inside of my sled. Have any of you seen it?"

We all looked around and then shook our heads. Nothing extra in our sleds. Marie-Josée's sled bag was gone. She was calm, but clearly disturbed.

"It contains everything I need for the expedition."

Josée and I tried to quickly assess the impact of the missing bag.

"I had one of the tents, and food, and a lot of my personal things. Not my camera and toiletries, but other stuff."

We split up to search. I took the stairwells and the trash bins. Marie-Josée went to the reception desk. Misha questioned some of the employees. No luck anywhere. A tent was gone, just as we were preparing to leave.

"I want you all to go skiing with Jen," Josée finally decided. "I'll stay here, and Misha and I will continue to look."

No expedition is without bumps, but we'd had several more than I had counted on before we even officially set out.

. ˙ . ˙

The sky was slate gray and threatening when we clipped on skis to cross the frozen Siberian bay. With backpacks and sleds in tow, this would be yet another test for us. It was colder—by about eighteen degrees Fahrenheit—than it had been the day before, and the wind was starting to kick up, but it wasn't too stiff at the moment.

Wielding backpacks and sleds that were loaded down dictated a slow pace. After an hour and a half, we'd traveled a little more than two miles. We were all starting to fully appreciate the challenge that this trek to the North Pole would be.

Jen skied up and down the line, checking on us. Was our clothing warm enough? Were we too warm? She stopped when she saw Kerri.

"Kerri, can you feel your cheeks?"

"Yeah, I think so. Why?"

"You've got a white dot in the center of each one, right in the middle of the patch of red."

Kerri looked at Jen, waiting for more information.

"Kerri, your cheeks are frostbitten."

It had taken less than fifteen minutes, but her face, exposed to the cold and the wind, had yielded to the conditions. Snug down the hood, bring the ruff in tighter, raise the neck gaiter. Protect the cheeks.

We went on for another two miles. Jen scouted ahead and found a little gully for us to slip into for a break. We had some hot liquid to share among us, and food from our snack bags, and it felt good to take off the backpacks. A little breather helped and made the next stretch easier.

We went nearly two hours more before stopping for our second break in the lee of a small hill that must be sandy in the summertime—whatever summertime looks like here. Off across the bay, to the southwest, storm clouds were grouping. Land in the distance was disappearing when we began to pick our way back along the edge of the small peninsula we'd been skiing. The wind preceding the clouds was coming into our faces by now, and it was coming with a vengeance. It had to be at least twenty-five knots, and the temperature was dropping.

"Ladies," Jen shouted above the rising wind, "we have to head back." I couldn't hear all that she was yelling, though I did hear "blizzard."

The team had been out for over four hours, and we were still more than an hour away from shelter, even if we cut right across the bay. And that would be into the teeth of the storm that dropped our visibility to less than fifty feet. We broke line and all headed for the town on the other side of the bay.

"Stay in line!" Jen was shouting as loudly as she could. "Don't get lost!"

We straggled back into some semblance of a line and shuffled directly into the blizzard and toward the opposite shore. It was an hour before we reached it, tugging the sleds and wiping snow off our eyelashes.

"Next time, don't get out of line," Jen cautioned. "What if one of you fell behind? A couple of you did fall down and had a hard time getting up. You've got to work as a team."

Her words hit home. In a moment of discomfort, we hadn't operated as a unit, and cohesion would be critical to our survival.

Fortunately, a truck that earlier had carried a load of freshly slaughtered reindeer came to our aid. The driver had watched the motley crew struggle across the last distance of ice, and waited for us at the top of the hill. We gratefully loaded backpacks and sleds and skis onto the truck's bed, and then walked back to the hotel, the cell of the storm having moved on.

. . . .

We had an invitation after dinner that night to meet with six women at the small civic building in town that also served as a library. They were part of a group that called itself "The Club of Interesting People." Notwithstanding the name, the club was more devoted to meeting interesting people than being self-congratulatory. We qualified as interesting people in their eyes.

They had prepared a lovely fare for us: cakes and chocolate, tea and wine, apple and orange slices, salmon, and a local favorite: frozen fish. The fish was literally frozen solid and then shaved, scales and all, down to the bone. The curlicue shavings were passed around, to be dipped in a mixture of salt and pepper and eaten. A Siberian sushi, and equally as tasty.

Vera, one of the women in the club, had earlier hoped to join us on the expedition, and I had offered to cover half of her expense. But she had been unable to raise the other half, and the weather in Khatanga that winter had been too hideous for any training: –94 Fahrenheit! She was pleased, all the same, to meet us.

I surmised that all the women were professional. Some were teachers, and one was a metallurgist. Another was connected with the airport. Through Misha's translation, we gave thanks for the gathering and exchanged gifts, Vera presenting me with a bead-and-rabbit-fur necklace the schoolchildren had made. It was a marvel to think how these women, some of them indigenous and others from elsewhere in Russia, made a life here. But they did, and it looked to be a good one.

On the walk back, Misha drew up alongside me.

"Phyllis had a problem today when you were out skiing. Did you not know that?"

"No." I had tried to give myself a little space from her. I needed to operate at a lower key.

"It is a serious problem, and I do not think she should go to the North Pole."

I stared at Misha in disbelief, not for the first time.

"Josée and I will come to your room and talk with you about it when we get back to the hotel."

"Thank you for letting me know. I'll be waiting.

CHAPTER TWENTY-FOUR

Frida was already in the room when I got back from the library and the Club of Interesting People. She was occupied with sorting and repacking gear. The latest buzz around the hotel was that the weather was lifting and we were flying out to Ice Station Borneo tomorrow—Tuesday, April 10. Frida and I greeted each other quietly. The day's ski on the ice, the dinner, and the evening's program had left us both tired, and our beds looked inviting, cluttered as they were. But they would have to wait.

"Frida, did you notice anything unusual while we were out skiing this afternoon?" I ventured, moving a pile of inner fleece off my mattress and wondering how it would all fit into my backpack.

"Yeah." She perked up. "It was really cold, and Kerri's cheeks went really fast." It was good to see her animated. "I've been around some cold in the U.P., but that was something. Do you think it's going to be that cold when we get to Borneo?"

The fabled Ice Station Borneo. May we soon see it.

"Boy, I hope not. That wind was wicked. But, was there anything else? Anything with Phyllis?" I was trying to imagine what had happened.

"No. She was struggling a little, but we all were at times. Nothing I can think of. Why?"

"Well, Misha said he wants to talk with me about her. Apparently there was a problem out there on the ice this afternoon and he's got some concerns. I don't know what it's about."

I didn't have long to wait. A knock at the door, and out of the darkened hallway emerged Misha and Josée.

"I'll just take off for a couple of minutes," Frida offered. She turned to me. "Make sure you lock up and bring the key if you leave." We were all a little skittish after Marie-Josée's sled bag had turned up missing—especially Frida, with several thousand dollars worth of video gear. Unfortunately, Josée's afternoon search for M.-J.'s missing items had uncovered nothing.

"Will do"—and I gave her a friendly squeeze of the shoulders as she moved around Josée and Misha to the door. "See you in a little bit."

Misha and Josée stood as a wall in front of me. Josée dove in.

"Phyllis has a serious medical problem, and I don't think she should go with us to the Pole."

It took a moment for this to penetrate my consciousness. I stared blankly back, and Josée continued.

"This afternoon, while you guys were out there, she wet her pants. It seems she's had a problem with this for the past few weeks, but she didn't tell anyone."

If Phyllis really was having difficulties, the news was distressing. The Arctic Ocean is no place for incontinence.

"Misha," I said, trying to grasp the consequences of what Josée had just said, "tell me from a medical point of view what this means."

He inhaled and pulled himself up. "It is not good. It is not absolutely dangerous, but it can be a big problem on the ski to the North Pole."

"Phyllis likes to mother," Josée rejoined. "She can come with us to Borneo and stay there with the Russian pilots. They would make her very welcome, and she could cook for them." She was forming the plan. "And then she could ride in the helicopter to the North Pole when they come to get us."

They both looked at me for an answer. I knew at that moment that I had the final say. If I concurred, we would eliminate a problem that could potentially slow us down, or even require an evacuation. If I concurred, I would eliminate a team member who was increasingly a source of irritation to me.

I could not concur.

"Misha, you have told me that it's not good to make decisions in the evening. It is better to make them in the morning." He recited the phrase to me in Russian. "And as challenging as this situation—and Phyllis—is, she's worked hard to get a shot at the Pole. If there is a way for her to handle this, I believe we should keep her on the team."

I stood there, understanding that my decision could come back to bite me. But it was the right decision.

"Let me go talk with Phyllis," Josée proposed. "And why don't the four of us get together in half an hour."

"As you wish," said Misha.

"That will work for me," I said, feeling a sudden drain of energy. I'd been presented with a solution to a personal problem, but had opted out. I hoped I wouldn't regret it.

. . .

A little more than thirty minutes later, Misha, Josée, Phyllis, and I gathered in Misha's room. I noticed that he had satellite TV. It pays to be a Hero of Russia.

Josée and Phyllis sat on the bed opposite me. Misha was near the window with his back to the wall.

Phyllis began, and then dissolved into tears. "I don't know what happened out there today. I don't know if it was the cold, or maybe the stress." She wiped her eyes. "I've been having little problems for the past couple of weeks. But I had surgery to take care of this." More information.

I needed to be well reasoned in my thinking. I was unhappy with her for not letting us know, and childishly unhappy with myself for not seizing this opportunity to leave her in Borneo.

Josée spoke up.

"If Phyllis goes with us, we need to talk with the rest of the team. It means that we'll have to divide up her weight. Perhaps the difficulty of pulling a sled is making this worse."

I agreed. "Phyllis, we need to call a team meeting to go over this, because it does have ramifications for the rest of the team. They'll have to buy into the idea." I paused. "It's important to go as a complete team, but we need to be wise as well. We've got a few days before we actually head for the Pole, so we can see what happens. Otherwise, if this remains a problem, you'll need to stay in Borneo for your sake, as well as the team's. Misha?"

"Mmm. It is a problem, but there are ways to take care of this. If we had known earlier, there is medicine. But diet is also important. And caffeine drinks."

"Phyllis, if you go and do need to be evacuated, the insurance may not cover you. It could run $5,000."

Phyllis nodded her head up and down, like an earnest child who has been presented a way out of a dilemma.

Josée put her arm around Phyllis, trying to soothe her. I was left feeling a bit like the heavy, delivering the tough messages. Misha and Josée were the ones who were ready to pull Phyllis just a little while ago, I thought.

"Okay, let's round up the team and meet in the lobby in half an hour." I got up and left.

Marie-Josée wrote later in her journal:

On our return to the hotel we have a meeting. One of the group members, while on our afternoon outing, had a hard time. Nerves and too heavy a load caused some incontinence. This happens when you push your body to extreme limits. Remember,

after all, this is the North Pole. Dr. Misha stated that there was no medical danger,
but that we should carry her equipment. We had to get this point across. We would
have to share the load of 120 pounds, which meant adding on to everybody's already
heavy load, 12 pounds or more. We all agree.

Josée borrowed as many rubles as she could from Misha and gave them to Jen. She led the search for disposable diapers in Khatanga. They bought the town out.

. ˙ . ˙

I read myself to sleep that night and woke up with the light on, feeling bad that it might have kept Frida awake. But she was deep in sleep. Stumbling over the bags that we'd pulled into the room for safeguarding, I slipped out into the hall and down to the bathroom. Somewhere on the floor there was a multilingual party in full force. Neither time nor the general physical state of the partygoers seemed to impede the international cavorting that took place in this Siberian hotel.

. ˙ . ˙

On Tuesday morning, we got definite word that we were in line for the next plane, an AN-72, out of Khatanga. Departure time, 1 P.M. local. That was 1 A.M. back in Michigan. I called Bonnie and let her know that we were set to fly out and filled her in on the day's difficult ski, though I didn't say anything about Phyllis. We had agreed among ourselves not to reveal this until after we returned. Most importantly, Alison knew that this information was off the record for the time being and respected that, as I knew she would.

Just before noon, we zipped up our bags for the final time in Siberia. Then dragged them down the stairs, along with our skis and sleds, and turned in our room keys. We'd all whittled down our piles of personal stuff even further from the sorting in Solotcha, and we tucked them in a storage room behind what passed for a meteorological station and control tower at the rear of the hotel. It was right before you got to the frozen reindeer carcass. There were stashes of us all over Russia.

A stake truck backed up to the hotel door to receive our gear. A couple of us jumped aboard and stacked the sleds and the rest of the gear as it was passed up to us. When the truck bed was filled to the brim, we jumped off and followed it the two hundred yards to the airfield terminal. We weren't the only ones planning to fly this charter to Ice Station Borneo. Some of the other teams who had been waiting along with us in Khatanga were flying out as well. They were dressed in their team uniforms, milling about amid the wooden benches and the odd dog.

It turned out better for us that we were departing later. The earlier plane had been stuck in Sredny, and several teams were literally cooling their heels there. We were told that ours would be a straight shot to Ice Station Borneo.

With the weather calm and the runway crack at Borneo repaired, this was to be the first "commercial" flight landing of the short season, and the cargo reflected it. The huge bay doors at the rear of the plane were opened, and along with all manner of Arctic gear loaded on were several dozen 55-gallon barrels of fuel that had been stacked on the ramp. As soon as we'd finished loading our baggage, we quickly got on board. There were only twelve passenger seats, and we were in competition with at least that many more paid customers. Musical chairs on a Russian cargo jet. But at least we were off to Borneo.

Phyllis, Frida, and I slid into the last row and hunkered down. This was to be a four-hour flight, and the accommodations were quite spartan. No in-flight meal here, unless the crackers tucked between the seats by previous passengers counted. Some of the younger team members found spots, or made nests among the bags and sacks that filled the back of the twin-engine. Their nests actually looked more appealing than our spaces, as they could stretch out. I dug down and found both ends of a seat belt, buckled it, and put my earplugs in. Did the pilots do weight and balance calculations as part of the preflight? Probably so, because they were as motivated to have a safe flight as the rest of us. Might as well grab some sleep if possible. I could read later.

The crackle of excitement woke me up. The plane was beginning to descend. I craned forward and pushed back a little cloth covering a window to find it was brilliant and white outside the plane. The light stabbed into the cabin in bright streaks, pure and undiluted by clouds or pollution.

Behind our last row of seats was a huge pile of cargo, overlain with the still-prone bodies of Arctic expeditioners, just starting to rise and take notice of the upcoming landing. It reminded me of going on a long drive with a young child, only to have the child wake up the minute the car pulls into the driveway. We were all alert now.

The plane flew over what looked like the helicopter crews' orange huts, and then continued on out. The pilot was probably taking a look at the runway to check its condition. After all, this was the first paid-customer landing at Borneo this year. A 180-degree turn, and the craft was positioned for a long final approach and the landing.

The plane was coming in with a fair amount of speed, but I really had no idea how much it needed to carry for the landing. The runway must be fairly long. ("Want it longer? We'll just bulldoze some more ice.") Landing and stopping on ice had to be tricky, though.

We touched down rather smoothly, and the pilot applied the brakes. Then, all hell—and the cargo—broke loose.

"Look out!" someone yelled from the back of the plane. "Stuff is shifting forward." There was a real urgency in the voice that conveyed the information. I quickly unbuckled and stood up. Big mistake. A sled was aimed right for my head, with the weight of fuel barrels powering it. I ducked down and yelled to Frida and Phyllis to do the same. We braced ourselves as the backs of our seats gave way to the mounting pressure from behind. Getting squished by baggage on the way to the North Pole was not how this story was supposed to turn out.

Another sled rocketed over our heads, and the force coming against us from the rear was mounting. The gap between the backs of our seats and those in front of us was getting smaller and smaller, so that I could no longer turn sideways. Finally, the jet came to a stop, and the cargo shifted slightly aft.

I checked in with Phyllis and Frida. They hadn't been shoved any tighter than I had, but none of us had much room to stir.

"You guys okay up there?" It was Diana. She'd ridden the shifting bags in the back. An aircraft dispatcher, she knew a lot about planes and the things they carried. We occasionally shared our impressions, and concerns, about Russian aviation. "Dave would love this," she'd exclaim about some aspect of flying. Her husband was a pilot in the U.S. Air Force, stationed in Germany.

"Yeah, we're okay," we all three said at once. "Hey, can you help us get some of this stuff off of our backs so we can get out?" Frida added. A little sobered, but no worse for the experience, we clambered out of our seats. Good thing we had our seat belts on. Right.

Outside the aircraft, the five-o'clock sky looked the same as the one-o'clock sky, which would look the same as the midnight sky—sunlit, and today clear of any clouds. The temperature at Ice Station Borneo was –22 degrees Fahrenheit. Who said the Russians don't have a sense of humor, at least when it comes to naming things like Ice Station Borneo . . .

The killer fuel barrels were rolled off the plane, and our equipment followed them. With sleds loaded and backpacks on our bodies, we set out for a campsite about four hundred yards from the runway, near the crews' tents. Misha guided us to a flat and fairly level space where we could put up our two tents for the two days we'd be there training. It was less than fifty yards from what looked like a white street that extended some way in either direction. Josée pointed it out to the rest of us.

"Yesterday, that was a lead. See where the ice is new and soft on top? The Russian pilots say they saw a seal there yesterday, before it froze over. Around here, you have to be careful where you step. It could be new ice." It hit me that we were really in a foreign—even an alien—environment now.

Today was April 10. We hoped to be flying to our drop-off point for the North Pole on April 12.

We fumbled around a little getting the tents out and assembled, but it didn't take too long for the memories of the January training in Michigan's Upper Peninsula to come flooding back for most of us. Of course, Alison, Marie-Josée, and Diana were new to our team since then, but the rest of us showed them tent rigging in short order. We self-assigned our sleeping space. The senior among us chose the smaller tent, where one tended to get a little more rest. Frida, Lynn, and I quickly bunked there.

Misha, who had now taken over his role as final trainer, outlined the rest of the day. It was nearly 6:30 in the evening.

"First, we have something to eat. Jen will light the stoves and prepare something warm. And then, we will all go for little ski."

. . .

In order to ski, we had to take the tents down, because our skis and poles were used to hold them up. Unsticking them from the hard ice in which we had planted them—there was little snow cover—the tents came down. There we left them—with our sleeping bags, all of our food, and our backpacks and sleds. After all, there was no one else at Ice Station Borneo except for the Russian helicopter crews. There certainly was no door to lock. We were probably hundreds of miles from anyone, except for a small handful of Arctic trekkers who were now, also, on their own quests. We would meet some before our expedition was over.

After our skis were fastened and our wind suits on, Misha headed us in the direction of a pressure ridge that had formed—maybe during the last winter—when leads refroze and pans of ice met up once more in a million-year-old dance. Freeze and light thaw. That was the cycle of activity near the eighty-ninth parallel, less than one hundred nautical miles from the North Pole.

"You must cross this pressure ridge." Misha waved his pole at the length of rubble ice nearly twenty feet high and hundreds of feet long. Then he clambered vertically up the pile and stood near the top. "But"—his voice now bigger as he called down to us mortals at sea level—"you will need to take off your skis to get to the other side."

No argument there. Kerri and I were standing next to each other; we nodded and began to unbuckle the straps holding our boots to our skis.

"No surprise," she said. "But this sure is a lot different from Petoskey, Michigan."

"Yeah, no kidding. They never taught us how to do this in ski patrol." I laughed, a little nervously. Once our skis were off, Misha called down again.

"Good! Now attack," Misha exhorted. Josée quickly amplified.

"Okay, girls, you need to form a human chain. Some of you get on top of the hill and a few on the other side. You at the bottom, pass up the skis and then the poles." Thankfully, they were all marked with our names, for this was not one-size-fits-all. "Then, the ones at the bottom start up, and the ones at the top move on over."

It took us fifteen minutes to transfer our skis and ourselves to the other side of the pressure ridge. Misha was disgusted.

"You did not even have sleds and backpacks. How do you expect to be Arctic explorers?" He was actually yelling at us. "You must do better. Go and put skis on. We will try again."

Windburned and shamefaced, we swiftly found our own skis and stepped into them. But Misha wasn't going to just settle for a better pressure-ridge crossing. He found a small lead, less than three feet wide, and directed us to cross it one at a time. He went first.

"Put your skis like so," he demonstrated, spanning the breech first with one ski and holding it in position while he brought the other one alongside it. Suspended directly over the lead, with only the tips and the tails of his skis on firm ice, he planted his poles on the other side and launched himself over.

"No, not there. Look where your ski tip is. It has to be firmly on the far side before you move the second ski." We all looked at the skis of the unfortunate who was suspended halfway. "Only after the first ski is secure do you move the second. Then you put your ski poles on the other side."

Some of the women never got comfortable crossing leads. For me, it was a matter of learning to trust my skis. If the skis could hold the weight of the big women wearing backpacks, then I, who was much smaller, ought to be just fine. Besides, there was no chasm, no great height to negotiate. The pressure ridges never reached thirty feet, no higher than snow piles at a shopping mall whose parking lot had just been plowed after a big dump.

Misha found another pressure ridge to test our mettle. "Decide where you want to cross," he instructed, "and then move fast. If you want to reach North Pole, you must be faster."

And this time we were, almost halving our crossing time. The Russian master was pleased.

After two hours of drill that seemed more like four, we skied the half mile back to our campsite and restored the big tops. With the tents up, the stoves were fired up once more, and we enjoyed the plat du jour: pasta and a stew made of reindeer, potatoes, onions, and mushrooms. There was enough for seconds, and we all had another round.

It was after midnight when one of the two Russian helicopter crews invited us for food and company. In this world where a sense of time is suspended, we bundled up in our down coats, put our boots back on, and walked the short distance to their brightly colored inflatable Quonset.

Only later did we come to realize that there was a rivalry between helicopter units for our attentions. We saw ourselves as polar trekkers, Arctic expeditioners. They appreciated us as a dozen women very close to the North Pole, an extremely rare commodity. Still, their actions and intentions were nearly all honorable. In fact, they became very protective of us, defending our honor and abilities against other naysayers. But they worried about us all the time we were on the ice.

The crewmen and pilots had food in great quantities, tucked underneath tables and overflowing shelves in their orange inflatable tent. Igor, Victor, Vladimir, Sergei, and Anatoli spread out a wonderful variety of food on the table in the center of their tent. I kept thinking, We're going to be the only team ever to go to the North Pole and gain weight! Sweet cakes and cookies, cheeses, and bottles of vodka. We sat on the cots that ringed the table and the stove and enjoyed it all. Best of all was the fresh, cool water that they ladled from a giant urn into glasses. With fuel, they had melted the polar snow and ice in a vast pot on the stove. When cool, it went into the urn. No water has ever tasted better.

Anatoli pulled out a guitar, and we began to speak the universal language of music. Sort of. Though his spoken English wasn't extensive, he knew a number of Western pop songs in English, including the Eagles' "Hotel California" —but only about half of it. When Anatoli got to the line about finding it here, he would let it trail out because he didn't know what followed. Embarrassingly, none of us could help him. Sorry, Glenn Frey. Your Michigan women failed you.

Finally—warm, full, and flush with companionship—we left the Russian hut at 2:30 in the morning and headed back to our cold tents and chilled sleeping bags. It was early morning, the sun was in full view, it was colder than hell, but we were primed. We were finally on Ice Station Borneo.

CHAPTER TWENTY-FIVE

Wednesday, April 11, and Thursday, April 12. These days are paired together in my mind.

To prepare us for a task that we hadn't undertaken before—namely, skiing for days in the Arctic toward a goal—Misha decided we would go on a two-day trip from Ice Station Borneo. The plan was to ski north for a day, make camp overnight, and then return to the ice station. Part test, part training mission, it was quintessential Misha.

It was well after noon on Wednesday when we took down the tents, loaded up the sleds, and headed north single file. Direction finding was still confusing. At this time of day, skiing north meant that the sun was to our backs. But it still eerily circled around our heads as we moved forward a mile or two an hour. Ring around the rookies.

The temperature was −18 degrees Fahrenheit—cold, but tolerable given the bright sun and little wind. With the urging and guidance of Misha and Josée, the merry band of neophytes glided forward.

Misha skied up and down the line the first hour, checking on our perspiration. He slid a hand up Susan's back, looking for dampness. No one was offended by his diagnostic gesture.

"Moisture is enemy in the Arctic. You must not sweat. If you are getting hot," he admonished all of us, "you need to take off your jackets." That meant skiing in our inner layers and fleece, something we'd done in the Upper Peninsula in January, but were less inclined to do here on the frozen ocean. Gradually, though, we either opened all the zippers on our wind jackets, or pulled them off.

The warmth that we managed to achieve while skiing on the icecap dissipated pretty rapidly whenever we stopped for a break, which was after skiing for about an hour and a half. The drill was to pick a site for a snack, put on our black down jackets as quickly as possible, step out of our skis, and pull out our thermoses and food bags—the ones loaded with high-calorie and high-fat items.

Misha either didn't have food that he liked in his bag, or opted not to extract it from his backpack. Instead, he would visit each woman, ostensibly to check on her condition. It was partly a ruse.

"Oh, what is this?" he would say, pulling out a porksicle or a piece of pound cake and sampling. "Mmm. It is very good."

He earned the name "Misha the Moocher."

"What does it mean, 'moocher'?" he asked of me. I was the chief translator of American idiom and culture for this Hero of Russia.

"It's not a bad thing, Misha," I said, to his relief. "A moocher is one who snacks off the plate, or from the food bag of another."

"Hrrumph." He feigned taking umbrage at such a nickname and moved on.

Having too long a break drilled the cold into some of us more than others. Throughout the expedition, the bitter temperatures seldom captured my feet, but my hands would ache and then feel as though dozens of needles had been shoved into them. The only way to grab hold of food was to take off a layer of mittens, increasing exposure. After that, no amount of relayering would stave off the sting of the Arctic on my fingers.

Susan suffered the worst from temperature swings and had to be continually encouraged to keep covered. Kerri kept watch over her friend from Northern Michigan and devised a little game to keep the circulation going—or start it running again—at the end of a break.

"One, two, three," Kerri would count in Russian, and with each number swing her arms, getting Susan to mimic the movement as Kerri counted all the way to twenty. The rest of us joined in, and learned our Russian numbers at the same time.

After about the fourth march of this first day of Misha's Arctic School for Young Ladies, fatigue from skiing and the previous short, cold night caught up with some of the team members. I was struggling with the extra weight I'd taken on in addition to my own share. It was a stretch not to fall behind.

Alison, Olympian and journalist, was getting a real awakening as well. Josée had laden her with some of the fuel canisters, the heaviest loads to be had outside of the radio equipment that Marie-Josée was carrying.

Alison started to cry.

"You are too used to having coaches tell you what to do, Alison," Josée challenged her. "It's time to think for yourself. If the weight is too much for you, you must say so, and not just struggle with it."

For most of the previous decade, Alison had just done what her coaches had told her to do, punishing her body for the greater good. The results had been two Olympic medals in rowing. But this was different. Polar Trek 2001 was not an Olympic event. Most of the team were ordinary women, working to make it to the North Pole.

When Alison filed her story with the *Ottawa Citizen* that evening, she was typically understated:

> *Clearly, I was unprepared. I had been perfectly happy for Josée Auclair, our team leader, to load down my sled with extras before we left Borneo. But the weight soon made my shoulders ache so much I could not go on, and Josée had to relieve me of the gas can I had added to my load. It was better after that.*

. . . .

We skied that day for a total of six hours, and barely made six miles. It was two hours before we were far enough away from Borneo that we couldn't see the two massive orange and blue helicopters sitting on the ice. The day had been long and sobering.

We fumbled around getting camp set up, and it was after midnight before we all huddled in the cook tent for supper.

We lined the walls of the tent, seated in camp chairs that also served as another layer under our sleeping bags when opened all the way. Food was passed around in plastic bowls, and we ate with plastic spoons, shoveling in chicken stew that Josée had prepared and dehydrated in her kitchen in Aylmer, Ontario. As an appetizer, the team feasted on a smoked Arctic fish.

There was discussion in the tent, prompted by Misha, that we continue on to the North Pole.

"We have already skied six miles, you see," went his reasoning. "We could all continue on from here." Marie-Josée and several of the other women were in favor of pressing on. I did not agree. As dear as Misha was to me, and as important as his counsel could be, we had created and promoted this as an all-women expedition. Honorary Woman that he was, Misha still didn't qualify. He could not be part of our forward progress to the North Pole. Besides, I wanted to return to Borneo to dump some of my excess gear.

Frida sat opposite me in the tent. She had been silent most of the meal and seemed to be withdrawing, maybe even "deconstructing," as I came to call it. She had passed on the smoked fish because of her allergy, and had only picked at her food. That was not a good sign in the Arctic where food, because of the energy it makes available, is critical. Frida, though, wasn't getting anything much in her. Her eyes were sinking into her head, and her body was melting into the side wall of the tent, backlit by the sun outside.

"Guys," she said in a quivering voice, "I don't think I can make it." Frida, dammit, don't give up on this now. You've come too far not to go forward. "I get cold, and I'm worried, and I miss Ron and the kids so much." There were tears pooling in her eyes.

Josée sensed that fatigue was a part of Frida's breakdown in confidence. "I know you are a long way from home, but you must be strong. Ron and your kids are very proud of you." She was working to find the right arguments to bolster Frida without babying her. "If you don't want anything more to eat, it is probably best that you get some sleep."

"I don't know if I can do that. I didn't sleep last night, and I haven't been able to sleep much at all. I'm scared." She was starting to shake. Lynn and I looked at each other. I cocked my head and motioned toward the entrance of the tent. Lynn turned to Frida.

"Where's your sleeping bag, Frida? We'll go over and get your bed ready for you. Get something to drink—Jen do you have anything for Frida to take?—and come over in a couple of minutes. It'll be all ready for you." Frida had been struggling with two days of diarrhea as well as reduced sleep, the components of a meltdown.

Lynn and I crawled through the tent opening and snugged it right behind us. We searched out Frida's sled and found her gear. Carefully, we laid out her mats in the other tent and fluffed her sleeping bag. Frida came over a few minutes later.

"I'm so sorry," she started to apologize.

"Frida, it's okay. Lynn and I have your bag ready. You just have to crawl in. Get some sleep."

"I just don't know . . ."

"You can't know right now. Are you warm enough? Okay."

"Frida," Lynn said as she zipped her in, "it'll be all right. Sleep will help. We'll be along in a little bit."

"Good night, Frida," I said, patting her. "I love you."

"You, too." I could hear the drowsiness in her voice. Lynn and I pulled the strings taut and went back to the cook tent.

. ˙ . ˙

The dishes and food were being put away for the night, and the team was settling back. It was time for me to work. I asked Kathy for one of the satellite telephones. She pulled out the U.S. Navy telephone she had dubbed "Phone A" and loaded warm, charged batteries into it. I dialed Bonnie. It was shortly before 2 P.M. back home.

The sound of Bonnie's voice bouncing off a piece of metal in space, thousands of miles above us, was clear and welcome. I filled her in on the events of the day—the long ski—and our plans for these two days. Some of the news I shared was cheerier. We had seen a sun dog, a celestial phenomenon where the sun appears to have a twin—two suns surrounded by a rainbow. I had never seen one before. We had all been pretty excited about encountering it.

Other team members wanted to add their news for Bonnie, the web, and the world. Kerri asked that Bonnie let teachers back in Michigan know that she and Susan would begin to make their scheduled calls to classrooms on Friday, April 13—Good Friday. Lynn said that if Tom called Bonnie, she could tell him that she was okay. In fact she was, though her lovely hair was starting to look as haggard as ours.

Then I handed the satellite telephone to Alison and she called her editor back home. It was 2:30 in the morning our Arctic Ocean time, already April 12.

. · . ·

Our sleep schedules were starting to get off-kilter, and that was disorienting. NASA research has shown that astronauts, left to their own devices, move to a longer day. Apparently, human circadian rhythms are better adapted to a twenty-seven rather than a twenty-four hour day. Well, the Polar Trek team could confirm that was true. Over the course of three days, we had already shifted our awakening by more than three hours. Adding to the sense of sameness, there was little to distinguish night from day except the time on our watches, and a careful examination of the sun's position as it swept around our heads.

Frida slept hard during the sleep cycle that passed for night. She joined us for breakfast somewhat refreshed and in a better frame of mind. The team had survived the first "polar meltdown" of a member. More, though, would come.

Most of the other women were sleeping better as well. We were really tired, which helped, and we had also figured out how to stay warm. For me, it meant stuffing a spare down vest around my feet in the bottom of the sleeping bag. Alison had discovered that a spare pair of mitts on her feet would push out the chill. Diana had a small metal hot-water bottle that went into the sack with her. Kathy simply wore everything she had to bed.

It was noon on Thursday, April 12, when we arose. Having determined that we weren't leaving for the North Pole from here, Misha decided to turn this day into a "serious training." The plan was an ambitious one. We were going to ski two marches north and then head back to Ice Station Borneo. It meant eight hours of skiing, with backpacks and sleds that seemed heavier with each mile. It meant twelve hours on the ice before we would next set up camp.

It was 6 P.M. local time when we finally headed out for our long day's journey through the night. But, of course, it was full sun.

Misha led the first march and Josée the second. Most of the team had rebounded following yesterday's minor disasters of weight, sweat, and meltdown. Susan was more attentive to her body temperature. Alison had resumed her cheerful nature, relieved of some of the excess weight that she had taken on. Frida was still quiet, but seemed to be less in a hole. Phyllis was managing her incontinence. I, however, was starting to flag.

"Sue Carter." Here it came. Some order or command from Misha directed at me, a calling to a higher level I wasn't sure was manageable.

"I want you to take the lead." I could feel my shoulders sag from the weight of my backpack and the assignment. We had just turned around from our northerly march and were headed back to Borneo. Our tracks lay in front of us and would be easy to follow.

"Sure, Misha." It was my duty to go first. I sensed that we'd all have a turn at taking the lead position. "Just tell me when you think we ought to leave."

"In a few minutes. Let the rest of the team finish their food. They must eat." Yeah, I know, "In the Arctic, it is better to eat than to sleep."

Tucking the thermos into my sled, I leaned down and buckled the skis onto my boots. This next stretch wasn't going to be easy, but it was critical to do my best. Misha and the others would be watching me.

We headed south, and the sun was now off my right shoulder, though I took little notice of it. My concern was to follow the tracks and not to fall, something that most of us did at one time or another. My tumbles just seemed to be a little more frequent.

Push and glide. Try not to shuffle on this icy surface, and don't walk. I kept reminding myself of the dynamics of cross-country skiing. My brain felt a little mushy. I tried to focus on pulling the sled and not slowing down too much, but things weren't going well. I failed to grab with an edge of my ski, slid on a small rise in the ice, and went down, stopping the entire line behind me. Frustration burbled up in me, as well as fatigue. Misha saw my predicament and motioned to Marie-Josée to take over. With a good spirit and a lot of energy, she skied into the lead.

"Thanks, Misha. I'm sorry I didn't do better."

"You must continue to attack. Do not stop." I wasn't about to stop, but I didn't know how much attack there was in me at the moment.

By the fourth break, I had recovered enough to take an air sample, using one of the vacuum tubes in my sled. These air samples were for two colleagues in the Department of Geological Sciences back at Michigan State University. They were interested in examining them for traces of nitrous oxide at high latitudes.

Nitrous oxide is a greenhouse gas that has three hundred times the global warming potential of carbon dioxide, though it is a thousand times less abundant in the atmosphere. In a newspaper article before we'd left Michigan, Nathan Ostrom, the professor overseeing the study, had explained:

> Within the last 10 years or so, stable isotopes have emerged as a powerful tool for resolving the sources of nitrous oxide. Thus, each source may have a unique chemical fingerprint by which the origin of nitrous oxide in air can be identified. We are interested in better defining the isotope distribution within nitrous oxide in a region [Arctic] in which local processes, primarily microbial activity, will be greatly reduced by the cold temperatures.

I had read Nathan's quote and realized that it was a good thing that he was the scientist and I was the mule in the field.

Taking off my ski mitts, and with only liners covering my hands, I pulled the tube out of the box. I opened it and counted to five, hearing the whoosh of air rushing into it. With the cap replaced, it went back into the box. I wrote the coordinates and the weather conditions, as well as the conditions under which the sample was taken (twenty meters upwind from team) in a notebook Nathan's lab assistant had provided me. All of a sudden my hands were really starting to hurt, almost bringing me to tears.

I hadn't taken off the final two glove layers, but the –11 degrees Fahrenheit temperature had gotten to me. With hands that were now no better than lobster claws, I dug into my pack for chemical hand warmers. Ripping open the package with my teeth, I shoved them down into my mitts, followed by my hands. Nothing. Flapping my arms across my chest and then windmilling them was no better. It was agony, and I was walking up and down among the sleds trying to get some circulation back, guided by a brain that was getting stupider by the moment. At least there was feeling, though it hurt like hell. Thank God I had some sensation.

We were ready to tackle the next march, and with real difficulty I buckled my boots into the ski footbeds. I could feel myself gasping a little now, trying to cope with the pain in my hands. Somehow, the ski-pole straps slid over my mitts, and I joined the line moving out, the sled jerking along behind me.

Please move faster, I prayed. The sting was now moving into my feet. Please hurry. I need to get warm. I looked down at the clock that was clipped to the lower zipper pull of my jacket. It read 11:22 P.M. Just twenty minutes and I'll be warm. I can make it that long, if I keep moving.

By now, if felt as though I was skiing on bloody stumps. There was feeling in my feet, but it wasn't comforting. They hurt too much. One ski in front of the other. Keep going, don't stop.

I wasn't particularly aware of the other team members around me, except that we were all moving forward in line. No one seemed to notice my agony, and that gave me some additional anxiety. Maybe they were all dealing with their own cold. There was no way my brain could sort it all out.

Slowly, and with the hideous burn of recovery, my feet and then my hands began to warm. By 11:45 P.M. they were almost tolerable, and the searing pain that had clouded my thinking had lifted.

You *have* to be more careful, the argument in my head went. Don't run the risk of permanently harming yourself.

. . .

When the pain finally lifted, I felt a huge sigh escape me. Misha would say, "In the Arctic, men are stupid." That applied to women as well.

. . .

On through the night we skied, though night was a relative notion. I was falling further behind the rest of the team each march. Jen stayed within hailing distance of me, but the next mile was always tougher than the last one. I wanted to sit down, to stop. I actually wanted to quit.

In the distance, the twin helicopters of Borneo popped up on the surface of the ice, looking disproportionately large. Based on the hours on the trail and the previous day's pit stops we had passed, the Russian ice haven lay at least two miles to the south. Ahead of me, the team was bobbing along, skimming across the frozen pan. It was all I could do to press forward.

I was apologetic to Jen for the sad duty she had—being the Border collie for the laggard lamb. There was nothing left to give, though. The cold, the weight of the sled and my backpack, the stressful weeks before we left were all claiming a chunk of me. For the first time, I was really worried about my ability to do what I had convinced others to attempt.

The tents were already up by the time I dragged into camp. About the warmest part of my body were my cheeks—from embarrassment. My equipment melted off of me, and I stumbled and crawled into the cook tent, as close to exhaustion as I had ever been. It was 6 A.M.

Supper was at 8 A.M. Friday morning. We had skied eight marches over twelve hours and covered almost ten miles. In a rare moment, Misha congratulated us for the skiing effort, though I didn't feel as though I should be included in the kudos. But, looking around the tent, I could see that several women of the team were a little tattered, too.

Diana had frostbite on her left middle finger. The dime-sized blister that blossomed from the tip made her look like E.T. flipping off the world. Alison had several blisters on her feet, including a rather extensive one on the bottom of her right foot. I had acquired frostnip on my right thumb and three other fingers. Little blisters were forming, and the sensation had left the ends of the digits.

It was time to call Bonnie, but I didn't have the strength left to do it, and asked Phyllis, who knew Bonnie better than any of the other team members, to phone in an update. I found my sleeping bag, removed my contact lenses, and slept for ten hours. Not even my bladder dared rouse me.

CHAPTER TWENTY-SIX

Friday, April 13, on Ice Station Borneo. We had gotten to sleep, mostly in a collapsed state, midmorning on Friday. Dinner had been at 8 A.M. It was nearly 8 P.M. Friday evening before we crawled out of the cocoons of our black bags, still chrysalises all. We were a far cry from monarch butterflies.

Over a meal of porridge, bread with cheese and butter, and coffee or tea, we took stock of ourselves following our twelve-hour ski the previous day. Misha was praising, but honest in his assessment.

"WomenQuest team continues to get stronger. You see that you can ski for a long time and continue to attack!" My chin slid a little down my chest. If I were the rear-guard action, we might be in trouble. "You had some problems, and you need to get rid of more weight, but you will be ready."

"Any idea when we might start?" Kerri asked. Her youth was no inhibition to asking questions. She was diligent about getting answers and information. On the whole, it was a pretty endearing characteristic.

"We must wait for the Weber-Malakhov team to arrive." That meant Richard, Josée's husband, and the five clients who would ski with Richard and Misha to the Pole. "I talked with Richard before going to sleep. They are in Khatanga now and will leave, maybe tomorrow."

Khatanga, the hotel, and the Pilot Café were fogged in distant memory now. It was strange to picture another group there. Richard would be busy with tasks, including finding a replacement tent for the one that was stolen from Marie-Josée's sled. My team had taken one that Richard had stored there from the previous year.

The ten-hour sleep had been most welcome, but we were a bit disoriented with respect to time. It was now nearly midnight, the end of Friday the thirteenth, and we were just getting going. The sun was of no help because it never set. Left to our own devices, we really were slipping into a different day length.

Josée had ventured out and visited the other tents at Ice Station Borneo.

Shaking off the last of sleep, the rest of us emerged. In the two days we were away, the camp had begun to grow. A team of huge Norwegians had arrived. Alison was delighted because, despite her height of more than six feet, they called her "small." The Italian Duke of Abruzzi and his group were also on Borneo. The duke was accompanied by the host of the Italian version of *Wheel of Fortune*. The whole team posed with the duke and TV host for video that would air the following week in Italy—while we would be slogging toward the North Pole.

Brigette, the self-appointed concierge of Ice Station Borneo, had her red and white tent up and warm. Each year, during the month-long existence of this frozen Brigadoon, she hosts guests and dignitaries from all over the world. More than a dozen French visitors occupied her at the moment. They had snubbed Marie-Josée when she spoke her French Canadian to them, looking down their long Gallic noses at her.

Viktor Boyarsky, a gregarious bear of a man, was there as well. Elsewhere, an expedition with sled dogs had staked outside in the –18 degree Fahrenheit cold. One of the dogs had gotten loose and was tormenting its chained mates. I was tempted to go after it, or try to find its owner. Where would it go, though? The dog was smart enough to stay close to food and fellow canines.

Surveying the icescape, one could see the makings of a real tundra town, except that it was floating on the Arctic Ocean.

"We girls have an invitation from one of the Russian crews to come for food," Josée announced.

The prospect of different food, warmth, and interesting people was a real draw. Spending time lingering over food, or just talking, was a significant part of life in the Arctic, an extension of life in Siberia. Without the normal distractions of our American life, there was time for conversation.

. · .

The gracious reception our team received from the Russian aviators will remain with me the rest of my life. Throughout our stay on Borneo, and during our time at the North Pole, they were very solicitous of their "American women," though it was clear that American men ranked much lower in their eyes. The Cold War dies hard.

In the heat of their tent this early Saturday morning, they pulled out all the stops—and the food, and the bottles of vodka, and delicious *chai*, Russian tea. Anatoli, the navigator, dug out his guitar and led another half round of "Hotel California," as well as "On a Wing and a Prayer." The song selection was such a curious mixture of American culture. How had it penetrated here, and why these selections? I wondered.

Inside, the tent was ten by twenty feet, a curved semicircle plopped down on the ice. The walls were a thick, double layer of heavy orange synthetic material, with several clear portholes along the sides, and a roof vent for the oil stove in the center toward the front of the tent. Behind it was a table for eating and work, with food and dishes stored underneath it. Iron beds lined the walls.

The door was made of wooden slats, like the cover of a roll-top desk. It, in turn, was layered by a heavy canvas flap. The interior was amazingly warm, to the point where we stripped down to our inner layers, and would have gone further but for the sake of propriety and odor.

The helicopter crews led an unadorned life, but a profitable one. They earned several times their regular salary shuttling the curious and the adventuresome back and forth to the North Pole.

. ˙ . ˙

After nearly four hours of eating, drinking, and communicating—in all the ways people who don't speak each other's languages do—we stuffed ourselves into identical black down jackets and became Michelin women again. It was all for the short walk back to our tents. No, we couldn't stay longer, but thank you. We have business we must do.

The sobering effects of the two-day march had settled in. It was time to think seriously about how much distance we could cover in the time we had, which was less than two weeks. The options ranged from twenty nautical miles to eighty, with no obvious solution emerging. It soon became apparent from the discussion that we were too tired to reach a comfortable consensus, and we decided to call it a night. Actually, it was eight o'clock in the morning. It was Saturday, April 14. Tomorrow was Easter.

. ˙ . ˙

Things felt unsettled from the group meeting we had had before getting some sleep, and most of us were up and out of our sleeping bags by one o'clock Saturday afternoon. Breakfast was at three.

Sitting around the walls of the larger cook tent, we drained the last of the coffee as Jen did the dishes. I envied her clean hands and unsullied nails. The team was now ready to decide on our drop-off point—and ultimately, the distance we would ski to the North Pole.

It was a very hard discussion for me. The mirror had been held up to my face during our two-day trek, with unflattering results. I wasn't capable of skiing the distance I had planned, and was hugely disappointed in myself for my failings.

Misha reprised the deliberation that had trailed off before the last sleep session. "We must decide today how far to ski. I need to tell Russian pilots so they can make proper plan for going in the helicopter."

The Weber-Malakhov team would be riding along with us to a drop-off point, and our plans had to mesh with theirs.

"We've said that we were going to ski two degrees, and I think we ought to stick with it," Susan jumped in. "Even if we don't make it."

"I agree." It was Kerri. "How can we go back and tell girls that we shortened the trek when we're telling them to push themselves as hard as they can?"

It was my turn to add a voice before the discussion got tilted too far in this direction. "I'm not willing to head out and not make it to the Pole. If we have to shorten the distance, so be it. We are going to get to the North Pole." I let the words hang there. "I also have to tell you, the longer distance is out for me. Yesterday was a real eye opener." I was feeling a flush rising, but was not willing to miss the goal of the North Pole by being unrealistic.

"I'm really disappointed," Marie-Josée said. "I came along because I wanted to be challenged. This won't be very hard at all."

"Me, too," Alison chimed in. "Personally, I want to ski as hard and as far as possible, and go home feeling exhausted."

Great. Now we're raised to Olympic standards. I didn't point out that Alison had been distressed to tears just a few days ago. As dear as she was to me, she was a latecomer and had less weight in the final decision.

"Guys, I hear what Sue's saying." Frida had been quiet up till now. "The North Pole is our goal. No one is going to remember how far we went, but whether or not we got there. We're just picking an artificial point to begin, anyway."

"Remember, we agreed to take Phyllis's weight back in Khatanga. And honestly, I'm going to need help with mine," I said. "I made a tradeoff that got us here. I spent too much time administering the details, and sacrificed some of my training time in the process." Admitting this weakness was so hard. This is not what the leader should be doing. "I can carry a reasonable load, but not if we go the full distance of 120 miles."

Josée leaned in toward the center of the tent. "Girls, you will find that a couple of things will happen. It always does." We focused on her, wanting to take in the value of her experience. Misha sat back in his camp chair and stroked his chin, rubbing the stubble.

"A couple of you will start out strong and then get tired quickly. Some of you will start out strong and stay that way. And the others, you will start out weak and get stronger." She looked around the tent. "I don't know who is who about this. But it does happen. You'll see."

From that point, we concentrated the discussion on the success of the mission, and what it would take to get there. And we compromised: we would ski fifty nautical miles in nine days, as the Arctic tern flies. This plan would allow for one or two days of rest, and would mean that we'd ski six marches a day, putting us on the trail for about nine hours.

It was less ambitious than what we had contemplated and announced, but would allow us to do all that we had planned: spend the time on the ice, and also call schoolchildren back in the States, and hook up with the crew from NASA for a webcast at the North Pole. It's just that some of us wouldn't go home exhausted—or so we thought.

. . .

The rest of the day was devoted to getting ready, now that the decision had been made about the point of departure: 89.1 degrees north. A manageable distance for the slowest of us, and enough to satisfy Diana, Alison, Marie-Josée, and the others.

My chief chore was to survey all of my gear and decide what I could leave at Ice Station Borneo, and what I absolutely needed for our march to the North Pole. The travel kit I had carefully packed with creams and wipes and deodorant and mouthwash was set aside. My personal items were boiled down to dental floss, a toothbrush, contact-lens solution and case, and a pair of glasses. Frida and Lynn agreed to bring enough toothpaste for our tent. No need for a hairbrush. I'd gotten a really short haircut before leaving Michigan, and, besides, with a hat on all the time, nicely combed hair wouldn't be much noticed. I did, though, keep a vial of scented oil—for no one in particular except me. Some touches of civilization couldn't be discarded.

The heavier camera stayed, as did the extra lens. There was ample video equipment among us, and I did keep a smaller Nikon. The two-day trek had shown us what clothing we really needed. The third pair of underwear got stuffed in a sack for storage on Borneo, as well as an extra hat and a third pair of socks. I did keep all the gloves and mittens I had.

The chemical hand warmers. Occasionally useful, but heavy, especially when any weight counts. I reduced the pile by half and stuck them into my backpack. The T-shirts would stay on Borneo, but I brought along Women-Quest patches. They would be treasures in the hands of others, having been hauled to the North Pole. The historical novel on Russia stayed behind. My hands always froze when I tried to read it in my sleeping bag. The story of Russia would have to wait until later to be finished.

The rest of the team was making similar decisions. Alison scoured her kit bag. Frida decided to leave a second video camera and bring a smaller one, which she would wear around her neck like a high school ring the entire time we were on the Arctic Ocean. Josée readjusted the weight of food in our sleds; I would start without any. However, I stubbornly clung to my Styrofoam box containing the six vacuum tubes for air samples.

It was Saturday afternoon, and we hadn't gone skiing in the two days since we had been in camp. After finishing the task of paring down our gear for the third time since we'd gotten to Russia, the whole team was a bit edgy, anticipating the possibility of leaving tomorrow. Before packing her larger camera away, Frida suggested we get some setup shots in—video of us skiing, as a team, pulling sleds, and going over the ice terrain. It's the kind of material videographers refer to as *b-roll*, videotape that will allow a bridge from one sequence to another, or cover a talking head.

Glad to have a reason to be active, several of us pulled on our wind suits, strapped on our backpacks, and glided along the ice near the tents and helicopters at Borneo. We were careful not to have them in the background of the shots. Back and forth we went as Frida got on her belly—on top of pressure ridges, on the back of a sled pulled by Alison—all to get the best shots. She's a great videographer, and it was fun to watch her work.

The exercise did us good and put us, as a team, in a better frame of mind following the hard discussion earlier in the day. Alison, Frida, Lynn, and Marie-Josée later made an attempt to crash the party in the red and white French tent, where champagne, mixed drinks, and a lavish buffet was being served. They got the bum's rush from a group Alison later identified as "snooty Parisians." Marie-Josée said it was quite the "icy reception."

. ˙ . ˙

The day before, on Friday, I had had a long talk with NASA Mike about looking for an alternate landing site for the Twin Otter that he, Dr. Clark, and the rest of the crew would be flying in from Canada. Our days on the Arctic Ocean had made me skeptical about finding the "level 2,500-foot landing strip" that the pilots from First Air required. Looking around, there were just too many pressure ridges to assure that we'd be able to guarantee a clear space right near the Pole.

The logical alternative was to land at Ice Station Borneo. It meant that our encounter wouldn't be at the North Pole, but the Borneo landing strip was in place, and it was certainly very high on the Arctic Ocean. We could meet the NASA team there after being plucked from the North Pole by a Russian helicopter. Mike said he'd check into it.

When I talked with Bonnie on Saturday, after our video session, we reviewed the possibility of a webcast at Borneo. Misha knew it was an option, and would make the arrangements with the base manager at Borneo if we decided to rendezvous there with NASA.

Bonnie was bubbly, even though it was fairly early in the morning on Saturday back home. "We're getting a lot of traffic on the website. We're over five hundred hits per day."

"That's fantastic, Bonnie. I hope that means that a lot of school kids are checking in."

"Well, if they are, they're getting some great pictures. NASA has made some of their satellite shots available. You can really see the leads. There are some huge ones out there."

That was not welcome news, but not a surprise either. Some of the pilots had reported on earlier flyovers seeing more than the normal number of leads. The leads could close and re-form with fair rapidity. They could also cause one to ski some distance out of the way before finding a point narrow enough to cross.

I signed off, sending my best to Bonnie and everyone back in Michigan, and turned the telephone over to Alison for her daily check-in with the *Ottawa Citizen*. She had written her story in her reporter's notebook, and filed as we all listened in. There was no privacy in the tent. Alison dictated:

Tomorrow night, we expect to take a helicopter to our drop-off point—which after much discussion will be 84 kilometers from the Pole, specifically N89.10 and E110 to account for the drift to the west, which is a little more than three kilometers a day in the direction of Greenland.

She continued on, laying out the guts of the discussion we had had earlier in the day about the distance we would ski to the North Pole. She reported her personal disappointment, and my frustration in not being as prepared as I should have been. It was uncomfortable to hear my own admission, knowing that it was there for all to read, but it was real. Journalism had taught me long ago that truth, not concern over feelings, had to be the superior value.

I questioned Alison's statement that we were leaving tomorrow night—

Sunday night. There had been talk that we were scheduled to fly out tomorrow, but I had my doubts. Tomorrow was Easter, for both western Christians and Eastern Orthodox—fairly unusual that they would fall on the same Sunday. Even though the helicopter crew grew up under Soviet Communism, there was still a strong strain of religion that was never far from the surface. It seemed unlikely they'd choose to work on Easter, but we'd know soon enough.

. · .

Nearly midnight Saturday, and Alison and I were outside with several others, gathering up our mats and sleeping bags for the night. She came over to me, the sun shining off her shoulder.

"I'm really sorry I had to write what I did about you not being prepared." She was feeling protective both of her work and of me at the same time. It raised a genuine conflict. For some reason, the twenty-year difference in our ages felt stark at that moment; she could have been my daughter. I sensed that she was looking for absolution from the team leader, who happened to be a journalist as well.

"I'm proud of you for what you did. It wasn't easy, but you told the truth." There were tears in her eyes. "Remember when we first talked? I said that you had my full support to report what happens on this trek, the good and the bad—and that includes me." My eyes were now misting up. "Sure, it's hard for me to admit those things, and to know they'll be put in a newspaper and on the web, but they're real." This tall, gentle woman standing before me, struggling, could also be my student. Tilting my head back, I looked her right in the eyes. "Alison, never stop telling the truth. It's your job as a journalist. And also, never make me cry in the Arctic. My eyes are freezing over."

She locked her arms around me and gave me a big hug. Whatever happened, she knew I'd be in her corner.

. · .

Happy Easter!

It was a time for celebration, for all kinds of reasons. We were operating more as a team now; we had a common goal, and a strategy we had agreed on. We were mostly healthy but for a few blisters, frostnips, a mild case of diarrhea, and some incontinence. Not bad for a bunch of women, some in their fifties, living in tents in −13 degree Fahrenheit temperatures. Plus, the sun was shining, no matter what time of day.

We had decided to limit our phone calls back home for two reasons. One, to make certain we had enough battery power for the satellite phones for scheduled and critical communication. Two, it was harder to concentrate on our task here on the ice if we were distracted, focusing our thoughts elsewhere. We got an example of that when we did make calls back home on Easter.

Susan had left two teenagers in Boyne City, Michigan: an older son and a ninth-grade daughter. Her daughter had been asked to the high-school prom, and several of us listened in as Susan tried to negotiate the terms of the date from several thousand miles away. She was later quoted in the *Ottawa Citizen*: "Since I'm 2,000 miles away, I cracked under the pressure." Yes, her daughter could go.

Frida reached the answering machine at her mother's in Marquette. Her mother, Fay, had undergone surgery and therapy for breast cancer the summer before, and Frida's attachment to her was all the stronger . No one was at home to answer the phone. "They're probably all at church," she said. Her mother, Ron, and the kids came back to a loving, weepy message.

I reached my father, who was amazed by the technology, and my mother, who was stunned to hear her daughter's voice and promised to call Amanda, whom I hadn't reached. Almost everyone either connected with or left messages for loved ones. It was a tender time on the threshold of our journey.

The Easter celebration continued throughout the day. Crewmembers from one of the Russian helicopters—including Igor, a pilot with more than 10,000 hours of flight time; Vladimir, the copilot; and Anatoli, the navigator—brought Easter treats to us. The centerpiece was Arctic char, fished from a big lake in the Tamyr Peninsula and flown in the day before, thanks to some of their family back in Siberia. The fish was frozen, and as Vera had done, Vladimir sliced the entire fish lengthwise, dipped the shavings in salt and pepper, and passed them around. There was also a traditional Easter cake, dyed eggs, chocolate, and vodka. We reciprocated with Canadian bacon and some of the jellybeans Phyllis had remembered to bring along. Anatoli had brought his guitar with him, and we laughed through half of "Hotel California" once more.

The path to our tent was becoming well worn. The crew from the second helicopter, not to be outdone, invited us over for an Easter dinner. The table in the center of the Quonset hut was literally overflowing with Russian Easter delicacies: reindeer dumplings, chilled borscht, salmon, a tomato and cucumber salad, orange slices, several kinds of breads, a bundt cake, and more Easter eggs. We brought Seven Crown and a liter of maple syrup, pouring some of each into a glass. They all took an approving sip.

The Russians taught us a game to play with the dyed Easter eggs. One person turns to the person on her left. Each holding her own egg, they smash the ends of the eggs together. One egg will invariable crack, and the other won't.

The egg smashing continues around the circle until there is only one unbroken egg left—the winner.

There was also ample vodka, tea, and refreshing cold water to go around. We passed on as many rounds of vodka as possible, though Marie-Josée found a way to handle her unwanted drink. We later learned that she had been discreetly pouring the vodka out of her tumbler into a corner of the hut.

Nicolai was the pilot of this crew, and he was supported by his copilot, Constantine, along with Eugene, Sergei, and Dimitri. Sergei pulled out his own guitar, and with hands as large as I had ever seen tackle strings, he went through his medley. It was a delightfully odd concoction that included "Bésame Mucho" and something that sounded like it was called "Mister Big." The songs always ended with "*cha-cha-cha.*"

I was still trying to grasp exactly how the sun moved through the sky—in reality, how the sun was seen as the Earth moved at this latitude, this time of year. In words and gestures, I asked Nicolai if he could explain it to me. Misha was there to help out.

He demonstrated by taking a fixed point and rotating an egg around it, as if the sun were skimming overhead. "He says it goes from ten degrees to forty-five degrees this time of year," was the translation. "Appearing to circle overhead."

That was very helpful. Our shadows really could be instructive as we tried to get bearings and time of day. If one variable was known, the other was accessible.

In an effort to return to a more normal schedule, we said our good-byes at 10 P.M. and headed off to our own tents. Away from the warmth and joy of the Russian huts, our nylon cocoons seemed cold and a little depressing. We had had a wonderful day, though, and were ready to leave. Tomorrow—Monday, April 16, 2001—the real adventure would begin.

CHAPTER TWENTY-SEVEN

Day Seven

April 22, 2001. Tired and edgy from yesterday's long and sometimes frustrating ski, we are roused to alertness by Josée shortly after 7 A.M. Khatanga time. The news on two fronts isn't good. Our tents have drifted half a nautical mile to the south while we slept. The Greenland Drift has done more than that, though. It has pushed us twelve degrees to the west. Our position is now N89.46 and E86.51. We are perilously close to the point of traveling too far west to successfully negotiate north and make it to the Pole.

The second piece of bad news only compounds the first. It is windy and snowy, and as Josée reads the sky, we have a storm moving in.

Eight and a half miles from the North Pole, with two days to get there, we are facing an increasing number of pressure ridges and leads.

It is clear to me that Josée is concerned about reaching our goal. Until now, she has done a great job of guiding on the ice—part encouragement and part exhortation. Now, with emotions starting to fray through exhaustion, it is time to get the team to dig deep. We have to ski hard today to counteract the drift. We have to ski east. Over breakfast, in unvarnished terms, she lays it out.

"I'll be barking at you today," Josée begins in fierce tones. "We are slow, and we have to get moving. You are all trying, but it's time to stop trying and start doing." She turns to her right and looks across the tent from me. "And, Phyllis, no crying today."

No one says a word. No rejoinder, no questions. We all know that we have one shot to make it. If we fail to measure up to the day's requirements, then we will have to be helicoptered back to Ice Station Borneo, as neither our strength nor our supplies will be enough to fight the ice plate's movement west. The Pole will be out of reach. All the planning and training and talking we have done back home will be diminished by the fact that we haven't managed to ski to the North Pole. The naysayers will be right. And the likelihood of meeting up with the crew from NASA for a live webcast will be all but gone. It is time to hitch up our bra straps and forge ahead.

The wind is still strong as we collect our mats, bags, and gear and pack them into our sleds and backpacks. With visions of part of the tent sailing off across the ice, I hold on extra firmly as we unstake it and shake off the crumbs and specks from the sleep session. Kathy's instruments show the barometric pressure dropping. It has ranged from 30.55 to 30.15 inches for most of our time on the ice, but it is now 29.60—low pressure, and a harbinger of bad weather.

Fog and snow surround us as we fall in line for a long day's ski. There is little value in thinking about how many miles, or how many hours, we have to go. The answer to the question is: "As many as it takes." We are dedicated to achieving the Pole and getting there as a team, intact, though that might prove to be a trek-ending challenge.

The routine—now ritual—of skiing, stopping, skiing, stopping provides a welcome opportunity to think. My mind leaves the ice that stretches out in front of me and skims over different landscapes: how beautiful it is here, how I will actually miss it, and how good I truly feel.

Surprisingly, the exhaustion I experienced the first few days after arriving at Borneo has faded. As Josée said, some of us would get stronger, and that is happening to me. Tired, yes, but not exhausted. The years of background training have helped. Having one of the lighter loads is a benefit. Of course, the other voice in my head replies, you're not thirty, and you're not an Olympian either. Walter Mitty and Ms. Reality debate the proposition for a while, and I happily ski on.

As usual, before leaving camp, I loaded my inner pockets with food for each break, with the fattiest and hardest to digest in the warmest place. Tucking in items close to the body is the only way of ensuring that they might not be frozen rock-hard. A wrapped porksicle went into my left breast pocket. In various other pockets, in descending order of eating, went the rest of the day's snacks. If it looks like I'll run out of pockets before we stop skiing, I'll dig into my backpack, pull out the food bag, and reload. How very central to the day eating has become. We are taking in more than five thousand calories a day, and I can feel myself shrinking. An interesting way to diet.

The morning fog remains outside my hood. The wind hasn't increased, but it still isn't certain that we'll avoid the storm. The difficulty now is seeing right in front of us. The sun is a 40-watt bulb straight ahead at the moment, but the icescape is flat and becoming tricky. For the first time, all of us take off our skis and walk. We will make more progress on foot than on ski, given the changing ice conditions and the lack of depth perception as the environment has visually flattened out. We tuck our skis into the side pockets of our backpacks, the tips looming straight over our heads. Josée takes the lead on the next march, carefully testing the ice before she sets foot on it. Skis spread a body's weight over a large area; a foot strike concentrates a lot of weight on a very small area and increases the possibility of breaking through. Water is a hazard, as well as the possibility of an ankle or knee sprain, or even a leg break.

What creeps into my mind is my concern about connecting with NASA. I still can't get all the pieces to fit, and communication remains a problem. In spite of multiple attempts, it has proven impossible to reach the NASA crew, now in northern Canada, by satellite telephone. The difficulty lies in connecting when someone is live at the other end. I have been able to leave voice messages, but don't know if the last five have really gotten through.

Bonnie has had much greater luck in connecting with the NASA crew, so I have taken to relaying news and coordinate information through her. Bonnie and I can read each other well with few words spoken. Her diligence back home in shepherding this webcast, in managing our own website, and in being the focal point for our families is without equal.

The chief problem is where to link up with the group coming from Canada. A complication is informing the Russian helicopter crews about the plan. Two factors add to the challenge: high-frequency radio contact is thoroughly unreliable, thanks to the solar flares, and none of us is very adept at speaking Russian, despite Kerri's earnest attempts.

Sitting around in the tent yesterday, we came up with a solution to one of the problems: a Russian speaker. Lynn knew a woman graduate student in East Lansing who might be willing to act as an interpreter for us. Lynn gave me her name, Olga Kritskaya, and Bonnie tracked her down through the student directory.

Yes, she would be happy to help, but whom was she going to talk with? The Russian helicopter crews didn't have a satellite telephone; they relied on either radio transmissions from Khatanga, or news brought in by the AN-72 pilots as they ferried passengers and supplies to Ice Station Borneo.

That was the answer. I got the Khatanga airport manager's name from Josée and passed it along to Bonnie.

"Have Olga call and ask the airplane crew to pass along a message for us," I said.

"What should she tell them?"

Good question.

"Have them tell the Russian helicopter crew that we'll need to be picked up at the North Pole by 3:30 A.M. on the morning of Wednesday, April 25." It is now Saturday, April 21. "They'll take us to a site nearby, say within a couple of miles, where we'll hook up with the group coming from Canada."

"Okay. Anything else?" Bonnie asked.

"And after that, we'll fly to Ice Station Borneo."

It is apparent that establishing Borneo as a meeting site isn't going to work, because of a bad past relationship between First Air (the Canadian charter) and the Russians at Borneo. The North Pole is the best option, though I remain unconvinced that I am going to find a stretch of ice long enough and smooth enough for a Twin Otter to land. Worry about that tomorrow, Scarlett. Just concentrate on getting the parties to the same general area at the same time.

I return from my mental interlude and look out from my fur-trimmed tunnel. The surrounding world is blue-tinged and featureless

We started at 10:50 A.M. It is now after 2:00 P.M. and we have just finished our second march—a rough slog. The break is welcome.

I unbuckle my skis and quickly dig thermos and down parka out of my backpack. Kerri and Lynn are turned in toward Susan, monitoring her reaction to the cold. I'll head over there in a minute and check on her. Leaning back against my sled, I remember that I am scheduled to take another air sample today. Now seems like a fairly good time. Later on, I might be tired, or need to use part of the break time to relieve myself, a proposition that takes some time with all of the clothing. Now is definitely the time to capture some more air in a tube.

Capping the thermos and stowing it, I take the top off my sled and open the Styrofoam container that has followed me around like a shadow during nearly two weeks on the ice. Loosening the band that keeps the lid on, I remove vacuum vial #105 (I've never understood the number sequencing) and pull the rubber stopper out of the tube. Unscrewing the valve that will let air into the empty container, I count to five, then plug the hole back up with the rubber stopper and turn the inner valve, but only finger-tight. With the tube back into the rack and returned to the box, I am ready for the next ski.

I am mindful of the earlier frostnip to my hands, which were covered only in liners and exposed too long while taking a sample. Blisters still cap several of my fingertips, as well as my thumbs. I've since learned to gather air samples speedily, with more protection to avoid that risk. We are dedicated to returning home with all body parts functioning. What would my fellow ski patrollers say if I came back with such a defect? Since joining the patrol in 1994, a number of the members had tracked my preparation for this expedition closely. A thoughtless injury would be hard to explain.

Kerri has Susan, Lynn, and Phyllis up and swinging arms in Arctic Aerobics, counting to twenty in Russian.

"Adeen, dva, tree, chyeetirye, pyat."

With each number comes a swing of the arms. Kerri, one of the team's youngest, is a great leader and an enthusiastic cheerleader. I join in, swinging away to ward off the cold that is starting to settle in.

Off to the side, Kathy and Josée take a position measurement. Even though we are skiing hard, mostly northeast, we are still not making the progress we need to.

"Okay, girls," Josée calls out. "We need to keep going to make the Pole."

Strapping on our gear, we head out.

. ˙ .

It takes several hours, but the fog finally lifts, and the sun resumes its brilliant position in the sky, now off my right shoulder. Most of the other women, and certainly the better skiers, have put their skis back on and are no longer walking. Lynn and I hold off another march, as we are making good speed without them. Josée is worried about a misstep, but following in others' tracks is working so far.

The skis go back on when we are confronted, again, by another lead. Whatever the cause, I am swiftly becoming a believer in the notion of global warming. Later, I will see the satellite photos of the ice we have covered and appreciate the tracery of veins that represent these stretches of open, or nearly open water. On the NOAA images, the leads are labeled "fractures." I am generating my own list of names for them.

Another lead confronts us. Again, packs and skis are unbuckled. Kerri, who is developing into a really strong skier along with Alison and Marie-Josée, is one of the first to cross this recently formed lead, in Josée's wake. The skim ice is precarious and can support two, maybe three skiers at once. Kathy follows them, but Josée stops her halfway and stations her to assist some of the other team members, who are a little skittish about traversing the barely frozen lead. Kathy anchors herself near what appears to be a fairly solid chunk of ice in the middle. The rest of us methodically trail along, shuffling rhythmically across the rolling ice that sways with each movement.

One at a time, Susan, Lynn, and Phyllis head across. Susan and Lynn quickly shuffle to the other side with continuous movements and ski forward onto the thicker ice. Whether out of tiredness or inattention, Phyllis tries to sidestep up in the wrong spot, and her foot goes in—well up her boot. The concern in Josée's voice is palpable.

"No, Phyllis, not like that!" she says, and several of the women on the other side reach over to pull Phyllis up and deposit her on more solid ice. I look at Diana, nod at her, and she steps down onto the ice and glides off, straps flapping at the side.

I follow, and Kathy and Jen bring up the rear. Phyllis is quickly putting on a dry sock when the rest of us get there. The shot of adrenaline we've gotten from a team member's misstep is strong. We soberly cinch our gear and head on.

The plan is to ski until 8 P.M., break for food, and then make an assessment as to our progress. But a wide, partially frozen lead changes those plans. We reach it just before 7 P.M. Our choices are east, west, or cross. West is out, as we can no longer afford to give ground in that direction. East is getting us precisely there—east—and we need to go north. I look at Josée to get a sense of what she wants to do. The burden of managing this part of the trek, it strikes me, is as heavy as the weight I encountered in getting us to this point. She had faith that I could handle my end of the management. I have great respect for her dealing with this end of the expedition, though I can see she is tiring—as I had.

"Let's stop here and get some food, some warm food," she says. "We're too tired right now to try to cross this lead, or to ski on." Besides, she has arranged to call Richard at 9 P.M., and I have told Bonnie that I will check in with her before 10 P.M. Everything back home is coordinated through her at the moment.

The cook tent is rapidly hoisted, and snow is gathered for Jen to cook with. With the Russian stoves blazing, we all crawl inside for a bowl of spaghetti. Josée reaches Richard.

She details where we are, having gotten the coordinates from Kathy, and explains that we are hitting major leads—unlike Richard and Misha, who are on a smoother patch of ice and nearly at the Pole. We have been out for nine hours and covered only 5.3 nautical miles, a lot of them to the east.

It is hard to tell what is being said from the other tent, but it is pretty clear that Richard is concerned that we are going to lose our opportunity, and that we need to cross the lead in front of us, semisolid though it is. Much further delay in skiing north and we will be out of the picture.

Josée is hesitant to take the team across the lead, despite Richard's urgings. She switches to French. Marie-Josée, Alison, and I all understand. "Il y a déjà quelqu'un qui a paniqué et est entré dans l'eau." Already, someone had panicked and gone into the water. Josée doesn't dare risk a repeat of what happened earlier. She wants firmer ice, but the question is how far we will have to go to find it.

Misha asks that I be put on the phone.

"Sue Carter, you know what you must do?" Misha says, more in statement than question. Before I can answer, he continues. "You must have two very long days of marches. It is time to attack. If you do not, you will not make it to the Pole. Do you understand?"

I am nodding my head, realizing that he cannot see me.

"What is required is to ski three or four marches to the east. Then you must sleep for a few hours. Leave your gear and go directly north to the Pole."

I look at Josée, wondering if Richard has given her the same counsel. Knowing her cautious nature, it is unlikely that she will be willing to separate from our gear—even in a last mad dash to the Pole.

Misha continues. "You have only one chance. It is like when we were training at Borneo. You must ski eight to ten marches or you will not arrive."

I am silent, absorbing this sobering admonition from a man who understands the Arctic as well as anyone alive. This is not pep talk to inspire us. Misha is deadly serious.

I say the only thing I can. "Misha, I understand, and I will tell the team what you have said. We will meet you at the Pole." I hand the sat phone back to Josée.

In the next call, Bonnie has good news for us. Olga has been able to call the airport at Khatanga and share our coordinates. She has also gotten the name and phone number of a man there who speaks English, and who will relay messages to Ice Station Borneo during the hour-long transmission window set up between Khatanga air-traffic control and Borneo. And she has reached the NASA team that is leaving Resolute Bay, Canada, for Eureka, a layover on the way north. The plan for meeting is now firm. We have arranged to shake hands at the North Pole.

But the task of getting to the Pole remains squarely in front of us. The urgency in Misha's English, along with the quiet from Josée, confirms what I have been feeling. We are not assured of hitting 90 degrees north. (In fact, I later discover that Richard and Misha have been fairly certain that we won't make it.)

Sleep is an activity for another day. As Jen repacks the pans from the spaghetti dinner, Josée and I address the team. Josée goes first.

"Listen, we've all worked too hard not to make it to the Pole. We have to reach back, really reach back now, and ski hard. Pull together for this last stretch."

I share Misha's suggestion of three to four marches due east, and then a turn north, leaving gear behind.

"I'm not so sure about that," Josée quickly adds. "I think we need to see where we are at the end of this next ski. I don't like the idea of leaving our gear, even though we'll come back for it." All attention in that tent—so thoroughly isolated on a pan of moving Arctic ice—is focused on her. "If something happens and we need shelter, it could be difficult."

"I agree with Josée," I say. "We can hold off making that decision, but it's a choice I'd rather not make. I think we can make it, and make it intact."

"Okay, girls. Let's go."

CHAPTER TWENTY-NINE

Day Eight

It is shortly after midnight on Monday, April 23. We have stopped less than four hours for a warm meal, rest, and communications. Before us is the biggest test yet: to nearly double in less than twenty-four hours what we haven't been able to ski in any previous day. We are just over eight miles from the North Pole, but we will have to pick up more than three miles going east before we can even make the turn north because of the leads. The team is looking at some eleven miles, plus whatever deviation is required, with no sleep. Time to attack!

Some clouds have moved back in, low-slung stratus clouds that flatten the environment. They also raise the temperature to +3 degrees Fahrenheit, which actually makes for warm skiing. Several of the team, including Kerri and Alison, pull off their wind jackets and ski in fleece, or even just layers of polypropylene.

The first challenge of the second long ski of the day hits us within an hour. Another bloody lead; they are spreading like cracks on an old piece of porcelain, confronting and taunting us mile after mile.

The expanse of ice ahead seems a bit gelatinous—hardly stable—and it is fairly wide. The pressure is on to ski east, though, and this lead is in the way. Phyllis has assumed her position behind Josée and is at the fore when Josée finally settles on a place to cross. She carefully slides down from the bank of the lead to the soft surface, in a motion we are all becoming familiar with.

"Don't go until I tell you," Josée yells back. She wants to scout the surface to make sure it is stable enough to cross. It reminds me of a wide suspension bridge with a little sway in it.

Suddenly, Phyllis starts out after Josée. Diana and I look on in surprise, wondering if she hasn't heard Josée's admonition. Her ski breaks right through the ice. Jen, on the near side of the lead, shoots forward to stabilize and get her across. What is going on? I wonder. Is she getting tired and not hearing instructions? We all are tired, but it isn't the time to let down. Not this close. She bears watching.

I am having my own problems, though. In the flat light, I lose an edge going over a little rise. Ordinarily it wouldn't present a difficulty, but fatigue catches me and I lose the inner edge of my right ski, smashing my right knee down hard on a very unyielding surface. The piercing pain brings a gasp from deep inside. I sit there for a moment, splayed on the ice, trying to collect myself and to assess any damage. I must have caught the inside of my kneecap because the pain starts to radiate outward from that spot.

Before I can twist to plant my ski poles and hoist myself back up, Josée is at my side.

"I've never seen anyone with a knee twisted like that." She is stooping over to look, and then to give a hand.

I can't allow myself to think that it has been injured. I look up and thrust my right hand up, a gesture for help. "It's hereditary. It's an old football injury," I say as she pulls me vertical. "I'm okay."

She laughs. "Well, just keep going. We're going to make it."

"Josée, do you really think so?" A level of doubt has crept into my thoughts after the conversation with Misha.

"Yes. I know that Richard and Misha are worried, but this is a good team that you've put together."

"And you're a good leader out here," I tack on quickly.

"Well, we'll see how good. Enough, now. Let's get going."

I hired the right woman.

. . .

It is 3:30 in the morning, and I have been looking down at the watch dangling from the bottom zipper pull on my wind jack altogether too often. Part of me is wishing this night to pass quickly. But I need to stop and take in the grandeur of being on the Arctic Ocean this close to the Pole, where few humans—let alone women—have ever been before.

At the next break, I catch up with Frida and sit next to her on the ice. Her quietness has continued for several days, and we haven't had much of a chance to talk about what she is feeling.

"Just think, Frida. You and I started this crazy conversation back in 1993, and now, we're almost there."

"Yeah, I look around and I think, 'Girl, you're a long way from Marquette.' And then I realize I'll be home soon."

"Are you glad you did this? Skiing to the North Pole?" It probably isn't the best time to ask the question, and maybe I already know the answer, but I want to bring her out into conversation.

"I think so, but it's been harder than I thought. I know I'm tired, and I know Jen and Josée are irritated with me."

"Stop," I say. "That's their problem. You and I are the organizers of this, and you, bless you, got me into this."

"But you made it happen, and they and some of the others don't appreciate it."

This touches a tender and still-hurting spot in me. "I think that's right, but there's nothing I can do about it, except to know that much of what I did got us this far, and hope that someday they'll see it." I put an arm around her shoulder. "But you know what? I got to know you, and you were an inspiration. Besides, we're going to surprise a lot of folks back at Borneo!"

My hands are starting to get cold. I push myself up from the ice and go to join Kerri's Arctic Aerobics.

. ˙ . ˙

During the next march, my mind shuttles back and forth between relief that our trek will soon be successfully over, and concern that we aren't going to have enough stamina to hit the North Pole. We still have some seven miles to go.

Lassitude is creeping up on me—and, as I look around, on the rest of the team as well. Lynn is soldiering on. Susan is intent and quiet. Even the usually ebullient Kerri has shut down and is concentrating on skiing. Weariness is evident in the number of spills we are taking. Even Frida, a lifelong skier, is occasionally falling prey to snow snakes, the critters that reach up and grab unsuspecting skiers and suddenly thrash them to the ground.

The burst of energy we crave comes from an unwanted source—adrenalin. There in front of us, and blocking our path for some distance, lies a wide, wobbly lead. Josée is taking no chances this time.

"I want you all to unbuckle your straps. And take your hands out of your ski-pole straps. Everything should be set to fall away if you go into the water."

If you go into the water. I am awake now.

"It's important that you go in pairs, and only when I say so. Do not stop on the ice."

Shuffle and keep going.

The shock of the last crossing's dipped ski has put us all on notice that we have to be particularly careful, given how tired we are. We have been up for twenty-two hours, on the trail for fourteen of those hours, and aren't as sharp as we could be. But, we are focused. Very focused. No missteps this close. We are going on together, even if we have to drag a teammate or two on her butt. I will not—we will not—fail now, having come so close.

It is the nearest to an uneventful lead crossing we have made to date. In tandem, with great caution, following every instruction.

On the other side, we take a short break.

"Let's go on until six o'clock," Josée suggests. That would be another hour—and it is possible, I think, looking around the group. The ice has smoothed out, and the sun is again filling the brilliant blue sky. One more hour before a rest.

"We'll put up the tents and sleep for a little while. That will be a good break."

Sleep is starting to sound enormously appealing. Even a few hours.

I recap my thermos and look off to my left to see Josée talking with Diana. Diana's shoulders are stooped and she is looking up at Josée. Josée then unhitches Diana's sled from her backpack and drags it over to Alison. I walk over to meet them to find out what is going on.

"Diana is having some vertigo and is having trouble pulling her sled. I am going to give it to Alison. She can hook it onto the back of hers." Josée already has taken Phyllis's sled and hooked it up to hers. She isn't asking Alison to do anything she wouldn't do.

"How about this?" I suggest. "Let me take Diana's sled, which is heavier than mine, and give Alison mine. At least it'll be less weight overall."

I can see the relief on Alison's face. She is immensely strong, but also has her limits. And I remember what happened during the training back on Borneo. Ages ago. Diana is fifteen years my junior and has been pulling a full sled, but she needs help at the moment. I take Diana's sled from Josée, and then go and retrieve mine and hand it over to Alison.

"Thanks, Alison. I really appreciate what you're doing."

She smiles in a wonderfully self-effacing way. It is easy to see how she was a champion.

I make the sled switch and then walk over to Diana, big white boots clomping over the ice.

"Hi, Diana." She is sitting down. "Are you okay?"

"I'm a little dizzy at the moment, and I had some vertigo back there on that last pressure ridge. It happens once in a great while, and this time it just snuck up on me."

A history I hadn't known about.

"Have you had something to eat lately? Maybe a little food would help."

"Yeah, I think I'll eat something. I'm out of drink, though." We hadn't had time to fill up many thermoses during the spaghetti dinner break eight hours ago.

I look around. "Let me see what I can find."

Lynn has some extra tea in her thermos, and I bring it over. "Here, this ought to feel good." She drinks, and I return the bottle to Lynn. It is time to strap up and head out.

. . .

Diana's sled is heavier than what I have been used to pulling, but not impossible. It just requires a firmer tug or two getting over the pressure ridges. It does make me more tired, though, and by 6 A.M. I am grumpy and feeling like toast. I am regressing into childishness, wanting to burst out, "Are we there yet? How much longer?" All right, Carter, stop it. This is no time for a polar moment.

At just after 8 A.M., Josée draws us together. "We're all getting a little tired, and we have some more leads ahead of us. We can't cross them when we are tired, so it's time to get a little sleep."

To a woman, we are all ready.

"Let's put up tents here and get right into our sleeping bags. We can eat something when we wake up."

With the dispatch that comes from practice, we rapidly lay out the tents in two circles, stake them out with skis and ski poles, and shove our sleeping pads and bags inside. We all are asleep within a half hour. It is 9:30 A.M., Monday morning, April 23, 2001.

CHAPTER THIRTY

By 2 P.M. the afternoon of April 23, six hours after we decided to stop for a rest, we are up and collecting gear to stuff into our bags and sleds for the final push to the North Pole. This is going to be it. The next time I crawl into my sleeping bag, it will be at the North Pole, at 90 degrees north. The final push is manageable. Not completed, but the North Pole is within our grasp.

Over a quick breakfast of oatmeal, we do a check around the circle in the tent. Yes, we have a haul in front of us, with easily six more miles to go. Our forward progress since we began yesterday morning hasn't been great, because much of the time was spent going east to counteract the drift that has been carrying us west. Now, we are better positioned to cut north. The leads have also been forcing us in that direction.

Susan has done a good job of avoiding hypothermia, with assistance from Kerri and Lynn. Diana's sleep has taken away her vertigo. Kathy and Marie-Josée are ready to attack. Frida and I are like retrievers smelling water. Phyllis is quiet.

Diana, Alison, and I sort out our sleds, and I clip mine onto the rope hanging from my backpack. The sleep and my good spirits make the sled feel extraordinarily light. Still at least six marches to go, but that should put us at the Pole by midnight—maybe one o'clock the morning of Tuesday, April 24, at the latest. Tonight, we sleep at the Pole!

Kerri is worried because we have had to scrub some of the calls to the schools, but there is no way to manage on the trail. We might try to reach Bonnie so she can post our progress, but that would be about all we can handle in the outdoors on the satellite telephone. The batteries degrade so quickly in the cold that we are fortunate to get ten minutes worth of time out of a battery that is good for a half hour under normal circumstances. But right now, we aren't even thinking about calling Bonnie. Our mission is the Pole.

It is surprising how much difference four hours of sleep and a little food make. The break proves to be a valuable refresher, because the path ahead of us continues to be strewn with leads and pressure ridges. Beautiful in their own right, but they are more than we want to contend with in our last dash to the Pole.

The pressure ridges have seemed to grow in height, but so has our ability to manage them. The drill is set: skis and backpacks off and sleds decoupled. Three women over to the other side, two or three on top, and the rest of the team feeding the bags and equipment up and over. And they are placed in rows, with a teammate's skis next to her backpack and sled so she can put them all on without having to hunt for them. Misha would be impressed.

The leads are also less daunting. Most of the team are now relatively comfortable crossing the breaks in the ice. With growing confidence, we even consider making a snow bridge to traverse those that seem too wide or unstable. Mercifully, though, we are able to cross each lead without paralleling it more than a few hundred yards.

As the Pole nears, our energy increases. The ice is still challenging in spots, and Lynn, Phyllis, and I opt to take off our skis and walk for a while. We can move as swiftly—and, more importantly, as surely—as the rest of the team on this harder pack we've encountered. In a line, all twelve of us snake north to our goal.

At eight o'clock in the evening of Monday, April 23, we are still nearly four miles from true north. During a break, I ask Kathy where the sat phones are. I need to call Bonnie so she can alert others on our movement.

"One's in the blue sack in my bag." She motions to it. "All of the batteries in that bag are good."

I find the blue stuff sack in her backpack, which still bears the airline's "HEAVY" tag on it. A nice touch of humor. Loading a battery into the base of the phone, I dial the access code, and then Bonnie's number back in Michigan.

"Hey, Bonnie, guess where we are? Less than five miles from the Pole!" The juice is really flowing in me now.

If I had to characterize Sue's tone, it would be euphoric. "We expect to be at the Pole by noon (Michigan time) tomorrow," she said. "Bonnie, you just can't imagine how amazing this is."

I give her our coordinates, and learn from her that the team from NASA has taken off from Resolute Bay and is some six hours away from Eureka, where they will spend the night before heading north to meet us in less than twenty-four hours. Call First Air at Resolute Bay, she tells me, to give them a local forecast so the plane can land as close as possible to the North Pole. I agree to get in touch with them once we have arrived and settled in at the North Pole. All indications are that everything will come together. A-OK.

I put the phone and battery back into the sack and return it to Kathy's backpack. There is just enough time for a bite of food and a drink of Earl Grey tea before the next march. Flapping my arms against my side, I walk over to my sled and pull the hot liquid out. From my left pants pocket, I dig out some beef jerky and a piece of chocolate. I am eating like a seven-year-old, but then maybe seven-year-olds are on to something.

The protein-carbohydrate hit, washed down with hot tea, works. I feel revived enough to tackle the next stretch. Frida is unwinding, checking the video camera that she wears around her neck like a talisman. It is never separated from her. I know that she is concerned about not having shot as much tape as she wanted for the documentary, but she has still captured a lot. It is stunning how much more difficult tasks are in the Arctic.

The mood now is so different from twenty-four hours ago, when we stopped for our spaghetti dinner and Misha gave his urgent warnings. Several miles still remain, but all is working in our favor. We feel reasonably well rested and fed, the sky has cleared to a magnificent blue, and the temperature is rather comfortable. There is also a caution. We have not yet reached our goal, and it is too soon to be self-congratulatory. It is time to get moving. We still have to attack

Richard and Misha tell the story of the one time they had a falling-out on their record-setting ski to the Pole and back from Ward Hunt Island. After a day's worth of marches, they were bone tired, but had nearly reached their allotted travel time for the day. At the end of a hard crossing, Richard said it was time to quit. No, Misha declared, they still had ten more minutes to go. No way, said Richard. We've done enough, and ten minutes more won't matter. Mr. Immoveable and Mr. Indestructible. There was an object lesson to draw from that exchange, though. Keep going until the task is finished.

Up we rise from our break—Lynn, Diana, Marie-Josée, and the rest of us climbing into our equipment for one of our final times. In the distance, we can see a large pressure ridge that extends right and left for some distance. It will need to be climbed, but we aren't there yet.

Earlier, Josée pointed out fresh ski tracks. "Those are Richard's!" she exclaimed, lifting up the bottom of her ski and pointing out the similarities. "See, they are fish-scale, just like ours. We're the only expedition that uses these skis." She put her right ski back on the ice. "They're ahead of us, but not by much."

It is hugely comforting to know that we are hard on the tail of a companion group. They'll be waiting for us at the North Pole when we arrive. In the meantime, we can lock onto their tracks and follow them due north. I feel a mixture of part Indian scout and part Arctic explorer with the discovery of the tracks. We are on an adventure, following the path of those who have gone before us. We, however, are doing it as a group of women.

Not everything, though, is working in our favor. The leads and pressure ridges pile on, one after another. We are mastering them generally well, but they slow our progress. Lynn, Phyllis, and I are still on foot, though Josée keeps a concerned watch out for us. The ice conditions can change rapidly, and it is not impossible to ram a foot through a thin crust, straining a tendon or spraining a ligament in the process. Josée also retains Phyllis's sled to ensure that she can keep up with the team. Progress is only as fast as the slowest, and she needs to be kept moving.

By 11 P.M. we know that we won't make the Pole by midnight. There are almost three miles left, and we are starting to flag. I mentally revise my projection to 2 A.M., April 24. That will be a Tuesday.

Still, an almost tangible feeling charges the air. Knowing that Richard and Misha have traveled here only a few hours ago makes the environment seem all the more alive. There is an energy that suffuses the atmosphere and touches us, even if we are fatigued. With only a few breaks, we've been skiing since Sunday morning, and it is now almost Tuesday. Somehow, though, this group of twelve women is going forward, is going to raise what now seems a historic banner.

Midnight passes, and we move through another march. Maybe arriving at the Pole by two o'clock Tuesday morning is a little optimistic, but not by much. I am willing to say closer to three. During a break last night, we all made a bet about the time we would arrive at the North Pole. The winner lays claim to the very first hot shower back in Khatanga. I had hoped for a midnight arrival, but guessed 2:40 A.M. I have a shot at being right.

One final lead, though, lies between us and Khatanga, the showers, and even the North Pole. Not as challenging as the leads we crossed earlier, but still one that requires diligence. Lynn, Phyllis, and I put our skis back on and get ready to cross the semifrozen gap.

Kathy, who is becoming increasingly adept as a skier, follows Josée, as does Kerri.

Then Phyllis sets out.

Inching her way, she carefully shuffles over the undulating ice, concentrating on her skis and on the other side. Kathy is again positioned midway to boost any team member who needs help; Josée is on the far slab of ice, just above the edge of the lead. Phyllis scoots to the other side, and then again tries to sidestep up at a place other than where Josée has indicated. The ice is thinner there. Phyllis again breaks through, and Josée, in a rush of strength, reaches down and grabs her off the icy lead and deposits her on the bank. Josée is shaken.

"Phyllis, you cannot do that. You must listen to what I tell you. Any mistake here and it can cost you. Even the smallest mistake can be tragic."

I have just started to cross the ice when Josée hoists Phyllis up. I can feel the tension building, and I concentrate all the more on my skis.

"You pushed me down!" Phyllis screams at her, gathering up her glasses and trying to wipe them off.

"No, I didn't." Josée is struggling to keep calm. "But you were about to go in, and I had to get you off the ice."

"Yes, you did!" Phyllis is now without restraint. She is crying in great gulps.

"Phyllis, stop it. Get a hold of yourself."

"No!"

I look up just in time to see her stomping off to the left and throwing her equipment on the ground, each piece coming off with a scream. My patience is thin, and I know Josée's can't be much greater. Several of the other team members have already started out again, following Richard and Misha's tracks. I know there is little I can do at the moment that will help Josée or calm Phyllis. I turn to follow Frida, who crossed shortly after me but is already skiing forward.

A few of the women on the team, including Marie-Josée and Lynn, hang back to help Josée recompose Phyllis. It is important for the rest of us to move on, as fatigue is setting in and we need to sustain our physical energy. It would be easier on a level emotional ground.

Gradually, the rest of the team, except for Josée and Phyllis, fall in line behind us. We are like horses to the barn at this point, following the tracks that Richard, Misha, and the rest of their team have scratched in the ice for us. This is as close to being on autopilot as possible on a ski to the Pole.

One o'clock passes, then one-thirty. Finally, I see the two women break over the horizon behind. Phyllis is on skis, and Josée—with a lone spare ski poking up like a huge feather—is pulling her sled and Phyllis's. We will all get there in some team order, but we are slowing down. The last outburst has cost us time and strength—and we have little to give at this point. I am frustrated by the diversion that has been created, but know that our gaze has to be focused forward for these last few miles. We'll sort the rest out later.

It is closing in on 2 A.M. Tuesday morning when the roar of a helicopter explodes from behind us, and the chopper sweeps over us and away. Frida, who is close to me, stands there stunned as I slide up beside her and watch in amazement. The helicopter—Russian, and surely from Borneo—stops and hovers over a spot. Then it lowers itself out of sight.

"Frida! Do you know what that means? It means that we're almost at the Pole. The helicopter must be going there. Why else would it be here and then land at that spot?" I am crying. "Frida, the Pole is right ahead!"

Her eyes are wide from sheer wonder, looking at the landing site and then at me. She wraps her arms around me.

"Yahoo! We've done it." I am jumping up and down, my skis clattering against the ice. "We can see the North Pole!"

Well, of course, we can't. We only figure that the helicopter has hovered over the spot designated, at this particular moment, as the North Pole. It is most certainly right, though. Flyovers and champagne flights are increasingly common. Rather than ski any portion of the way to the North Pole, wealthy patrons hire the Russians, or the Canadians, to take them the distance by air. (We later learn that is exactly what occurred here—the Sharaf of Dubai had chartered the chopper and flown in for a toast. Tent set up, he donned his robes and made a brief appearance at 90 degrees north. Then flew out after less than an hour on the ground.)

The appearance of the helicopter is an immense lift to the team, though. We can't be more than a mile and a half away, as we have all but seen the aircraft touch down. We are virtually there with our eyes.

I am struck for a moment by two thoughts, one from the Old Testament and one from the New. Standing there, perched on a little pressure ridge, I have some small inkling of what Moses must have felt as he looked off in the distance at the Promised Land. Unlike Moses, though, I have every intention of getting there with my little band. The second thought is of the Star of Bethlehem, guiding the Three Wise Men—even though the analogy arguably breaks down there. But, like the Star, the helicopter hangs in the sky over the special location. All we have to do is head in that direction.

Frida and I are now hip to hip. We have endured much for a long time, and we are going to lead this group in together, right to the North Pole.

Behind us, the line has started to stretch out again. Kerri, Susan, Kathy, and Diana are close by, but Alison and Marie-Josée have slowed down. Josée and Jen are back with Phyllis.

Suddenly, Marie-Josée comes ripping up from behind. Before she catches up with us, she dumps her backpack and her sled.

"M.-J., what's happening, what's going on?" Frida and I ask.

"It's Lynn and Phyllis. They're just about at the end of their rope. Josée told me to go get Misha and Richard." And she is off.

Lynn is nearing exhaustion. She has handed her sled over to Alison. Phyllis is in no better shape, and Josée is still pulling both of their sleds.

Marie-Josée's speed is impressive. She has tapped a critical reserve. Frida and I muster on, following the tracks of Susan and Kerri, who have pulled ahead of us, watching Marie-Josée disappear into the distance. The best thing we can do is to get ourselves there. Help is on the way for Lynn and Phyllis.

It is less than a half hour before I see two strong figures skating in profile across the horizon in front of us. By their styles, they can only be Richard and Misha. Marie-Josée had arrived, calling out for them. She rapidly explained that Josée needed help getting these two into camp, and they hurriedly strapped on their skis and rocketed out of the camp. Without stopping to congratulate M.-J., they swiftly were gone, leaving her to turn around and collect her backpack and gear from Jen, who gathered them along the way. Richard and Misha pass us on their way. Quick hugs from both of them, and they speed on.

Frida and I encounter Marie-Josée as she is backtracking from the camp. She is winded, but has gone the full measure at the end. What an impressive woman.

Richard and Misha's camp is easy to spot. The other five members of their team come out of the tent and surround us with hugs and warm drinks as we peel off our equipment and packs. From somewhere inside our sleds, they dig out the two tents and get them set up—the design is familiar to them, as Josée made their tent as well. Warm water and tea and a down jacket, and Frida and I start to understand that we really have arrived at the North Pole.

But we aren't all there.

Misha and Richard are bringing up the rear, helping Josée and Jen shepherd Phyllis and Lynn into camp. Lynn is closer to collapse than I had realized. She looks wan and depleted; she is cold and emotional and degrading fairly quickly. She is quickly ushered into the other team's warm tent. Misha and Josée are escorting Phyllis, by her side, helping her the last half mile. Less than one hundred yards from the camp, Phyllis collapses into a heap and starts screaming and thrashing. I look away. I have held up my end of the bargain. She has gotten to the North Pole.

Lynn and Phyllis are quickly hustled into their sleeping bags, and they sleep round the clock. The dual skiing stretches—fifteen hours, followed by twelve hours—has taxed them seriously. Josée later tells me that "if this had happened earlier, I would have had Phyllis helicoptered right out." I reflect on my decision back in Siberia whether or not to let her remain with the team. The decision had been the correct and principled one, but we have paid for it.

Standing there in the camp that marks the North Pole, I am bone tired, but elated to the point of punchiness. In that last stretch, Frida and I have discovered a profound sense of joy and release for the team's accomplishment, and for ours. We have arrived at the North Pole—not exactly as we had expected, but we've all gotten there. It is 4 A.M. Tuesday, April 24, 2001. We have traveled more than eighty miles on the Arctic Ocean.

CHAPTER THIRTY-TWO

Day Nine: The North Pole

All is silent in the tent when I unstick my eyelids and manage to focus. My left arm, the one with the cheap, clunky watch, snakes up from the cocoon of my sleeping bag, and with my right hand I peel back the layers of fleece and check the time—5:20. It must be evening because it doesn't feel as though we have slept around the clock. From the amount of daylight, though, it is impossible to tell.

Time to move. Nothing inside me, though, wants to stir. Nothing particularly aches, but I have little sensation either. Just five more minutes, please, and maybe the desire to move will be there. At this moment, though, I'm not sure—and care even less. What is left to give?

Still, there is unfinished business. Mark, the airport manager at Resolute Bay, is expecting my call at 7:30 A.M. his time, and that is a little more than an hour from now. I pray that we have finally worked out our times correctly. It should be easy to figure. But with my Arctic-chilled brain, it all seems a bit confusing now. I am so tired.

I force myself into a sitting position. Now, pieces of the body start to hurt. The right kneecap and the right hip groan out their complaints from yesterday's last hard fall. There is probably enough ibuprofen in the world to quiet them, but not here—not at the North Pole.

"Sue?" Frida whispers out from the opposite side of the tent.

"Yeah, I'm awake," I reply. "You getting up?"

Frida is already starting to unzip her sleeping bag. "Yep, I hear voices in one of the other tents. I'm dying for a cup of coffee." It does sound as though our cook tent—or possibly the Malakhov-Weber tent—has stoves going, and maybe warm water for food and coffee.

"I'm right behind you," I say softly to Frida as she slips on her camp boots, unlashes the two strings that cinch the tent's opening, and tumbles out the entrance, drawing the strings behind her.

Reaching down into my sleeping bag, I retrieve my contact-lens solution. The case is in the pants pocket to keep the contents from freezing. Lenses in and teeth brushed, I undo the cords to the enclosure and crawl out, shuffling through the entrance on sore knees.

I have no sense of how this day will turn out. The past week still hasn't resolved exactly where, and at what time, we are going to meet the crew from NASA for a live webcast.

It had seemed from that first day on Ice Station Borneo that it would be impossible for me to find a 2,500-foot landing space close to the Pole where First Air's Twin Otter could land for our hookup with NASA. And the other choices had their own problems.

The most logical solution was to land at Borneo. The ice strip could accommodate the airplane, and it was already set up. Besides, Borneo is only about one hundred miles farther than the North Pole. That distance is small compared to the hundreds of miles the plane will be flying from Eureka, the layover between Resolute Bay and the Pole. I encouraged NASA to push for this alternative. I figured they were in a lot better position than I was, sitting in a tent on the polar icecap, to make the argument.

It was technically feasible, but flatly unacceptable. Great. Apparently, First Air flew into Borneo several years ago, but a dispute over landing fees to the Russians arose. The two operations were in competition for North Pole clients, and that didn't help.

Despite the previous troubles, Misha had gotten assurances of a flat landing fee from the Russians—to quell the Canadians' fears that they would be gouged as a consequence of the earlier dispute. There remained the question of fuel charges on Borneo, even though the Canadians could arrange for fuel caches en route and avoid the need to buy from the Russians. Nonetheless, the Canadians absolutely refused to consider Borneo as an option.

The remaining choice is risky. The pilot from First Air flying to the North Pole has to find a suitable landing spot within a few miles and then radio us the coordinates. At the same time, the Russians will send a helicopter from Borneo, gather up the Polar Trek team as well as the Weber-Malakhov team, fly to those coordinates, land, and we will stage a live webcast. The timing has to be precise. The window isn't quite as narrow as a Shuttle launch, but it feels pretty close all the same.

Since our first discussions, NASA Mike and I have settled on April 24 (U.S. time) as the day for the webcast. Having established the day, the time for the webcast is critical, as we will be using the EOS Aqua Observatory satellite, a circumpolar satellite that gives us a link time between 4 A.M. and 6 A.M. our time, which is 4 P.M. to 6 P.M. back home. It will already be April 25 for us, April 24 in the States.

All of this is churning through my mind as I head for the Weber-Malakhov tent, where steam is already venting from the top. Down jacket off, snow and frost from the night dusted off, I get set to enter our neighbors' tent.

"Incoming," I signal before untying the drawstrings. "Okay, c'mon in," is the faceless reply. I loosen the cinch and crawl in, careful to miss the stoves that are heating food and providing warmth. Misha, already in the tent, swiftly closes the opening behind me.

Richard is there along with Misha, as well as Josée, Jen, Frida, and several of the Weber-Malakhov team. It is their tent, after all. I spot Ray on the far side of the tent and crawl over to an open camp chair next to Mats, a Swede, on the opposite wall.

"Coffee?" Richard offers. I mumble thanks and also take a bowl of porridge. Frida, next to me on my left, is finishing her cereal and cradling a cup of coffee.

"You should have seen him," she says, clearly excited. "His feet were unbelievable. I shot some video of them. And his face—"

"Who do you mean?" I interrupt. Aside from the nineteen of us, who else is here at the North Pole?

"Borg Ousland, the Norwegian guy who's going it alone from Russia to Ward Hunt Island." It sounds a little familiar. "He's the one with the dry suit."

The dry suit. I remember now. Borg is on a solo transpolar trek and is just about halfway there. He's been out forty-five days and is planning on journeying a total of ninety-five days before arriving in Canada. Borg puts on the dry suit whenever he comes up against a lead that is too wide to ski across. Even being a scuba diver, I find it unimaginable to consider getting into these waters.

"It's the craziest thing," adds Richard. "He stops at a lead, puts on the dry suit, swims across pushing his gear in front of him, and then gets out." Once out, Borg takes off the suit and gets back into skiing mode. As it turns out, his campsite is less than a hundred yards away, on the other side of the pressure ridge that backs up against our three tents.

Talk about Borg continues on a little while as my thoughts drift toward today's task. It is now 6:10 P.M. our time, and I need to call Mark at Resolute Bay shortly, with a local weather update. I also have to deal with Misha.

Misha is a visionary in many ways. So it has been hard to understand why he has a fair amount of resistance to our meeting NASA at the North Pole. Yes, it is clearly another complication in an environment where life succeeds when it is simple. But the chance to have the space agency share satellite photos and weather data, as well as 'casting live from the North Pole, is simply too good to pass up. It will really expand our reach to schoolchildren, a big part of our mission. Perhaps his reluctance stems from the fact that this involves an American agency. Maybe it stems from the fact that it wasn't his idea.

After all of the wrangling about landing sites and times, we have agreed that First Air will land as near to the North Pole as practicable, and that the Russian helicopter will ferry us to the site, then continue on to Borneo once the webcast is over. The Twin Otter left Resolute Bay yesterday, and the crew, including Dr. Clark, spent the night on Eureka. They are poised to take off for the Pole once I pass along the weather conditions. Yesterday, shortly after we arrived, a Twin Otter from First Air on a North Pole tourist flyover spotted a landing site less than three miles away. The coordinates, of course, will change, as the ice pack is moving, but the site will drift along with our camp.

There is still a huge problem. We haven't been able to directly verify our schedule for pickup and meeting with the Russian pilots. Working through Bonnie and Olga, we have left a series of messages and gotten assurances that our plan to join NASA for a polar webcast early on the morning of the twenty-fifth, local time, had been received. Olga has talked with the flight director at Khatanga, who relayed the information to Borneo. But it is still second-hand information. We need to confirm with Ice Station Borneo, and we haven't been able to raise them. The solar flares that interrupted communication with Borneo last week must be continuing.

It is almost time to call Mark with the "field" conditions.

"Ray"—I turn to the far more experienced pilot than I—"what should I tell Resolute Bay about present conditions?"

A big grin spreads across his face. "It's a fantastic day. Call and tell them 'CAV-OK.'"

It is a new term to me. "Tell me what it means."

Ray explains that "CAV-OK" is shorthand that commercial pilots use for "ceiling and visibility okay"—well within tolerance limits.

"'CAV-OK.' I got it. But I feel like I should give more information. What does it look like to you?"

"Well"—he turns to Mats, who is tucked between us—"what's our position?"

Mats has maintained a very thorough record of the Weber-Malakhov team's progress during their trek. I hand my notebook to Ray as Mats gives him the coordinates. I haven't been able to shake my fatigue and appreciate their help. Ray writes: N89.58, E25.22. "The temperature is right about −20 Celsius, [−4 Fahrenheit]," Ray continues, "with a barometric reading of 1005 millibars." That translated to 29.68 inches of mercury.

"And the wind," I add, "is slight. Wouldn't you say 'variable at five knots'? CAV-OK?"

Ray smiles. "CAV-OK."

Misha, meantime, has no luck in reaching Ice Station Borneo on the radio. Each team has carried a high-frequency transceiver, but the Weber-Malakhov unit has been down since just before leaving Ryazan for our journey to Siberia and the North Pole. "Maybe the other radio will work," Richard offers. He heads for the Polar Trek cook tent and returns with the set we have used, checks the battery, and hooks up.

"Borneo, Borneo, Malakhov calling," Misha directs into the microphone in Russian. No answer. Jiggling the wire, he calls again. Some static, but no answer.

Misha gives me a foreboding look that says he is unconvinced we will be able to reach the Russian crew. It also is chastising. Had we left one of our two satellite telephones at Borneo, as he suggested, we would not have this difficulty communicating. He had warned me that any communication problems would be my responsibility because of my decision to keep both phones with us. "You must accept responsibility, Sue Carter. Do you understand?" I had understood quite well, and also knew that I couldn't leave a second telephone on Borneo. Calls to schools and U.S. media, as well as politics, had ruled that out.

It is past time to call Mark. I ask Richard to hand me one of the satellite telephones we have brought into the tent to warm up for the call. I start to dial.

"Sue Carter, you must tell them not to send the plane." I look at Misha, stunned.

"Misha, I can't tell them that. The plane is already in Eureka. It's left Resolute Bay."

"We haven't reached the pilots on Borneo. You must tell them not to come."

"But Misha, Bonnie and Olga have told us that they have direct confirmation that the helicopter pilots on Borneo know. Yes, it would be good to confirm with them, but I believe they already know."

The tent has gone silent. Mats and Ray look from Misha to me and back. Richard holds his own counsel in another corner.

"Then you must tell them to delay by two hours."

My heart sinks at this struggle. A two-hour delay will blow the satellite window for the live webcast. There is a possibility that it can be videotaped and shown later, but the live webcast is an important feature of this event. We have a U.S. senator waiting to talk with us live. We can't do that on tape. So much of what we have planned for will be lost. A major dent in a $20,000 investment.

Misha looks at me, waiting for a rejoinder. My fatigue and his persistence have pushed me up against the wall. I start to feel closed in. I face him across the tent.

"Give me a minute to think this through, Misha." And I turn away from him to Ray, sitting two people over. "Ray, help me think this over." It is a chance to buy time, and to get another view from someone whose opinion is very valuable at this moment. "Can we pull this off? I mean, getting the Russian helicopter here, and then hooking up with the NASA plane?"

Ray ticks off the difficulties. In addition to reaching Ice Station Borneo to confirm that a helicopter will be arriving, there is the challenge of coordinating the pickup location, the drop-off point, and the time. The Twin Otter can stay at the Pole a maximum of two hours. Because of the cold, the plane must keep the engines running the entire time, and longer than two hours will start to compromise the amount of fuel needed to return. If the helicopter is late, there will not be enough time to get picked up and delivered and to access the satellite. If the First Air plane is late, the same problems arise. In this weather, each craft has to arrive at nearly the same time, or the plan won't work.

"It's a bit of a long shot, but it can be done."

"Thanks, Ray." I turn to Misha. "I'm not going to stop it. We're going forward."

Misha shrugs his shoulders, as if to say, "It's on your head." He tries to raise Ice Station Borneo again.

I dial the number of the airport director at Resolute Bay. Mark answers the telephone. I quickly give him the local conditions. He confirms that Annie, the pilot flying the Twin Otter yesterday, has indeed found a good spot to land near us, and the crew is set to take off.

"There's just one problem, Mark," I add. "We haven't been able to make a final confirmation with the pilots on Borneo."

"Well, that is a bit of a problem," he shoots back. "If they don't arrive, then none of this will work."

"I know, but we have a couple of hours to reach them." I swallow hard. "Go ahead and send the plane from Eureka. We'll be there." And I hang up.

I hand the satellite telephone back to Richard. There is still no answer from the radio shack at Ice Station Borneo. In eight hours, the plane from First Air will land. We need to allow at least three hours for the helicopter to warm up, go through preflight, and fly to the Pole. That gives us a maximum of five hours to contact the crew—to do something we haven't been able to do for nine days: reach them by radio.

Richard moves in toward the center of the tent. "Misha, we've got

Brigette's satellite-telephone number, don't we? Maybe we could have her relay a message to the helicopter crew."

Brigette, the unofficial concierge at the ice station. Her tent houses all manner of folks headed to the North Pole. When we saw her last on Easter, she was putting up three members of the Russian Duma who were on an official visit. Misha finds the number and Richard dials. Brigette answers. I hold my breath. Richard talks into the handset softly for a few minutes. This is going to work.

"*Au revoir,* Brigette," Richard signs off. "That was Brigette," he says as he turns to the rest of us in the tent. "She's not on Borneo. A couple of days ago she moved to the weather station." A scientific weather station has been set up after a hiatus of several years. "She doesn't think the Russians know that they are supposed to pick us up for this meeting."

How can we come this close and not make the final connection? We are here on time, after two very difficult final days of skiing, and the weather is perfect. This has to happen.

"Brigette did have a suggestion, though," Richard continues. "She said to try Philippe. He may be at Borneo. She gave me his satellite-telephone number." Philippe is one of the organizers of the ice station. An entrepreneur, he has helped launch a number of expeditions from Borneo.

"*Bonjour,* Philippe," Richard begins. He then sets out the reason for calling and quickly hangs up. "He's there on Borneo. He said to call back in five minutes. He's going to talk with the helicopter pilots right now."

I swirl the remainder of cold coffee in my cup. In five minutes, we will know.

"Misha, if you talk to the pilots, tell them that we need to be picked up at 3:30 to get the gear loaded and meet the NASA plane by four o'clock." Reaching the ice station is the first step. We still have to make sure we make the connections at the right time.

"The plane from Resolute will probably be late," Misha counters, perhaps from previous experience. "I do not want the Russians waiting too long. We can have them come a little later."

"But Misha"—I am pressing now—"we need to meet the plane at 4:00. We've got a short time on the satellite, and we can't be late."

Richard has dialed and Misha now turns to speak. Philippe is bringing one of the Russian pilots to his telephone "I will tell them 3:45 to 4:00 to come and pick us up."

I can feel the heat rising in my face, but there is little I can do about it at this point. "Thanks, Misha," I say. Somehow we will make this work.

CHAPTER THIRTY-THREE

Outside the Weber-Malakhov tent, the sky is a huge, inverted basin. Beautiful and all-encompassing, it leaves one feeling a bit like a pheasant under glass, only cold.

The three tents—two for our Polar Trek team and one for the other group—are backed up against a pressure ridge. On the other side is Borg with his gear, tent, and dry suit, resting before attacking the second half of his journey. I learn later that he is making this trip for the second time.

Most of the women from our tents are awake, and a number of them are outside, sorting and arranging their own sleds and backpacks, getting ready to leave the North Pole to make the trip home. The exhaustion we felt setting up the tents some sixteen hours ago, after the hard final push to get here, has left a jumble reminiscent of a yard sale. We'd gotten food and shelter, but tidiness had not been a high priority. There is time now, before the helicopter arrives, to straighten things out.

Inside our cook tent, another breakfast is waiting. I decline the oatmeal but take a cup of coffee. Kerri turns to me. "So, what do we know about the helicopter?"

I hand the extra satellite phone I've brought back from the Weber-Malakhov tent to Kathy, along with batteries I have been keeping warm in my armpits.

"We reached the Russian pilots, and they're going to pick us up by 4 A.M. Then they'll fly us to a site where the plane with the folks from NASA has landed, we'll get out, do a webcast, and then get back on and head to Borneo."

"What time is it now?" Susan asks.

"It's about 9:30."

"Morning or night?"

"Nine-thirty at night." It is a relief to know that someone else is disoriented as well.

"Okay," Susan continues, "so we've got a little more than six hours, right?"

"That's right." And secretly I hope that it will all come together as confidently as I am stating it. The pickup, the drop-off, the webcast. God, I hope it will be that straightforward.

Lynn sits forward. A resilient, strong-willed woman, she has endured good-natured comments about her lovely hair turning haggard during the past two weeks, as well as her own self-doubts about being the oldest and one of the weaker team members. Only slightly younger, and not a lot stronger, I have felt a common bond. Several days ago, on one of our breaks following a march, she and I pulled up our sleds a little away from the others. I needed quiet and a sounding board, and she apparently wanted to debrief as well.

"So, look at you two over there," Josée had cajoled. "You don't want to join in?"

I was tired, and hadn't felt particularly appreciated for a day or two. The strain of taking group time in the tent for extended communications back home in trying to arrange our NASA hookup was showing. Some of the others were unhappy with my time on the phone. But I knew I had no choice.

"Nah, this is the Old Ladies Club. You have to be at least fifty to join."

Josée looked at me, somewhat in disbelief. "You're fifty?"

"Yeah, I'm fifty," I nodded, feeling every inch of it.

At this moment in the tent, though, Lynn is at the center and wanting to offer some closure in the quiet moments before our final explosion of energy.

"I have a poem and a peace candle," she begins. "I want to read it; it was given to me by some of my close women friends back home." In East Lansing. "And I think we should the light the candle and each say something about what we've experienced and what we're feeling."

Jen reaches into her kitchen kit and pulls out a match. The candle is in a little cup that has a peace symbol on it. Lynn lights the wick, and the candle springs to life in the full daylight of the tent. She reads first.

Then, with the candle cradled in her hands, Lynn offers her reaction to the trek and the arrival at the North Pole. "I am glad we all made it."

Each woman in turn takes the candle. Frida is thankful for her family and can't wait to get home and gather up everybody in bed—Ron and Eryka and Ian—and just hug them. "I know that they'll say, 'Mom, we gotta get out of bed. We have to go to school!' But I won't let them." She has missed them more than she had anticipated. "I'm gonna keep them there with me for a month."

When the candle comes to Marie-Josée, her eyes moisten over. This amazingly strong woman, a real teammate who came on board late, chokes back a word and just shakes her head "no."

"It's okay, M.-J.," we encourage her. "Take your time."

Holding the candle in both hands between her knees, she dips her head and then looks up. "I am glad to be here with you guys," she says in her French Canadian accent. "It has helped me to find what I am looking for."

I try to take in what Marie-Josée has meant. Here is a woman who, to all appearances, presents a complete picture. I am touched that she has been affected by these women and the trek.

When the candle reaches me, I wonder what to say. Certainly, I am thankful that we have all gotten here and reached the Pole safely. I'm not ready for closure, though. That will come only after the helicopter lands at Borneo. "I am really pleased," I offer distractedly, "that we all made it."

In the few hours remaining before the helicopter's arrival, we have some final business to take care of. In addition to striking camp and packing up all the gear, we want to take Official North Pole photographs. We all want one taken with our own cameras. Clem, a member of the Weber-Malakhov team, cheerfully obliges as we line up against a mass of ice rubble, decked out in our red and blue wind suits. With all of our cameras stuffed in his various pockets, he pulls out one at a time and shoots nearly a dozen pictures. Then there are the photos with the various national flags and sponsor banners. And Frida wants separate headshots of us for her video.

There are two things left I need to do, and I quietly slip off to take care of them. One is to gather the final air sample for the Department of Geological Sciences back at Michigan State University. I've taken some grief for carrying the Styrofoam box filled with six vacuum tubes on my sled, but I have been determined to use my time on the ice in as many ways as possible. A little gathering of scientific data is one way.

The final task is to take the fifteen Nalgene collection bottles and fill them with snow from the North Pole. They will be a hard-won souvenir. Sell them on eBay? Maybe. But more likely they'll be shared with my family and dear friends. From the bottom of my backpack, I retrieve a plastic bag with the bottles. Each is filled from a clean patch of North Pole snow.

At 3:15 A.M., now the morning of April 25, the sound of an aircraft bursts over the horizon. This is an airplane. It can only be the Twin Otter belonging to First Air. It has to be carrying the team from NASA.

It passes over our camp and then turns away in a direction that feels southeast. It is hard to tell, though, for the ice we have been perched on has moved more than a mile since we arrived nearly twenty-two hours ago. Ray scampers up on the ice rubble and watches as the twin-engine flies toward its landing site. From twenty-five feet above the ice pan, he has a clear view.

"Looks like they're going to land over there!" he shouts down. "They're on their third pass right now." On the fifth try, the plane touches down. A huge cloud of snow rises in the air and hangs there.

"Up here," Ray calls to me. "I've got them marked. You can still see the plume from the landing."

I clamber up to a gap in the pressure ridge and see the results of the touchdown in the air above the landing site. With no wind to speak of, the cloud remains.

Down below us, Misha is marking a huge arrow in the snow with his foot. It points right in the direction of the landing. Though we can't see the plane, we calculate that it is less than three miles away.

Ray follows me off the ice rubble and stops at the bottom.

"That was a really strong thing you did with Misha back in the tent," he says.

I look at him quizzically, and then realize my face is flushing. I hadn't wanted to be confrontational with Misha, given my respect for him as a friend and a mentor.

"Thanks, but I guess I really didn't have much of a choice. At this point—in for a penny, in for a pound." I realize at that moment how valuable it had been to have Ray to turn to. "Besides, I am awfully glad that you were there to help me think it through."

We are partly there, but that is all. The Twin Otter from Eureka is on the ground, but it is early by about an hour. In addition to the visual sighting, Mark has given me coordinates for the landing location that the pilot selected yesterday. At least we have that piece securely nailed down.

The early arrival is a real problem. As the Twin Otter can stay on the ground a maximum of two hours, it means the plane will have to depart for Canada at 5:15 A.M. And the helicopter isn't due until 4 A.M. By the time we load the chopper, take off, and land, we'll have only about half an hour for a webcast. That is far less than the hour and a half that we have been counting on. It isn't all right, but it will have to be okay. Still, having come this far and this close, it is frustrating to know that we won't get the full measure. I'm not sure what will have to be trimmed, but I don't want it to be the senator.

Four o'clock passes, as does four-fifteen. It is now four-thirty, and there is no sign of the helicopter from Borneo. I am too stunned to do anything but stare in the direction of the ice station. The plane with the crew from NASA lies on the Arctic Ocean only a few miles away. Too far to ski in the time remaining, but close enough to see the takeoff when the time is up. And that time is rapidly nearing. The Polar Trek teammates are hovering over their gear, tents down and everything packed. We wait quietly as my anxiety brims over.

At 4:45 A.M., with only a half hour of the Twin Otter's time on the ice remaining, the Russian helicopter comes thundering over the horizon. It isn't clear why it is late, and at this point it doesn't matter. It has arrived, and there is a chance to salvage some of the operation after all.

As soon as the helicopter is down and the wheels firmly planted, I jump on board, grabbing as much gear as I can. We quickly form a human chain, and skis, backpacks, and sleds fly into the cavernous interior. I yank sleds into the back and reach for more. Clem and Lynn press to shuttle the equipment in with me.

The gear in, members of the WomenQuest and Weber-Malakhov teams swiftly pile in. The ladder is pulled in and the door slammed shut. We lift off, with several of the others searching my face for an indication of our chances. I shrug my shoulders and smile.

In the body of the helicopter, there is little chance to see the landscape. Misha and Richard are standing toward the front of the cabin. Ray pulls up the jump seat between the pilots. Misha passes along to the pilots the coordinates I have written on a slip of paper for him. They are the ones Mark gave me for the Twin Otter. I repeated them twice and am confident they are correct.

I dig my watch out from underneath several layers of jackets. It is five o'clock. We'll be there in five minutes. We can dash out and maybe do something that will pass as a webcast. There has to be a way to salvage this. Lemons, lemonade.

Five minutes turn into ten, and the roller coaster in my stomach takes another dip. "What's the problem? What's going on?" I murmur. "Why aren't we there yet?"

Then, the helicopter begins to climb, and everything we have tried to do to make this connection seems fruitless. When aviators are lost or can't find their targets, the response is to climb. Greater altitude logically gives a wider view. We are lost.

We climb, and then start to circle. Dammit. How can we have missed them? We saw where they landed!

One of two things is going to happen first, and neither one is good. Either the Russian helicopter will give up its search, or the First Air plane with the crew from NASA will be forced to leave, having used up its allotted time on the ground. I am beyond tears. I turn to the porthole that is rudely jammed up against me, and numbly have to accept that we have done the best we could. We have gotten within three miles of each other, on the same day and at the same time—and it still isn't good enough.

With a lurch, we suddenly start to go down. If it is true, if we really are descending, then the pilots have spotted the plane. It might actually happen after all. Well, maybe not a webcast at this point, but at least we could make the connection. It would be an emotional salvage, even if we have to settle for a taped segment instead of a live 'cast.

Down the helicopter shoots. In less than two minutes, we are on the ground, wheels planted, and ready to open the door. Somehow, I melt through the teammates in front of me and bound down the ladder. The plane is there on the ground, and the NASA cameras are set up and ready to go. Kathy Clark comes running over, grabs me, and lifts me up.

"Where have you guys been?" she says. "We saw the helicopter, and then watched it go in the other direction!"

"I don't know what went wrong. We saw your plane land and knew the direction to head. I couldn't see from inside the helicopter."

"Never mind about that." She squeezes my shoulder. "Come on over here; we're all set up and ready to go."

I whoop, and motion to my teammates. "Hey, guys, let's go do a webcast!"

As we jog over to the site where NASA Mike and the rest of the crew are waiting along with Morgan, the producer from *Good Morning America*, Kathy tells me we have lots of time. I stare at her, not fully understanding.

"You got here early, and the plane's been on the ground for almost two hours. Don't you have to leave soon?"

"No, as it turns out, because it's so mild—relatively speaking," she chuckles. "And because there isn't any wind, the First Air pilot was able to shut the engines down." This is an unbelievable stroke of luck. "If it gets colder, he can start them up again right away. In the meantime, we can stay here for quite a while."

Kerri, Susan, Josée, Lynn, and the rest of the team circle around the camera. When the helicopter landed, the prop blast had nearly knocked it over, and had filled the lens with snow. It is clear now, and Kathy motions me to join her in front of the lens. Working off of one mic, we talk for several minutes about our journey to the North Pole, and about our desire to connect with young women and girls.

Mike then motions to us and says that Senator Stabenow is ready to talk with us and wants to congratulate the entire team, half of them from the state she represents in Washington.

This is truly a spectral, out-of-body experience. Here, talking with a U.S. senator at the North Pole via satellite. Ten minutes ago, I was certain that this had all been lost. Deep down, there is the satisfaction that Debbie Stabenow and I had been students at Michigan State University at the same time, thirty years ago. Now we are reflecting on preparing the way for the next generation of women, especially to encourage them to take on challenges that involve math and science. Maybe, just maybe, they'll improve on what we have been able to do.

With seemingly all the time in the world, we move from a conversation with the senator to the webcast. Kathy gives us questions that webcast viewers have phoned or e-mailed in.

"From a viewer in Haslett (Michigan): How is Lynn's knee?" It has to be Tom, her husband. He's figured out a way to take a look at her. Lynn steps up to the mike, says it is fine, and the whole team smiles. We all know how devoted Tom is to Lynn.

"For Kerri, where's the banner?" Has to be someone from North Central Michigan College, where she's an instructor.

"Alison, tell us about the porksicles." Alison troops to the mic, and Kathy, who is six-foot, registers surprise. "I can look you right in the eye." Alison, at her full six-foot-one, smiles graciously, proceeds to thank the viewer for reading, and explains the porksicles.

One at a time, team members of Polar Trek 2001 come forward to answer questions. As a group, we all ring the discussion and relax in the Arctic sun. I slip away and grab Misha.

"You are our trainer and a great supporter of ours, Misha." I pull him by the arm to get him in front of the camera before the webcast ends. "You should be part of it, too."

After the satellite is gone and the webcast is over, we stay in place for interview questions from Morgan, and to hold up a banner for Ripley's Believe It or Not. Finally, the folks from NASA, who have been on the ground almost two hours longer than we have and who are not used to the polar environment, begin packing up gear and saying good-byes. Mike has brought Hershey's chocolate bars, our first in a month, and pins and patches for all.

While the team has been occupied with the webcast, the crews from the Russian and Canadian ships have staged their own gathering. The Russians have brought two stools, upon which they have placed a container of hot tea and a bottle of vodka. The aviators, along with the members of the Weber-Malakhov team, have had their own celebration. It turns out to be the First Air pilot's birthday, and one of his final flights. It also turns out that he and Misha are good friends and pleased to see one another. Any tensions that existed between these competitors are gone for the time being.

Our team, along with the others, piles back on board the helicopter for the ride back to Ice Station Borneo. Kathy, NASA Mike, and the rest of the crew from the States moves to the Twin Otter as the engines start to warm up.

We've met at a common point, and now are flying off in fairly opposite directions—our journeys completed and our missions accomplished.

The Russian helicopter takes off before the Twin Otter. As it lifts off, it rocks back and forth, waving good-bye. Inside, I lean against a porthole. I don't mind being crowded.

Josée Auclair. A Canadian ski champion, Quebec native, and wife of Arctic
expeditioner Richard Weber, Josée captained the Polar Trek 2001 team to
the North Pole. Her emotional strength and physical stamina, along with
her detailed planning, were critical to the expedition's success.

Lynn Bartley. An associate principal at Haslett High School, Lynn was the oldest member of the team. Her husband Tom's contact with Senator Debbie
Stabenow led to NASA's participation. She good-naturedly took much
ribbing over the rapid decline of her lovely hair.

Kathy Braegger. A financial analyst with a major telecommunications company,
Kathy's heart was in the outdoors. Though living in San Diego, this Idaho
native was a strong skier and the team's communication specialist.

Jen Buck. A nurse and outdoor enthusiast, Jen assisted Josée Auclair in the Polar
Trek 2001 preparation and on-ice execution. She is Japanese Canadian.

Sue Carter. WomenQuest founder and team leader, Sue organized the expedition, hired Josée and Jen, and assembled the team. Her responsibilities on
the ice included media and finalizing the webcast at the North Pole with
NASA. She was the second-oldest team member. ("Media" included communicating with print and broadcast journalists as well as developing a
public relations plan.)

Diana Ciserella. A late addition with Antarctic and mountaineering skills,
Diana added strength and support to the Polar Trek 2001 team through
her steadiness and patience. She was captivated by Russian aircraft
because of her training in air-freight dispatch.

Kerri Finlayson. The youngest team member, Kerri was a college instructor in
northern Michigan. Strong and mature, she was very important in organizing on-ice communication with school children.

Phyllis Grummon. A university administrator who also served as team treasurer, Phyllis struggled with the physical demands of the polar expedition

more than the other team members. She worked hard to achieve her goal, supported by the rest of the team.

Alison Korn. A Canadian Olympian who had medalled twice in rowing, Alison was the biggest, and one of the strongest team members. She also served as the journalist, reporting on Polar Trek 2001 for her employer, the *Ottawa Citizen.*

Susan Martin. A middle-school science teacher from northern Michigan, Susan worked closely with Kerri in linking with schools, and helped Kerri and Sue in creating the online curriculum for the expedition.

Anne Sherwood. A freelance photographer, Anne participated in the final training in Michigan's Upper Peninsula, but was unable to make a timely final payment in order to secure her place.

Marie-Josée Vasseur. A late but important addition to the Polar Trek 2001 team, M.-J. brought strength and a willingness to be challenged. A French Canadian, she managed the radio communication efforts with Ice Station Borneo.

Frida Waara. A founding member of WomenQuest and the Polar Trek 2001 team, Frida was the expedition's videographer. Her spirit, generosity, and Yooper laughter from Michigan's Upper Peninsula made her an important sparkplug. She and her husband, Ron, hosted two team-training sessions.

Carter Walker. An early member of WomenQuest and the Polar Trek team, Carter was a freelance journalist, EMT, and firefighter with quiet strength. She opted out of the expedition just prior to departure and was sorely missed by fellow teammates.